WINDSOR CASTI

Olwen Hedley was formerly assistant to the royal librarian and resident in Windsor Castle. She is the author of *Round and About Windsor and District*, *Royal Palaces* and *Queen Charlotte*, and various other titles, including *The Queen's Silver Jubilee*, *Buckingham Palace*, *The Princes of Wales* and *The Royal Foundation of Saint Katharine, in Ratcliffe, 1984*. She now lives in London.

WINDSOR CASTLE

OLWEN HEDLEY

ROBERT HALE · LONDON

ISBN 0 7090 5413 0

Robert Hale Limited
Clerkenwell House
Clerkenwell Green
London EC1R OHT

Printed in Great Britain by
St Edmundsbury Press Ltd, Bury St Edmunds, Suffolk.
Bound by WBC Bookbinders Ltd, Bridgend, Mid-Glamorgan.

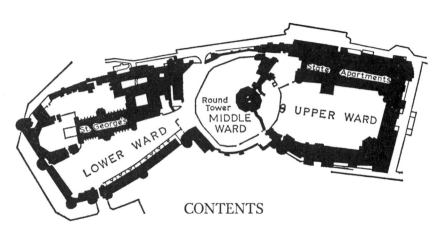

CONTENTS

ILLUSTRATIONS

> Numbers 7, 10, 11, 12, 17 and 19 are reproduced by
> gracious permission of Her Majesty the Queen; 14, 15
> and 16 are reproduced by permission of the Dean and
> Canons of Windsor.

PLANS

The plans of the Castle are based on those published in Hope, *Windsor Castle*, 1913, and drawn by T. R. Allen and K. J. Wass.

AUTHOR'S NOTE

It is my desire to record my gratitude to Sir Owen Morshead, G.C.V.O., Royal Librarian Emeritus, for help and advice, and also my debt to his book, *Windsor Castle*, and his monograph, "Royalist Prisoners in Windsor Castle". It was he who investigated, in the former, the restoration of the Castle to its primacy by King George III, and established the relationship between the modern appearance of the Curfew Tower and that of the Tour de la Peyre at Carcassonne—two examples of the rewarding work of research which amplifies and illuminates Sir William St. John Hope's great architectural history of the Castle. My own interest in the annals of the Upper Ward and Royal Household had its impetus in the assemblage of data originated by Sir Owen during his years at Windsor.

I wish also to acknowledge the kindness of Oxley & Son (Windsor) Ltd., in allowing me to consult the files of the *Windsor, Slough and Eton Express*, a rich storehouse of information unavailable elsewhere.

O.H.

1

THE FOUNDING OF THE FORTRESS

The story of Windsor begins at that far-off point in time when the Romans were making themselves masters of England. In A.D. 44 the Second Legion "Augusta" marched up the Thames Valley, and some historians have suggested that the chalk cliff on which the Castle stands lent itself to encampment by the invading army. Since it was outside the direct lines of communication the theory is perhaps idle, but one may take leave to suppose that Roman soldiers climbed the long slope, curious to know what view it had to offer. From its northern heights, a hundred feet above the Thames, they would see outspread the landscape which the world now flocks to see: the broad valley closed by the blue rim of the Chiltern Hills, of which the cliff is a lonely outcrop in an area of London clay.

Under the established order Romans called the district their home. Coins minted as early as A.D. 69 have been dug up in local gardens, while tombs found at Old Windsor in 1865, and assigned to the fourth century, reveal the presence of a settlement there.

After the Romans had passed out of the picture the Saxon invaders made a domestic niche in the district. Perhaps as early as the seventh century there was a Saxon settlement at Old Windsor, between Staines (the Roman Pontes) and the cliff three miles upstream. Here, at the manor-house of Kingsbury, Saxon sovereigns held court, and from its shelter rode out on their hunting expeditions in the royal forest away on the south and west. Edward the Confessor, whose death in January 1066 was the signal for the Norman invasion of England, kept many festivals there. Tradition places this Saxon palace near Old Windsor Church, in a riverside meadow fronting "The Priory", and excavations have tended to confirm the story.

The cliff stood, not in the great royal manor of Old Windsor, but in that of "Clivore" (now Clewer). The hamlet of Clewer nestled on the shore a mile further up the Thames, and apparently had a church, since traces of Saxon origin have been noted in the ancient building which lifts its spire beside the water today.

The foundation of a castle on the barren cliff-top had its starting-point in the Norman victory near Hastings on 14th October, 1066. After his coronation at Westminster two months later, on Christmas Day, William the Conqueror ordered the Tower of London to be built, and this was followed by the erection of strongholds all over England. Thus he subdued and controlled his new kingdom. Some of his castles, like the Tower, were royal. Others were held by his followers.

To guard London he surrounded it with a ring of outlying fortresses, and Windsor was one of these. On the north he placed four castles of which only the ruins now remain: Berkhamsted, Hertford, Ongar and Rayleigh. Rochester on the south-east still has its stone tower, set at the point where the Medway joins the Thames. The southern approaches were protected by the castles of Tonbridge, Reigate and Guildford, all now ruined. Twenty-five miles west of the capital he closed the ring at Windsor.

The chalk cliff presented a favourable site, since it overlooked the main waterway to London. Moreover, the river had in primeval ages ground its northern face into perilous slopes which formed a natural defence. As a focus for militarist development it satisfied William the Conqueror's most searching needs, and he must have congratulated himself on finding such a viewpoint adjacent to the amenities of a royal manor-house and forest. Kingsbury continued to serve as a residence after the Norman Conquest, but was presently deserted for the new castle. It was probably part of William the Conqueror's plan to secure a palace as well as a fortress on the cliff top.

Windsor has thus been a royal castle since its foundation. The year in which it was begun is uncertain, but the date is believed to have been about 1070. The earliest reference to it is in the Domesday Survey of 1086, in the entry relating to the manor of Clewer, which reads: "Ralf the son of Seifrid holds of the King CLIVORE.

Harold the earl held it. Then it was taxed for five hides. Now for four hides and a half, and the castle of Windsor is on the (other) half-hide."[1] It stole both the importance and the name of the Saxon palace although the cliff stood in the manor of Clewer and had no previous connection with the old royal residence. William the Conqueror rented the site from the lord of Clewer for twelve shillings a year, and payment continued until 1572.[2]

The early castle was built of wood, for the Normans were in haste to erect their defences, and the forest provided plenty of timber. They cut down the trees, trimmed them to shape, and rammed them into banks of chalk and earth to make a continuous fence enclosing thirteen acres of the cliff top. Outside the fence they dug a broad ditch which surrounded the Castle except on the long northern side, where the steepness of the slopes made further defence unnecessary. Within their massive stockade they laid out two courtyards separated by a high, broad mount bearing the keep or great tower. This was the chief feature of Norman castles. The keep, also called the *donjon*, was intended to be the final retreat in case of siege, and the king himself might have to seek its shelter. Several examples appear in the famous Bayeux tapestry, which illustrates William's preparations for the invasion of England and his final triumph. He set up camp at Hastings as soon as he landed, and one of the embroidered panels shows workmen with picks and shovels building the mount and keep of a castle, possibly the very one whose ruins now crown the steep crag overlooking the town.[3]

Just such a scene took place at Windsor a few years later. The Normans impressed local labour, and so men already living in the district must have cast up the mount on which the Round Tower stands. They did this by digging a great circular moat and heaping up the displaced chalk in the centre to a height of 50 feet—in the same way as a child builds a sand castle on the sea shore. The moat was left dry, since the Normans lacked skill to raise water to such a height, and it would in any case have drained away through the porous chalk. To secure a supply of water within the keep they had to sink a well. They bored through the 50 feet of the mount and continued through the solid chalk to the level of the Thames, a total depth of $164\frac{1}{2}$ feet.

The higher of the two courtyards, the Upper Ward, was laid out

Windsor Castle in Norman times

on the flat top of the cliff east of the mount. The long slope of the hill below the mount became the Lower Ward. Almost at the bottom of the Lower Ward, near its south-west corner, was placed the entrance into the Castle. Here the ditch was crossed by a drawbridge worked up and down by chains from a gatehouse.

Only one path led from the Lower Ward to the Upper. It rose in a north-easterly direction round the moat encircling the mount until it reached the Inner Gatehouse, set at the narrowest point between the mount and the steep slopes on the other side. Here it became a passage compressed between the defences of the Gatehouse, which covered the steps leading up to the keep. To this day the Inner Gatehouse remains a stricture, as the Normans planned, but the roadway that passes through it is less sharply inclined, and the ground level of the Upper Ward several feet lower than in former times.

A cross-ditch dug at the top of the Lower Ward completed the defences. It extended from the north edge of the cliff to the fence on the south side, and so a small middle ward was formed between this line and the mount. Over the cross-ditch stood a drawbridge which like the one at the entrance was worked up and down by chains from a gatehouse.

The plan and scale of the Castle led Sir William St. John Hope, author of its architectural history (1913), to suggest that it was laid out by William FitzOsbern, ruler of the Isle of Wight, who died in 1072. He is believed to have been the great military engineer who planned the castles of Arundel, Carisbrooke and Rockingham. With Windsor, these formed a class almost by themselves, being among the largest and most skilfully planned of the Norman fortresses.[4]

William the Conqueror himself may never have lived in his hilltop castle. For the first forty years it served as a fortress and prison. In 1095 his son, King William II, surnamed Rufus, led an army to the far north, where Robert, Earl of Northumberland, was in open rebellion, and when eventually the Earl was captured, ordered him "to be brought to Windsor and to be kept in the castle there".[5] He is said to have remained a prisoner for thirty years. Down the ages many hundreds of captives shared his fate and were immured in its high towers and rough chalk dungeons.

The early Norman kings made frequent use of the palace at Old

Windsor for festivals and hunting expeditions. The Saxon forest had been largely barren waste, with here and there cultivated areas, which supported small settlements and herds of swine. William the Conqueror planted more trees, paying no heed to the Abbot of Abingdon's lament that he was turning "the habitations of men into the lairs of beasts". To deter poachers, harsh penalties were introduced. In a recital of oppressive measures *The Anglo-Saxon Chronicle* emphasizes the King's jealous concern for his hunting-grounds.

> He made great protection for the game
> And imposed laws for the same,
> That who so slew hart or hind
> Should be made blind.
>
> He preserved the harts and boars
> And loved the stags as much
> As if he were their father.
> Moreover, for the hares did he decree that they should go free.[6]

The Castle had been provided with royal apartments by the Whitsuntide of 1110. King Henry I, having summoned all his nobles, celebrated the festival by holding his court "for the first time at the New Windsor". The site of this early palace is not recorded, but may safely be guessed at. The royal chambers would not have been in the keep, which besides being a defensive retreat was a lodging for state prisoners. Nor is the King likely to have wanted to make a home in the Lower Ward. The position was insufficiently secure for the King's palace. The surroundings too would not have been altogether acceptable, since it must have served as a compound for stables, storehouses and barracks. There was also a gaol-house, of which mention was made in 1184. It was known for centuries as the "Colehouse" and used for offenders dealt with by the Castle court, which had to enforce the laws relating to Windsor Forest.

The appropriate site for the new palace was in the Upper Ward, along the northern edge of the cliff. This was the highest and therefore the safest point, overlooking the perpetually beautiful panorama of the Thames valley. It is occupied today by the State Apartments, which served as the royal residence from the end of the twelfth century until the nineteenth. The timber lodging of King Henry I probably formed the earliest foundation of these superb first-floor galleries. Their position is a reminder that in medieval palaces the kitchens and offices were on the ground floor and the royal quarters above.

His new buildings included a chapel. Here he married his second Queen, the beautiful Adeline, daughter of Godfrey VII, Duke of Lower Lorraine and Count of Louvain, on 22nd February, 1121. The wedding had been delayed because of a dispute between the aged Ralph, Archbishop of Canterbury, and the Bishop of Salisbury, both of whom claimed the right to officiate. The Bishop insisted that the privilege was his because the Castle was in his diocese, but a council decided that the sovereign was a parishioner of the Archbishop of Canterbury. As Ralph was infirm and feeble, he appointed the Bishop of Winchester to perform the ceremony, but startled everyone by appearing in the chapel himself after it had begun. It was customary at the time for the king to wear his crown during a state ceremony, and when the Archbishop entered Henry was already invested with his regalia. The Archbishop asked who had crowned him. The King replied that he had not taken much notice, and could not say, whereupon the Archbishop took the crown off his head and put it back himself. He then proceeded to marry the royal pair.[7]

In the same year the monks of Abingdon waited on the King at "the town commonly called Windsor". This was the earliest notice of the future royal borough of New Windsor. The settlement was probably no more than a thin fringe of houses at the south-west angle of the Castle, which provided homes for royal officials, traders and dependants.

The growing consequence of the Castle is reflected in a state function which took place at Christmas in the year 1126. "This year," says *The Anglo-Saxon Chronicle*, "King Henry held his court at Windsor, and David, king of Scots, was there, and all the chief men, both clerics and laymen, that were in England. And there he caused archbishops and bishops and abbots and earls and all the thegns that were there to swear to give England and Normandy after his death into the hand of his daughter Athelic, who had been the wife of the Emperor [Henry V] of Saxony."[8] King David swore fealty to the widowed Empress in the character of an English baron. The crowning of King Henry at this Christmas festival was made a point of contention between William, Archbishop of Canterbury, Ralph's successor in the primacy, and Turstan, Archbishop of York. The latter made an attempt to perform the ceremony, but was prevented from approaching the King by onlookers, who turned his cross-bearer out of the chapel.

Athelic, who is better known by the name of Maud or Matilda, was shortly remarried to Geoffrey Plantagenet, Count of Anjou. After her father's death in 1135 her cousin, Stephen, Count of Blois, secured the succession, and civil war followed. Although the Castle was unaffected, its importance to the safety of the realm was stressed in a treaty made at Wallingford in 1153. In this agreement King Stephen acknowledged Maud's son, Henry Plantagenet, Count of Anjou, as his heir. He also entrusted the "tower of London" and the "mount of Windsor" to Richard de Lucy, the chief justiciar, who pledged himself to return them to Henry after Stephen's death.[9]

In 1154 the Count succeeded as Henry II, first of the Plantagenet kings. His court was ever on the move, as a much-tried retainer narrates: "If the King has decided to spend the day anywhere, you may be certain that he will get off early in the morning, and this sudden change will put everyone's plans into confusion. You may see men running about as though they were mad, urging on the packhorses, driving chariots one into another. His pleasure, if I may say so, is increased by the straits to which his courtiers are put." Nor did he mind if they found themselves at nightfall in an unknown forest, where they had to wander for miles to find a hovel in which to sleep.[10]

Despite this eccentric behaviour, he spent enough time at Windsor to carry out an ambitious programme. In about 1170 he started to build the stone walls and towers which enclose the Castle on the north, south and east fronts. Altogether he replaced with masonry nearly half a mile of his great-grandfather's wooden defences. Winchester Tower, which stands like a tall stalk of stone midway along the northern heights, was first built at this period. The two square towers to the west of it, at the top of the Hundred Steps leading down the North Slopes, also made part of King Henry II's new works. Along the south and east sides of the Upper Ward his stone wall linked a series of shallow watch towers.

He also began to build the Round Tower, for by now the mount had hardened into a compact mass, nearly 300 feet in diameter at the base and 100 feet at the top, and was sufficiently firm to support the weight of a stone keep. Probably its shape dictated that of the tower, which is not a perfect circle but nearer in form to a rounded square. From this period too dates the ascent on the south side of the mount, which was originally a continuation of the mural defences.

Although it is convenient to call it the Round Tower, the name properly belongs to a later period. At first it was referred to as "the tower of the Castle", and afterwards by the successive names of the Great or High Tower, the Dongeon Tower and the Keep. It is not a solid structure, but a shell-keep with an open centre. The stone "apron" or gallery around the base had a purpose in those days of primitive warfare. Supposing an enemy were to penetrate into the Castle, he would have to fight uphill under the fire of bowmen stationed on the gallery as well as behind the arrow slits in the keep itself.

Lead for the roofs of the new buildings had to be brought from as far away as Cumberland, but the other materials were not so far to seek. The cliff provided chalk filling for the outer walls, some of which are 13 feet thick, while the heath stone to face them came from Bagshot about ten miles south of Windsor. Then and later the account rolls included references to stone obtained from "Collingley in Windsor Forest", a name which may be identified with Collingwood a mile south-west of Bagshot. The outer walls and towers built by King Henry II are still substantially intact, and if today the Castle does not give a complete impression of remote antiquity, the durability of this heath stone helps to account for it. It never betrays its age, for being a silicate and crystalline substance it is cleansed and refreshed by every shower of rain.

When the King died in 1189 the outline of the Castle was defined in solid masonry, and half-way down the Lower Ward, on the north side, he had built a Great Hall about 70 feet long and 40 feet wide. It was massively constructed in chalk and stone, and is thought to have been divided into a nave and aisles. The *Domus Regis* or "King's houses" in the Upper Ward formed by this time a rectangular, two-storeyed block against the north wall. The King's hall, with pantry and buttery, his great chamber, wardrobe and chapel stood around three sides of a cloister or herb garden, which was closed along the western side by the Queen's lodging. East of the King's chambers the great kitchen extended along the north wall, on the same site as the royal kitchen today, and overlooked a courtyard appropriated to domestic use.[11]

Henry's personal life was saddened by the turbulence of his sons, among whom were the future King Richard I and King John. Legend says that in a chamber at Windsor he caused to be painted an eagle, with four birds, three of which were attacking the old eagle, while the fourth was scratching at the old eagle's eyes. "This old eagle", the King said, "is myself, and these four birds are my four sons, who cease not to pursue my death, and especially my youngest son, John."[12]

2

A PALACE BEYOND COMPARE

The defences of the Castle were first put to the test in King Richard I's reign. While he was fighting in the third crusade his brother John plotted against him, arranging for his capture by Leopold of Austria on his return journey in December 1192. He was imprisoned in a castle on the Danube, where according to a favourite legend his minstrel Blondel finally tracked him down. Meanwhile, at home, Prince John garrisoned Windsor Castle. This was resented by the barons, who remained loyal to their King, and in March 1193 a large force of knights attacked it under the leadership of Walter, Archbishop of Rouen. The besiegers were said to be "not very earnest" because the Archbishop had friends within, but in April the Castle surrendered and was delivered into the hands of Eleanor the Queen Mother.[1]

When he became King, John was frequently at Windsor. He is said to have loved the Castle "above all others", but the only traits he impressed on its annals were the cardinal sins of anger and gluttony. His psychopathic temper was packed on one occasion into an act of hideous savagery. A quarrel with William de Braose, who had formerly enjoyed the King's favour, led to William's flight oversea in 1210 and the transference of John's revenge to his wife and son. The victims were shut up together in a tower at Windsor, with a sheaf of wheat and a piece of raw bacon for their sole sustenance. When their prison was re-opened eleven days later both were dead. Lady de Braose was "sitting upright between her son's legs, with her head leaning back on his breast, whilst he was also in a sitting position, with his face turned towards the ground. Maud de Braose, in her last pangs of hunger, had gnawed the cheeks of her son, then probably dead, and after this effort she appeared to have fallen into the position in which she was found."[2]

John's greed is implicit in accounts swollen with the items of a monstrous diet. He entertained lavishly, and the quantities of wine, beans, bacon, chickens, pheasants and partridges which arrived at Windsor provided only basic requirements. Butchers and cooks co-operated in 1210 in the slaughter, preparation and salting of 375 pigs. Sometimes there was so much food that it became an embarrassment and was thrown out. Festivals offered opportunities for concentrated voracity. Before spending the Christmas of 1213 at Windsor John ordered the sheriffs of the surrounding counties to supply, in all, 15,000 herrings, 3,000 capons, 1,000 salted eels, 400 head of swine, 100 pounds of fresh almonds, 20 pounds of white bread, spices for seasoning, 500 pounds of wax, 1,000 yards of cloth for table napkins, 20 large casks of "good and new wine" for his household and 4 casks of the best for himself.[3]

From the Castle John rode out on 10th June, 1215, to the riverside meadow of Runnymede, three miles downstream beyond Old Windsor, to meet Stephen Langton, Archbishop of Canterbury, and some baronial envoys. Following a revolt by the barons against the tyrannous King, a truce had been arranged until 15th June, and meetings were to take place daily to discuss their demands. The barons had their base at Staines, while the King made the Castle his headquarters. It was a trim pastoral scene that the negotiating parties invaded, for the season was early and the commoners of Egham had cut their hay. Against the green mantle of summer the demands were duly presented, and the King submitted to them. On 15th June, when the truce was due to expire, the parties assembled in great numbers, and agreement was reached on all the points embodied in Magna Carta. This day was regarded as so significant that when the Charter was finally drawn up it ended with a dating clause: "Given by our hand in the meadow which is called Runnymede, between Staines and Windsor, on the fifteenth day of June, in the seventeenth year of our reign." The meetings continued until 19th June, by which time the formal document had been engrossed and sealed.[4]

Peace did not long prevail, for John sent to Rome so malicious an account of what had happened at Runnymede that on 24th August the Pope annulled the Charter, and the barons again rebelled. They obtained aid from King Philip II of France by offering the crown to his son, Prince Louis, who brought an army to England in May 1216. Leaving the Castle garrisoned by sixty knights and their followers, under the command of the Constable, Engelard de Cygony, who was reputed to be "a man very skilful in the art of war", John set out to meet the invaders. He never again set foot in his castle of Windsor.

The French soon made themselves masters of southern England, and all the castles in the counties around London submitted to them except Dover and Windsor. Prince Louis himself led the assault at Dover. At Windsor the barons assembled a great army, under the leadership of the Count of Nevers, and, in the words of Roger of Wendover, who wrote the earlier part of the *Flores Historiarum*, "laid siege to the Castle with engines of war, which they brought close up to it, and fiercely attacked the defences." The weapons which they hauled into place in the main streets of Windsor are not enumerated, but one was a *petraria*, an engine used for hurling great stones.[5]

For nearly three months the barons continued their battery against the Castle, meeting spirited resistance from Engelard de Cygony and his company. "They were there long, but did little and were in great jeopardy," continued Roger of Wendover. Twice the beam of their *petraria* was cut by Engelard's raiding parties, who crept out through secret passages emerging in the Castle ditch. In September the siege was abandoned. The chroniclers maintained that the Count of Nevers was bribed to retire, either by the King or the Constable, and that the barons withdrew on his advice. They then went off in pursuit of the King, who was ravaging East Anglia and Essex.[6] A few weeks later, on 19th October 1216, John died at Newark "from a surfeit of peaches and new cider", and the war ended with a settlement made at Windsor. The regents of the young King Henry III confirmed the great Charter, which in 1225 was reissued by the King himself under the Great Seal. This was Magna Carta in the final form, word for word, in which its stands today as the earliest enactment on the Statute Rolls of England—"the starting point of the constitutional history of the English race", in the words of the jurist and statesman, Lord Bryce. To men of the Middle Ages it represented hard-won liberties: continual confirmation made it the palladium of liberty in the modern world.

King Henry III was a child of nine when his father died. He grew up to be a man of taste and culture. Westminster Abbey was rebuilt by him, and at Windsor he not only repaired the damage caused by the sieges but completed the defences. In 1223–4 two new towers were placed along the south front. One, which bears his name, stands at the top of the Lower Ward. The other, now miscalled King Edward III Tower and formerly known as the Devil's Tower, gives emphasis to the westernmost point of the Upper Ward. Like the Round Tower, whose lesser neighbour it is, it was long used as a state prison, and inscriptions carved by captives have been found on its stone walls.

In contrast to the older square towers, these two are D-shaped, and represent an advance in military architecture derived from the experience of Crusaders in the Holy Land. Similar towers may be seen at the Krak des Chevaliers, the Syrian fortress built early in the twelfth century by the Knights of St. John of Jerusalem.[7] The space between the two towers was sealed by a curved wall with a curious deep indentation in the middle.

King Henry III set a smaller example of his D-shaped towers half-way down the south front of the Lower Ward. Then in 1227–30 he carried out the work which most notably commemorates him at Windsor. He walled the west end of the Castle, placing along it three towers which turn conspicuous, rounded fronts towards the town— Salisbury at the south-west corner, Garter in the middle, and the Curfew, or Bell Tower at the other end. Since they were built in the original ditch, a new one was dug which swallowed up some of the homes on the Castle boundary. Payment was made by the King in 1242 to "our honest men of Windsor for the damage which they have sustained owing to the pulling down of their houses, on account of the ditch which we have caused to be made." A year later an order was issued for "the ditches about the Castle to be enlarged as far as the houses of the town outside or their ruin allow", and further compensation to "our poor men of Windsor" followed. The final breadth of the ditch was about 80 feet. The barbican, or outer fortification of the Castle gate on the town side of the ditch, was completed in 1249, and in 1260 a portcullis, or running gate, was ordered for the great gate, and timber procured from Windsor Forest to repair the drawbridge, across which was placed a strong iron chain.[8]

Thus the outer defences were completed in equal might and majesty. The Castle at that time would have looked more forbidding than it does today, because its outer walls contained no windows, but only narrow slits through which bowmen could shoot their arrows. The regular garrison in the year 1242 consisted of four knights who were paid two shillings a day, eleven soldiers at ninepence a day, seven watchers at twopence a day, and "certain crossbowmen, each of whom takes sixpence a day".

Behind the massive walls civilizing influences were at work. In 1236 Henry III brought to Windsor a young wife from the shores of the Mediterranean, Eleanor, daughter of Raymond Berenger, Count of Provence. She made the best of her new home, always seeking to cajole the unfriendly northern light with warmth and colour. Workmen hastened to put two new glass windows in her great chamber on the side overlooking the King's herb-garden, and another painted with the Root of Jesse in the gable at the south end, but she was not satisfied. Two years later she had the room rebuilt. In 1239 she gave birth to her eldest son, the future King Edward I, and there were nurseries to be planned. The domestic picture gradually takes form, only to shrink and tremble in 1251 under the fury of a summer storm, against which the royal lodging seemed as defenceless as a dolls' house. Matthew Paris thought the cataclysm worth reporting. On 19th May at one o'clock in the morning the royal household were awakened by approaching thunder. Out of a blackened sky it rolled towards Windsor, and "coming nearer, with the lightnings, one stroke more dreadful than the rest, and as if the heaven were hurling itself upon the earth, fell upon the bedchamber of the Queen, where she was abiding with the children and her household, crumbled the chimney to powder, cast it to the ground, and shook the whole house."[9]

Four years later the rebuilding of the Queen's lodging began. The rectangular block of the royal apartments must already have been extended westward, so that by this time her suite and the nurseries enclosed a second cloister with a herb-garden. The arrangement represents the basic plan of the State Apartments today. The Queen's new great chamber, unlike the half-timbered room it replaced, was apparently raised in stone, and in an elegant style of architecture, for it was graced with stone pillars. In 1262 one thousand boards for panelling the Queen's great chamber were ordered, indicating that she had decided to have it completed in the same way as the adjoining rooms. All of them, including her new chapel and the nurses' quarters, were wainscoted and delicately painted. The room next to the great chamber was coloured green with gold stars, and this was the favourite device not only at Windsor but in every one of King Henry III's palaces.[10]

The basic provisions of the royal lodging did not change. Whenever the Court left, the cesspools under the various apartments were cleaned out ready for the next visit. Water was laboriously drawn up from wells sunk through the chalk, of which there were several. The Norman well in the Round Tower figures in the accounts from time to time, as in the year 1245, when two good and thick ropes and two buckets were ordered for it. In the middle of the courtyard in the Upper Ward was the "great well". It was worked by means of a wheel, though whether this was operated by human agency or by a donkey, like the famous one at Carisbrooke Castle, is uncertain. The kitchen and bakehouse had a well to themselves. In 1256 King Henry wanted water from the great well to be led down to conduit heads in his cloister in the Lower Ward. This was on the north side of a chapel dedicated to St. Edward the Confessor which he had built in 1240–8 (on the site of the present Albert Memorial Chapel). It enclosed a grass plot laid out at the same time and now celebrated as the oldest lawn in England. From there the water was continued down to his grandfather's Great Hall. Rain water provided a further source of supply and was carefully conserved. In 1243 an order was issued for a cistern to be placed "on the mount of Windsor to receive all the rain water".[11]

To simplify domestic arrangements in the palace the King introduced a gate on the south front of the Upper Ward. A drawbridge led over the Castle ditch to the new entrance, which was first mentioned in 1260. It adjoined the Devil's Tower and was called the Rubbish Gate. The name clung to it throughout its history, but since it was a convenient approach to the palace it was also known as the King's Gate. On the other side of the ditch were the royal garden and vineyard, which had been named in the Castle accounts since 1156.

The Great Hall in the Lower Ward had already been renovated and bore on its gable a stone lion added in 1237. King Henry, who steadfastly practised religious observance and was lavish in his charity, opened it at Christmas 1239 to poor people, whom he fed and clothed "to the glory and honour of God". In the lesser hall which made part of the palace in the Upper Ward the poor were welcomed on St. Stephen's Day, and at Epiphany, and poor clergy were feasted and clothed on St. Thomas's Day, and poor boys on Innocents' Day. Again in the year 1241 the King commanded his stewards to cause "the hall of our Castle of Windsor, and also the hall within the tower of the same Castle, to be filled with poor folk on Good Friday and to feed them, and a maundy on Maundy Thursday of twenty poor folk."[12]

Very different was the reception accorded in 1265 to forty deputies seeking pardon for the City of London, which had taken part in a revolt against the King. Henry kept them waiting outside the gates until evening, and when at last they were admitted, clapped them in a tower, where they enjoyed "small cheer and worse lodging". Nor was he in haste to let them go. Some of them remained in their prison for four years.[13]

The Great Hall shared in the colourful beauty with which Henry gradually invested the Castle. In 1250 he ordered for the dais a new throne "painted with the image of a king holding a sceptre adorned with gold", and ten years later the windows on either side were filled with painted glass. Leading out of the hall at the north end, and reaching to the Castle wall, were chambers which included a royal withdrawing-room on the first floor. It was gracefully appointed, with arched doors and windows and a fireplace, and decorated with elaborate wall paintings.[14] On the west a covered alley led to the kitchen and the penthouse where the tablecloths were kept. A well for the kitchen, six feet in circumference, was sunk in the chalk in November 1252.

The adornment of the hall brought it into accord with the chapel and cloister. The devotional setting was completed by yet another royal lodging which extended as far as the Norman cross-ditch, enclosing the cloister on the north side. On the west a beautiful Porch of Honour (now blocked at its inner end) opened into the ceremonial route to the chapel door. Covered alleys enclosed the grass plot ordered in 1240, and against the three inner walls of the cloister ran a bench of freestone which the King desired to be made six years later. In 1248 the cloister was paved and panelled, and then "painted with the Apostles" by Master William the King's painter, a monk of Westminster. The cloister offered a path for processions when festivals of the church were celebrated, and a sheltered retreat for discussion among the clergy. The stone bench must have been a resting-place for generations of pilgrims, but it was not used for repose only. At intervals along all three sides were scooped out sets of shallow holes, in lines of three by three. They were for the medieval game of nine-holes, which resembled "noughts and crosses" played with marbles or counters. Looking at them today, one can feel very near to the players who made merry around the cloister lawn on summer evenings long ago.

The dedication of the chapel to Edward the Confessor recalls Henry III's devotion to the saint, upon whose shrine his new plan for Westminster Abbey was based in a literal sense.[15] At Windsor he confined his ambition to a minor though no less careful achievement. The chapel was small, but lovely, as surviving fragments declare. The north wall of the present Albert Memorial Chapel, which belonged to it, displays a series of arches rising from stone and marble shafts planted in groups on the bench where nine-holes was played. Recorded details help to fill in the picture. Metal left over from the great bell of Westminster made four small bells which hung in a stone turret on the front, above the triple arcade of the west entrance. William the monk painted the chapel, which had "a high wooden roof after the manner of the roof of the new work at Lichfield, so that the stone work may be seen", and four gilt images added seemly splendour.[16] One of these was probably the "Virgin of Windsor", a silver-gilt statue of Our Lady, weighing over a hundredweight, which Henry had to pawn at least once in order to pay his bills.

He was often in financial straits, for the new works proved costly, but in return for his outlay he procured for himself a palace beyond compare. The writer of the continuation of the *Flores Historiarum*, commenting on the garrisoning of the Castle by Prince Edward with alien troops in 1263, describes it as "that very flourishing castle, than which, at that time, there was not another more splendid within the bounds of Europe."[17] The fulfilment of King Henry's purpose left the Prince with few obligations at Windsor after his accession, and his Welsh and Scottish campaigns in any case allowed him scant time to frequent the place. Himself a famous builder of castles, he added to its renown only by holding a great tournament there on 9th July, 1278. This celebrated event took place in "The King's Park in the Forest of Windsor", later called the Great Park to distinguish it from the "Little Park around the Castle", which was yet unformed. It had been enclosed before 1086, and had a moated manor-house where the royal family sometimes stayed, but several centuries were to pass before it was directly linked with the Castle. The route to it lay along Windsor High Street, which was sometimes described in deeds as the *Via Regia*, and then down Sheet Street and King's Road.

Many of King Edward's most distinguished knights took part in the tournament, including a number who had soldiered with him in the crusades. Such military sport was often so realistic as to be dangerous, but on this occasion the events were "jousts of peace" devised at the King's expense. The helmets issued to the thirty-eight combatants were made of boiled leather, their shields were of light timber, and their sword blades of whalebone and parchment, silvered.

Although it was a pageant of horsemen rather than an exercise in arms, it was not the less effective on that account. The knights of highest rank wore helmets covered in pure gold at a cost of twelve pence each, while the rest were silvered at eight pence each, and pure gold was used on the hilts and pommels of the mock swords. Silk to make the long, sleeveless surcoats worn over their armour came from Lucca. It was specially ordered by Adinett the King's tailor, who also bought eight pieces of diaper, a costly fabric flowered with gold thread which ornamented the exposed parts of the armour. Among many accessories procured for this historic extravanganza were 800 little bells for the horses' bridles and harness, and furs from Paris to make the Queen a mantle.[18]

With this picturesque flourish the history of the Castle in the thirteenth century closed. Ahead lay the full flowering of the Middle Ages: the upsurge of national pride, the birth of the English language, the foundation of the Order of the Garter. All these took effect in the reign of the King's grandson, Edward III, in whose dynamic story Windsor bore a spectacular part.

3

THE ORDER OF THE GARTER

The Castle was the birthplace of the third Edward. He was born on 23rd November, 1312, and was the first child of King Edward II and his seventeen-year-old wife, Queen Isabel. So delighted was the King that he granted an annuity of £20 for life to John Launge, the Queen's valet, who brought the news to him. The Prince was baptized in the chapel built by his great-grandfather, King Henry III, and from the place of his birth was known as Edward of Windsor.

An ancient horoscope, or "astrological scheme" of his nativity, painted on glass, is still preserved in a window of the Royal Closet in St. George's Chapel. Although this magnificent building was not begun until a hundred years after King Edward III's death, history unites its fame with his, for it is the spiritual home of the Order of the Garter, which he founded in 1348.

Of all the orders of chivalry, this is the oldest, and the chief in majesty, honour and fame. It had its origin in the warring patriotism of King Edward's reign. Jean Froissart, who spent his life recording contemporary events, shrewdly summed up the national character at the time. The English, he wrote, "will never love or honour their king, unless he be victorious and a lover of arms. They delight in battles." Edward III amply fulfilled the heroic role expected of him. He laid claim to the French crown in right of his mother, who was the daughter of King Philip IV, and in 1337 the Hundred Years War began.

He himself was present when the English merchant navy won the battle of Sluys in 1340, and after this great victory claimed lordship of the English sea. In the same year he added to his own royal title that of "King of France". It was borne by every succeeding King, and the golden French lilies were quartered with the English royal arms until in 1801 King George abandoned both the title and the lilies.

The idea of forming a brotherhood of knights, dedicated to the service of God and the maintenance of valiant traditions, was in the King's mind as early as 1343. From the beginning he intended the shrine and meeting place of such a company to be at Windsor. With this in view he arranged to hold "noble jousts and great feasts" there in the presence of guests both from England and abroad. Accordingly, on 1st January, 1344, letters of safe conduct were issued, granting the King's protection to knights and gentlemen of all countries who wished to attend.

About three weeks later there arrived at Windsor a great host of people ready to enjoy this great occasion. They included a large number of earls, barons and gentlemen, and many knights from oversea. The King's consort, Queen Philippa, and his mother, Queen Isabel, were there, and also the Lady Isabel, daughter of Edward and Philippa. Nine countesses arrived, and so many baronesses, ladies and young girls that they filled the Great Hall, where the King himself showed them to their places, setting them in order of rank. The young Prince of Wales and all the male guests had to sup outside, and a tent was set up in the courtyard.

For three days the jousts continued, the King himself winning three of the six prizes, and each evening the guests returned to their feasting. A local historian, Adam de Murimuth, Rector of Wraysbury, who was evidently present since he recorded all these details, described the banquets as expensive and abounding in the most tempting of drink. The minstrels provided sweet music and other joyous entertainment, and afterwards the company joined in a variety of dances. The most popular seems to have been a ring-dance in which kisses were exchanged.

After the jousts on the third day it was announced that no lord or lady must depart, as the King desired the presence of his guests next morning. On the following day he appeared in "royal and festive vestures, and he had on uppermost a mantle of very precious velvet, and the royal crown placed upon his head." Accompanied by the

Queen, who was also most nobly adorned, he led the company to the chapel to hear mass. After the service a solemn procession was formed. Henry of "Grosmont", Earl of Derby, Steward of England, and William Montagu, 1st Earl of Salisbury, Marshal of England, walked before the King, who carried the royal sceptre. The two Queens, Edward Prince of Wales and all the guests followed.

At the assembly place the King laid his hand on the Bible and took an oath that he "would begin a Round Table, in the same manner as the lord Arthur, formerly king of England, appointed it, namely to the number of 300 knights, a number always increasing, and he would cherish it and maintain it according to his power." Then the trumpets sounded and the company hastened to a final feast, where there was all manner of rich fare and overflowing abundance of drinks. "The delight was unutterable," concluded Adam de Murimuth happily, "the hilarity without care."[1]

In February a circular banqueting hall 200 feet in diameter was begun in the courtyard, or Quadrangle, of the Upper Ward, and fifty-two oaks brought from woods near Reading to make a "Round Table" within it. Then, a fortnight before Easter, the busy scene was halted. As November frosts closed in, the half-built hall stood deserted under a protective covering of tiles, and there its brief story ends. Furred robes of red velvet were made for the King to wear at a feast of the Round Table in the following spring, but if it ever took place it was the last. The Arthurian revival faded like a dream, perhaps because King Philip VI of France, jealous lest it attract foreign knighthood to England, began building a Round Table too.[2]

To glorify his intended invasion of France, King Edward III also founded in 1344 a brotherhood of Knights of St. George. Herein was the origin of "The Most Noble and amiable Company of St. George, named the Garter", but four years passed before the plan matured. In 1346 the King sailed for France, and it was as a result of his victorious campaign that the Order assumed its final and exclusive form.

On 26th August, 1346, he defeated the French at Crecy. In this battle the sixteen-year-old Prince of Wales, more famous as the Black Prince, commanded the right wing of the English forces and proved himself a brave and skilful soldier. A week later the King laid siege to Calais. While he was thus engaged the Scots took advantage of his absence to invade England. They were defeated at Neville's Cross on 17th October, 1346. Credit for inspiring this victory was accorded to the King's young cousin, Joan, Countess of Salisbury, the celebrated "Fair Maid of Kent". She was the daughter of Edward I's younger son, Edmund Earl of Kent, and wife of William Montagu, 2nd Earl of Salisbury, and was then about eighteen, exquisitely beautiful, gracious and gay, but also highly sensitive and the friend of the poor and unfortunate. Chaucer's irresistible Criseyde is accepted as the best study of her character. Before the battle she rode among the soldiers, urging them to be of good heart and "recommending them to God and Saint George". As a result of their triumph she held as her prize the Scottish king, David Bruce. He was taken to Windsor and remained a prisoner there for eleven years at a cost of 3s. 4d. a day.

The Countess was immediately summoned to join the King and Queen in their luxurious camp before Calais, where a great feast was given in her honour. Her presence dazzled the King, who was seized, in the words of Froissart, with "a sparcle of fyne love that endured longe". (The term "*fine* love" indicates ardent but unfulfilled emotion.) Calais surrendered on 2nd August, 1347, and it was at some celebration of this event that the incident occurred which traditionally led to the founding of the Order. Joan was dancing with or near the King when, to her confusion, her blue garter fell to the ground. The King picked it up and bound it around his own leg, then, turning to some courtiers who rashly ventured insinuating jests, rebuked them with the words which became the motto of the Order, *Honi soit qui mal y pense*—"Shame be to him who thinks evil of it." The Countess's garter, he added, should soon be held in supreme honour.

His return to England on 12th October was the signal for a series of triumphal tournaments. The King selected a team of twelve knights to take part with him in these events, one of whom was Joan's husband, the Earl of Salisbury. Before holding a tournament which took place at Eltham Palace not later than January 1348 he ordered for himself a surcoat, mantle and hood decorated with garters, and for his team of knights twelve blue garters embroidered with the words *Honi soit qui mal y pense*. The royal wardrobe accounts show that robes and dresses were also adorned with garters, and there is a reference to "making a bed of blue taffeta for the King, powdered with garters, containing this motto."[3]

The earliest authority for the story of the fallen garter is the historian Polydore Vergil, who came to England in 1502. In his version it was "the Queen" who had dropped it. The learned John Selden, in the seventeenth century, named its owner outright as "Joan, Countess of Kent and Salisbury". Later historians dismissed the tale as a "vain and idle romance", a mere "vulgar invention", and accused Selden of inaccuracy on the ground that Joan of Kent "was never married to the Earl of Salisbury". Lawfully she was not, but unlawfully and publicly she was his wife for several years. At the age of about twelve she had secretly married Thomas Holand, a young Lancashire squire who early distinguished himself in the French wars and then sought further fame in Prussia. In 1341, while he was still absent, the King and other relatives forced her into formal marriage with William Montagu, and Holand on his return found himself unable to claim his bride.

She was not present at Windsor on 23rd April, 1348, when St. George's Day was also Garter Day for the first time. Holand had appealed to the Pope to annul her marriage to Salisbury, and the Earl had retorted by putting her under lock and key. On 3rd May the Pope ordered her release, and in the following year she returned to her lawful husband, who became Earl of Kent and died in 1360, leaving her with a young family. She was as lovely as ever, and her widowhood was brief. A charming story relates that the Black Prince undertook to present an offer of marriage from his friend, Sir Bernard Brocas, whose name is perpetuated in the Brocas Meadow at Eton and whose majestic tomb may be seen in Westminster Abbey. To this proxy proposal the Countess responded with tears. The Prince kissed them away, and was rewarded by an intimation that her heart was already his. Their marriage on 10th October, 1361, in the chapel at Windsor made her the first English Princess of Wales. She was often called "the Queen" after Philippa's death in 1369. Polydore Vergil's account therefore represented accurately the lady who was to become the most famous in the annals of chivalry.[4]

A more sinister explanation of the story was suggested by Dr. Margaret Murray in *The Divine King in England*, published in 1954. She associated it with the "Old Religion" of witchcraft and devil-worship. The Countess's confusion, wrote Dr. Murray, arose "not from the shock to her modesty—it took more than a dropped garter to shock a lady of the fourteenth century—but the possession of that garter proved that she was not only a member of the Old Religion, but held the highest place in it." Had it been so, Joan would have been in deadly peril. Witches, then and long afterwards, were held in abhorrence and dread. A century later, in 1432, the notorious Margery Jourdemain came as a prisoner to Windsor and was later burned to death at the stake.[5] Dr. Murray concluded that by redeeming the Countess's garter King Edward III saved her life, and she expanded her theory by pointing out that the number thirteen, which originally dominated the destinies of the Order, was that of a witches' coven.

There seems no need to regard the story so unfavourably. A garter was associated with sentiments of gallantry, and knights often wore a lady's favour, such as a glove or riband, at their jousting. A replica of Joan's blue garter was being worn later in 1348 by a second team of twelve knights, led by the Black Prince. Among them was Thomas Holand. As the Earl of Salisbury belonged to the King's company, the two teams no doubt contended as rival claimants for possession of the disputed Joan.

As such they may have taken part in the tournaments held at Windsor on 24th June, 1348, the Feast of St. John the Baptist, to celebrate Queen Philippa's "up-rising" after the birth of her son William. The Scottish king was a guest at these elegant rejoicings, for which new apparel and furnishings were as usual prepared. The Queen appeared on the eve of the festival in a blue velvet mantle over a tunic "worked with birds of gold, each bird being within a circle of large pearls", and on the day itself in a red velvet robe and a gown "worked with oak and other trees, and in each tree a lion formed of large pearls."[6]

The institution of the Order took place shortly afterwards, the founder members being the twenty-four knights who had formed the two teams, with the Sovereign and the Prince of Wales bringing the number to twenty-six. The Order was exclusively military in origin, but it was also Christian, and the King's first care was to arrange for observance both of solemn ceremonial and daily worship. For these a setting of appropriate splendour had to be prepared.

By letters patent dated 6th August, 1348, he caused the chapel "wherein we were washed with the water of holy baptism, magnificently begun to the honour of St. Edward the Confessor . . . to be finished at our royal charge, to the honour of God Almighty, and of his Mother the glorious Virgin Mary, and of the Saints, George the Martyr and Edward the Confessor."[7] The re-dedicated chapel was accordingly furnished with new painted windows and Garter stalls, over which hung the swords and helms of the Knights. It was henceforth called St. George's Chapel, and a large wooden figure of England's patron saint clad in armour was placed within it.[8]

Eight priests already served the chapel. The King increased their number, forming an establishment of twelve canons under a dean, and thirteen priest-vicars, or minor canons, as they were later called. Furthermore, he elected to add twenty-six resident Poor Knights, soldiers of gentle birth who by reason of age or infirmity were grown more fit for prayer than war. To them, or rather to the few who were actually appointed, was assigned the duty of praying daily for the Sovereign and Garter Knights.

The affairs of the Order were entrusted to three officers: the Prelate, the Register and the Usher. Chief among them was the Prelate. The office was first held by William Edyngton, Bishop of Winchester, and thereafter by his successors. The Dean of Windsor usually held the office of Register in early times (and since the reign of King Charles I has always done so). The office of Usher was granted to the Gentleman Usher of the Black Rod, an official of the House of Lords, created in 1350. In the picture too were the heralds attached to the royal household, who had an important role in medieval pageantry. Their business included the organizing of state ceremonies and tournaments, in which armory (or heraldry) played its greatest part.

The first service for the King and the twenty-five other Founder Knights of the Order was held on St. George's Day 1349. Their attire was a capelike blue mantle worn over a surcoat, and a hood fastened about the shoulders. To add distinction to England's staple industry, the wool trade, the mantles were made of fine woollen cloth. On the left breast, over the wearer's heart, they bore "one large fair Garter, containing the Motto *Honi soit qui mal y pense*", and within it was embroidered the red cross of St. George on a silver ground. A train distinguished the Sovereign's mantle from those of the other Knights, who were called the Knights Companions.

For a long time after the foundation of the Order the surcoat and hood were "garnished or powdered all over with little Garters, embroidered with silk and gold, in each of which was neatly wrought the Motto." The first surcoat and hood worn by King Edward III were adorned with no less than 168 of these embroidered emblems.

The blue Garter, worn on the left leg, just below the knee, bore not only the motto but also embroidery of gold and silk. Blue and gold, colours of the arms of France, are believed to have been chosen by King Edward III in token of his claim to the French throne.

Every year the Knights of the Garter assembled at Windsor to keep the festival, and a sequence of religious and secular observances was established which is best described by the seventeenth-century historian of the Order, Elias Ashmole. He states that "the Feast of St. George takes up three days—part of the 22, all the 23, and part of the 24 days of *April*; yet the 23 day [the day of St. George] is the *Grand Day*, wherein the chiefest and most solemn Ceremonies are celebrated."[9] The festival opened on the eve with a procession from the royal apartments to the chapel. The Sovereign and Knights Companions first entered their chapter house, where they held a chapter, or general meeting, the door being guarded throughout by Black Rod. Their business done, they proceeded to their stalls in the chapel for the service called "first evensong" or "first vespers", after which the procession returned through the Castle grounds to the royal apartments for supper.

On the Grand Day, or Feast Day, the King and Knights Companions assembled early and walked in state to the chapel for mattins. After breakfast the religious rites were resumed, a grand procession being followed by high mass, at which offerings of gold and silver were made. The Company then returned to the royal apartments, where a magnificent banquet awaited them. When it was over, they went back to the chapel for the "second vespers". If the banquet had been prolonged, and dusk was falling, the processional route was lit with torches. Throughout all these ceremonies the Knights constantly wore their robes, a statutory obligation being laid on them not to put off their habit "from the beginning of first Vespers, on the eve of St. George's Day, to the second Vespers on the Morrow inclusive."

The morning of the third day directed their minds to the end of all human pomp. They walked again to the chapel in their mantles, but without any demonstrations of grandeur, to attend a requiem mass for the souls of deceased members of the Order, and on this solemn valedictory note the festival ended. With such intensity was the theme fixed in the medieval mind that whenever any Knight died the King ordered one thousand masses to be said for him.

Changes took place in the religious ritual after the Reformation, but the general procedure remained the same for nearly three centuries. For the first two hundred years the festival was held annually, except when interrupted by wars at home or abroad. There were times when the Sovereign could not be present, and on such occasions authority to conduct the proceedings was vested in a deputy. This was also commonly done when a new Knight was installed in the chapel at Windsor. "Installation feasts" were distinct from the festival and frequently took place at other times of the year, the Knight elect being fully invested and led to his stall in the course of a stately little service, during which he swore the Sacred Oath to uphold the statutes. Special chapters summoned for elections and formalities not directly connected with the festival were often held at other royal palaces. One instance was the ceremony at Greenwich on 27th March, 1504, when the Cardinal of Rouen's gift to King Henry VII of "the right leg of St. George" was received.[10]

Ladies were admitted to the Order and wore the Garter on the left arm, just below the elbow, as may be seen in effigies on their tombs. The first Lady of the Garter was Queen Philippa. The King bestowed the honour upon her in 1358. Their daughter Isabel was the second. She married Ingelram de Coucy, later a Knight of the Garter and Earl of Bedford, at Windsor on 27th July, 1365, and herself became a member of the Order in 1376, after her mother's death. These are the only appointments of Ladies of the Garter known to have been made by the Founder himself.[11]

4

"FAIR AND SUMPTUOUS WORKS"

Four years after the foundation of the Order King Edward III built a chapter house and vestry for its use, placing them on the east side of King Henry III's cloister, along the Norman cross-ditch and against the north-east corner of the chapel. They adjoined the Deanery, of which they now form part. At the same time he rebuilt in the Decorated style the stone arcade around the garth.

The canons and minor canons, like the Dean, had to be accommodated nearby, for medieval routine included eight daily services. The College of St. George, to give the community its historic name, was thus pledged to the chapel from dawn almost to the moment the curfew bell signalled the hour of retirement. The Dean and Canons, who formed the Chapter of St. George's, were men destined to hold other high offices in church and state. The canons therefore needed deputies who would be always resident. This obligation was fulfilled by the minor canons. Their special duty was to chant the services, and for this reason a fine voice has always been requisite in a minor canon.

In 1351 work began on the Canons' Cloister, a picturesque enclosure of timber-framed houses on the site of King Henry III's lodging, which had been partly destroyed by fire in 1296. As medieval clergy were not allowed to marry, the members of the College required only single apartments. The Canons' Cloister was originally built like the colleges at Oxford and Cambridge, with bachelor rooms all round the rectangular courtyard. The minor canons lived on the ground floor, and the canons in upper chambers which oversailed the cloister arcade. The canons were granted the use of the Great Hall and its kitchen, and the clerical domain was further equipped with bakehouse and mill, roasting-house and brewhouse, and a well in the eastern half of the courtyard in the Canons' Cloister. Far below, at the foot of the cliff, was placed the canons' burial ground. In 1353 steps were made down the steep side of the slope from the cloister to the cemetery. They were the forerunner of the Hundred Steps which lead down to Thames Street today.[1]

The famous William of Wykeham, chaplain to the King and later Bishop of Winchester, came to Windsor as clerk of the works in 1356 and stayed for five years. Among the buildings created by him in the Lower Ward was the square tower half-way up on the south side, which he built in 1359–60 as a detached campanile for the chapel bells. The curtain (or outer) wall between his new belfry and King Henry III Tower he lined with houses for the singing-men of the chapel.

All this part of the Lower Ward King Edward III allotted to the Dean and Canons as their freehold. They also enjoyed many other privileges, from which the needs of the body were not excluded. The clergy had to eat much fish, and in 1352 the borough of Yarmouth granted them yearly "a last of red herrings, dry and well cleaned". (The document, with its double-sided seal of green wax, is preserved among the records of St. George's Chapel.) Sometimes the herrings were lost on the way, and sometimes stolen, and often they were so unsatisfactory that in 1728 the canons decided to do without them.[2]

Venison pasty made an agreeable variation, and the early canons, it seems, used to caper forth into the Great Park with bow and arrow to shoot the royal deer. Their behaviour not unnaturally offended the King. He did not consign them to the Colehouse, like the Abbot of Chertsey, who once found himself there, along with Thomas de Hamme, Richard, "the abbotes cosin", and John, "the abbotes plomer", following a quiet hunting expedition. Instead, he compounded with the canons that provided they left his deer alone, he would give them venison twice a year. This perquisite lasted until the Second World War, when the herd of red deer was removed from Windsor.[3]

In 1356 the Black Prince crowned his military exploits by winning the battle of Poitiers. He took prisoner King John of France, who joined the Scottish king at Windsor. King John was permitted to hunt and hawk, and take what other diversion he pleased in the neighbourhood. The French lords remained in London, but visited the King whenever they pleased. David Bruce, who was married to Edward III's sister, Joanna, returned to Scotland in the following year. There is a pleasant story that while riding with Edward the two kings urged him to rebuild the Upper Ward, and he replied that he would devote their ransoms to the purpose.

Whether this is true or not, in 1359 he embarked on an ambitious programme. Two hundred years later Holinshed recorded in his chronicles:

> In this year the king set workmen in hand to take down much old buildings belonging to the castle of Windsor, and caused divers other fair and sumptuous works to be erected and set up in and about the same castle, so that almost all the masons and carpenters that were of any account within this land were sent for and employed about the same works, the overseer whereof was William Wickham, the king's chaplain, by whose advice the king took in hand to repair that place, the rather indeed because he was born there, and therefore he took great pleasure to bestow cost in beautifying it with such buildings as may appear even unto this day.

Such was the priority accorded to the royal scheme that hardly anyone else, it was said, could obtain the services of a good craftsman except in secret. There was no opting out of the King's employ, for the workmen were impressed, and measures taken to prevent defection. The sheriff of Yorkshire, according to the testimony of the Exchequer (King's Remembrancer) accounts, found it necessary to issue masons sent to Windsor with red caps and liveries, "lest they should escape from the custody of the conductor."

Hundreds of loads of stone began arriving at the Castle for the work. Some came, as in earlier days, from "Collingley". Large quantities were brought, too, from Reigate in Surrey, and at Taynton in Oxfordshire 35,000 feet of stone were quarried for the King's use. So much timber was called for that a whole wood at Farnham in Surrey was bought, and another at Shottesbrook in Berkshire. The accounts show that at least 600 oaks were worked into the new buildings. Thousands of paving-tiles, quantities of heavy ironwork and boatloads of glass appear among the purchases,

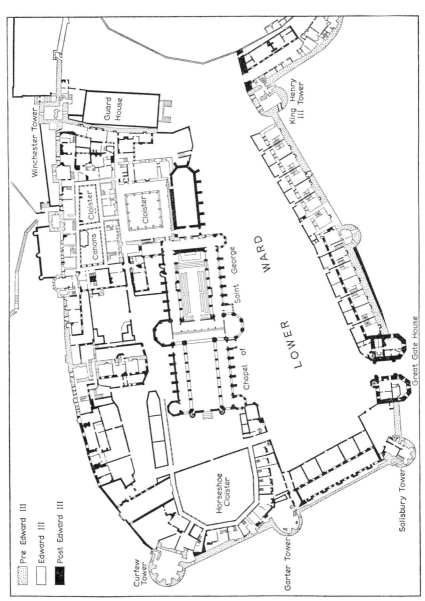

Pre Edward III

Edward III

Post Edward III

Winchester Tower

Guard House

Canons Cloister

Cloister

King Henry III Tower

Chapel of Saint George

LOWER WARD

Horseshoe Cloister

Great Gate House

Curfew Tower

Garter Tower

Salisbury Tower

Windsor Castle, Lower Ward before the nineteenth century

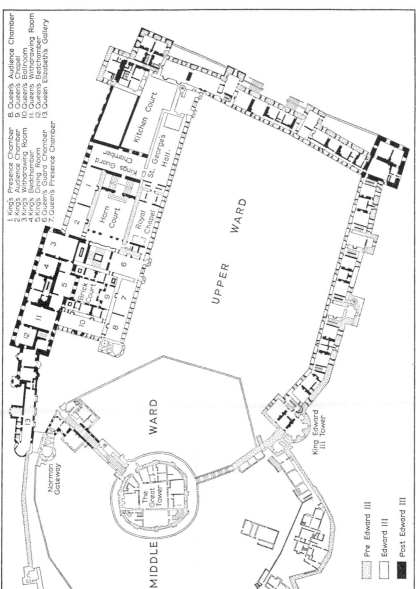

1. King's Presence Chamber
2. King's Audience Chamber
3. King's Withdrawing Room
4. King's Bedchamber
5. King's Dining Room
6. Queen's Guard Chamber
7. Queen's Presence Chamber
8. Queen's Audience Chamber
9. Queen's Chapel
10. Queen's Ballroom
11. Queen's Withdrawing Room
12. Queen's Bedchamber
13. Queen Elizabeth's Gallery

UPPER WARD

MIDDLE WARD

Norman Gateway

The Great Tower

King Edward III Tower

Kitchen Court

Kings Guard Chamber

St. George's Hall.

Horn Court

Royal Chapel

Brick Court

Pre Edward III
Edward III
Post Edward III

Windsor Castle, Middle and Upper Wards up to about 1790

and from Nottingham in 1367 came a reredos of alabaster which required eighty horses and ten carts with twenty men to transport it. Alabaster was a material newly come into fashion, very few works having been executed in it apart from some royal tombs. It was valued less for its beauty than for the ease with which it could be sculptured when fresh from the mine, and according to contemporary practice the reredos, which was placed in the chapel in the Lower Ward, was gilded and painted.[4]

According to tradition, William of Wykeham directed the work from Winchester Tower, which he had already rebuilt in 1356-8 and which was long known as "Wykeham's Tower". A story popular in later years says that he inscribed on an interior wall the words *Hoc fecit Wykeham*—"Wykeham built this". William Camden, the sixteenth-century antiquarian, recorded it in his *Britannia*:

> It was alledged by his enemies who envied him, as if Wickham arrogated to himself all the honor of the building. The King resenting this, and reproaching him with it, he replied that he had not assumed to himself the honour of such a magnificent and royal building, but that he owed his own advancement to the building. "I," said he, "did not make this Castle, but this Castle made me, and raised me from a low rank to the king's favour, to wealth and honor."[5]

Five centuries later, when Sir Jeffry Wyatville was restoring the Castle for King George IV, he too lived in Winchester Tower, and finding the inscription almost obliterated, renewed it on the north front.

The new palace was built with handsome ground-floor vaults which still exist in the present State Entrance Hall and part of the kitchen quarters. In plan it preserved the ancestral pattern, the royal apartments being grouped as before around the two cloisters or herb gardens, with the kitchen and kitchen court on the east. A floor of marble was laid in the covered alleys of both the King's and the Queen's cloister. The herbs which grew in the garths of these cloisters were not the kind which live in jars on the kitchen shelf today, but sweet-scented flowers—roses, violets, gillyflowers, lavender and a host of others. Our ancestors used them to freshen their undrained homes and ward off plague, and the royal household included a herb-woman whose duty it was to strew them daily in the royal apartments and chapel. The way to the two cloisters from the Quadrangle was through an arched state entrance flanked with two towers. It replaced a gateway with an iron portcullis, and was called *La Spicerie*, a name which probably derived from the herb gardens.

Although the rooms opened one into another, and the various pieces of furniture do not suggest much comfort, the seats being benches or stools, and the tables mere boards laid on trestles, the new palace displayed a degree of stylishness superior to anything recorded before. There are references to a "bath-house", and Queen Philippa's four rooms, which together with her chapel were grouped around the smaller cloister, included a "Hall of Mirrors" and a "daunsyngchambre". The graceful pointed windows of the King's and Queen's apartments contained 923 feet of coloured glass, with borders of the King's arms. The vivid effect of the new buildings is illustrated by the decorations of King John's Tower, which formed part of the royal lodging. It was erected in 1362–3 at the south-west corner of the block, and was then called "La Rose" on account of the rose-embossed ceiling which still remains in its principal chamber. Colours of red, green and blue were bought for it, together with "1,400 of gold leaf at 6s. a hundred".

Among the most important of the King's "fair and sumptuous works" was St. George's Hall, which he built along the south side of the Kitchen Court, in line with a new private chapel at the western end. This lofty room, lit with pointed windows overlooking the Quadrangle, was the scene of Garter banquets, and "had on the dais at its upper end three tables, placed apparently end to end, on four trestles, and in the body five tables down each side, with an eleventh table, probably for carving at."[6] The south and east fronts of the Upper Ward shared in the reconstruction. In 1367 King Henry II's shallow watch towers and connecting walls were lined with residential chambers, and a year later the Rubbish Gate was rebuilt on the plan of the other gatehouses, with a portcullis and a prison room above.

While their new palace was being prepared the King and Queen went to live in the Round Tower, which had already undergone change. Within the ring of stone a two-storeyed timber residence enclosed the courtyard, making it into a trim little square. The accounts show that 170 oaks were used for the massive framework of this building, which was begun in 1354 and included a great hall or armoury. The arrow slits in the outer wall of the keep had been replaced by pointed windows opening on to far-distant views, and more windows overlooked the courtyard tucked away inside, where rain-water cisterns were installed to eke out the supply of water from the well. To increase the effect of light the rooms were whitewashed before the King and Queen moved in. Probably the only sound that broke the stillness of their high retreat was a great clock placed there in 1351. It does not appear to have had a face, but it had a bell which chimed the hours.

King Edward III was able to turn the Round Tower to domestic use because the need for a militant purpose had declined. At the same time, he could not afford to neglect his key defences, and the works begun in 1359 included the rebuilding of the Inner Gatehouse, now miscalled the Norman Gateway. Its vaulted passage and twin drum-towers were erected in 1359–60 over dungeons cut in the chalk rock. At the entrance the grooves for the heavy portcullis may still be seen, and overhead gape three mouths through which unpleasant liquids such as boiling oil might be poured on to enemy heads. Entirely new was the little square tower along the twelfth-century wall adjoining the Norman Gateway. It was built in about 1358, and used in later times as an ammunition store or "powder tower". To this it owes its modern name of the Magazine Tower.

The King endowed the Castle with a further amenity by enclosing "The Park of Lydecroft" on the north side. He bought the land bearing this name from the Abbot of Reading in 1368 and it formed the first tract of the "Little Park" which presently embraced the upper part of the Castle. He also enlarged the Great Park by taking in the manor of Wychmere at Old Windsor, and thus brought its green acreage nearer to the extent familiar today.

Ardent as was his devotion to Windsor, the King did not elect to found a royal burial place there. Even if he ever thought of doing so, Queen Philippa's preference for Westminster prevailed. Froissart, her countryman and faithful secretary, touchingly records the wish she made when dying. "The good Queen of England, that so many good deeds had done in her time . . . fell sick in the Castle of Wyndesore, the which sickness continued on her so long, that there was no remedy but death. When she knew this, she took the King's right hand and said, 'Sir, now I pray you, at our departing, that you will grant me three desires.' " One was that he would be buried beside her in Westminster Abbey, and the King, weeping, gave the required promise.

Then, continues Froissart, she made the sign of the cross and "yielded up the spirit, the which I believe surely the holy angels received with great joy up to heaven. Thus the good Queen of England died, in the year of Our Lord 1369, in the vigil of Our Lady in the middle of August."[7]

5

LANCASTER AND YORK

Geoffrey Chaucer, the first great English poet, drew inspiration from Windsor. He was the devoted servant of Princess Joan and her son, King Richard II, and many references to celebrations of the Order of the Garter have been traced in his poems. The "Knight's Tale" and the "Squire's Tale", both of which are included in the *Canterbury Tales*, are believed to be among those which were intended for Garter festivals.[1]

On St. George's Day 1374 King Edward III granted him a daily pitcher of wine. King Richard II, who succeeded his grandfather three years later, at the age of ten, allowed him to exchange it for money, probably in acknowledgment of the poet's graceful devotion to his beautiful mother. This was only a week before she was admitted to the Order on St. George's Day 1378. In preference to blue, scarlet robes lined with fur were usually issued to medieval Ladies of the Garter, of whom she was the third, and so she appeared in the chapel at Windsor in "a mantle of scarlet covered with garters in blue taffeta".[2]

Chaucer was clerk of works to Richard II, who in 1390 appointed him for three years to restore "our collegiate chapel of St. George within our Castle of Windsor, which is threatened with ruin and on the point of falling to the ground, unless it be quickly repaired." By that time Princess Joan was dead, and in 1394 Richard's first wife, Anne of Bohemia, died too. His second wife, Isabel, daughter of King Charles VI of France, was barely eight years old at the time of their marriage in 1396. A parrot sent to her by the Pope is the first known pet to make its appearance in the palace at Windsor. It was a rare possession, and the child Queen probably preferred it to the frontlet of rubies and pearls which accompanied it.[3] She seems to have been an affectionate and sensitive little girl, and a charming devotion grew up between her and the King who was her husband in name only.

As sovereign, Richard was becoming increasing unpopular. The violent ending of his reign was foreshadowed by an event which took place at Windsor on 29th April, 1398. It was the "Court of Chivalry" appointed to judge between his cousin, Henry Duke of Hereford, later Duke of Lancaster, and Thomas Mowbray, Duke of Norfolk, who had accused Hereford of treason. King Richard heard the case himself, seated on a dais in the Quadrangle. A decision to refer the quarrel to the arbitrament of single combat at Coventry on 16th September, 1398, was revoked at the last minute by the King, who banished both Dukes from England. They took their leave of him at Windsor on 3rd October. Norfolk died in Venice, but Hereford returned within a year to crush his cousin and to be accepted by Parliament as King Henry IV.

In connection with the Garter festival of 1399 King Richard "proclaimed through his realm and in Scotland that a grand tournament would be held at Windsor by forty knights and forty squires, clothed in green, with the device of a white falcon, against all comers." When it took place, either on St. George's Day or on 24th April, the eleven-year-old Queen was present, in resplendent robes, and a host of ladies with her, but despite all the attractions the attendance was poor.[4] On 25th April the King rode out "in fatal pomp" to visit Ireland. As the hour of his departure drew near, the little Queen became frantic with grief. He petted her, and arranged that she should have a new governess. The Lady de Couci, who had accompanied her from France, was proving too extravagant and imprudent to have charge of such a personage as the Queen of England. She had eighteen horses and employed as many dress-makers, embroiderers and furriers as the King and Queen themselves. The King decided to pack her off home, and appointed his niece, Eleanor Holand, widow of his cousin, Roger Mortimer, 4th Earl of March, to the office of lady of honour and governess.

This done, he took the Queen affectionately by the hand and led her through the Castle grounds to the chapel, where the canons "brought St. George's mantle to the King, and the King wore it over his shoulders, as is the custom of the country." When the canons had "chaunted very sweetly", and the King himself had chanted a collect and made his offering, he took Isabel in his arms and kissed her many times. The poor little Queen began to cry again, imploring him not to leave her, and the King, his own eyes full of tears, replied that she should follow him. Then they went to the Deanery for wine and sweetmeats, and before mounting his horse he lifted her once more in his arms and kissed her at least ten times, saying "Adieu, Madame, until we meet again." With that they parted, and the historian who described the woeful scene added, "Great pity was it, for never saw they each other more."[5]

On 30th September, 1399, Richard was deposed by the cousin he had banished, and in the following February he died. The new King's reign was menaced by threats against his life, some of which were planned to take effect at Windsor. Sir Bernard Brocas, son of the Black Prince's friend, was among several plotters executed for scheming to assassinate him and his sons early in 1400. The deed was to have been done at a tournament arranged at the Castle for Twelfth Night. A few months later a weapon called a "caltrap" was said to have been discovered in the royal bed at Windsor. It was made of iron, "with three branches so sharp that whenever the King had turned him it should slay him." Rumour gave out that it had been put there by a member of Queen Isabel's household.[6]

Henry claimed the throne through his father, John of Gaunt, Duke of Lancaster, fourth son of King Edward III, but he had two young cousins whose claim challenged his own. They were Edmund Mortimer, 5th Earl of March, and his brother, Roger, sons of Queen Isabel's governess, Countess Eleanor, and grandsons of Philippa, Countess of March, the daughter of Edward III's third son, Lionel of Antwerp, Duke of Clarence. When Henry IV deposed Richard II they were no more than children, and the new King treated them kindly, bringing them up with his own younger son and daughter, but keeping watchful custody of them. They were staying at Windsor when a daring plot was made to kidnap them on the night of 13th February, 1405, the instigator being named as their cousin, Constance of York, Lady Despencer. The story is narrated by John

Capgrave, an Augustinian friar who died in 1464. "In the fest of Christis Nativite, certeyn men let make keyis of many dores in the castelle of Wyndesore. Ther entered thei by nyte, and took the eyres [heirs] of March, and let them owte. Summe say her purpos was to lede them into Wales, that, be the power of Glendor, thei myte rejoyse the crowne, as the rite eyeres of Yngland. But thei were pursewed, and some were slayn and summe fled." The boys were brought back, and the smith who made the keys had first his hands and then his head cut off.[7]

Queen Isabel left Windsor early in King Henry VI's reign and lived for a time at Sonning, higher up the Thames. Attempts were made to persuade her to marry the new Prince of Wales, later King Henry V, but this she obstinately refused to do. In 1401 she returned to Paris, a pathetic little figure robbed of her jewels and dowry. Shakespeare in *Richard II* sums up her exit from England:

> The Queen to France: from whence, set forth in pomp,
> She came adorned hither like sweet May;
> Sent back like Hallowmass, or shortest day.

She did remarry, for she became the wife of Charles, Duke of Orleans, only to die in childbirth in 1409. When Henry V renewed Edward III's claim to the crown of France, Charles of Orleans, the head and general of the French nationals, was among his opponents at the battle of Agincourt in 1415. He was captured by the victorious English and taken to Windsor, where he remained for some time. A poet of restrained and courtly grace, he composed a number of ballads during the twenty-five years of his imprisonment in England. One is a lament for a dead princess, so full of tender remembrance that it can commemorate none but the lost Isabel.[8]

There were other royal prisoners at Windsor in this springtime of poetry. King James I of Scotland, captured at sea in 1405, when he was a child, was moved there after the accession of King Henry V in 1413. He was shown every courtesy and according to tradition had apartments in the Devil's Tower. It overlooks the south side of the Round Tower moat, which being always dry had early become a green wilderness. In 1319 five women were paid one penny a day to mow the nettles. Soon afterwards, if poets are to be believed, it was trimmed and made into a garden. Chaucer probably had the Round

Tower and its moat in mind when he wrote in the "Knight's Tale" of Palamon, imprisoned in

> The great tower, that was so thick and strong,
> Which of the castle was the chief dungeon.

From his window Palamon saw and fell in love with Emily as she walked below in a garden "full of branches green".

In about 1423, while still at Windsor, the young Scottish king wrote a poem called "The Kingis Quair" (the word Quair means a book). This is believed to record a love story in real life, for the verses indicate that he first saw his future Queen as she walked in the moat garden, and straightway fell in love with her, like Chaucer's Palamon with Emily. The girl who captured his heart was Lady Jane Beaufort, daughter of the Earl of Somerset. His description of the moat accords with Chaucer's, and is still more interesting because he gives added details. The picture he draws in "The Kingis Quair" is of a formal garden, with trees and hawthorn thickets where nightingales sang.

A ruler who visited Windsor not as a captive but a guest of state was the Emperor Sigismund, King of Hungary and later of Bohemia, brother-in-law of the dead Richard II. An alliance with him against France formed part of King Henry V's skilful diplomacy, and the Emperor was elected a Knight of the Garter in 1415. He was not the first foreign sovereign to become a member of the Order. As early as 1400 King Henry IV had conferred the Garter on King John I of Portugal, husband of his sister Philippa, and the inclusion of foreign rulers dated from that time. When it was not possible for them to come to England, the insignia was carried oversea by officers of the Order, and the new royal Knight was installed in the chapel at Windsor by proxy.

Sigismund was among the kings who were personally installed. He came to England for the ceremony in 1416, bringing with him as an offering to the chapel the "Heart of St. George". The Chronicle of London describes his arrival: "This yere, the vij day of Maij, came themperour of Almayne, Segismundus, to London; and the fest of Seint George was deferrid til his comyng, and then solempnely holden at Wyndisore; and at the procession the King went on the upperside of themperour and so alle the masse tyme stode in the

higher place, and at mete he sate on the right side of themperour."
According to the chronicle known as the Black Book of the Order, "the
Finery of the Guests, the Order of the Servants, the Variety of the
Courses, the Invention of the Dishes, with the other Things delightful to the Sight and Taste, whoever should endeavour to describe,
could never do it with Justice." Fortunately an attempt was made to
detail some of the splendours of the occasion. At the Garter banquet
elaborate confections called 'soteltes" or "subtleties" were served
which so effectively combined culinary and artistic cunning that they
inspired a particular account. "And the first sotelte," says the
Chronicle of London, "was oure Lady armyng Seint George, and an
angel doyng on his spures; the second sotelte was Seint George
ridyng and fightyng with the dragon, with his spere in his hand; the
third sotelte was a castel, and Seint George, and the kynges doughter
ledyng the lambe in at the castle gates. And all these soteltes were
served to the emperor and to the Kyng, and no ferther."[9]

The Heart of St. George, which the Emperor brought in a silver-
gilt reliquary, was placed with other treasures in the chapel.
Thereafter, whenever the Sovereign and Knights Companions were
present at service, each in turn reverently kissed the relic, which was
offered to them "decently wrapped up in knapkins and coverings".
This custom was observed as late as King Henry VIII's reign.

At the time of the Emperor's visit King Henry V was approaching
the peak of his renown. In 1420 he was recognized as heir and regent
of France and married King Charles VI's youngest daughter,
Princess Catherine. After her coronation at Westminster in 1421 he
took his wife to Windsor, where memories of her dead sister, little
Queen Isabel, still lingered. The apartments of the King and his new
consort were of rare beauty, being hung with tapestries, many of
which were brilliantly embroidered in gold. They included "a gold
arras of St. George, a gold arras of The Three Kings of Cologne, and
a gold arras of the Salutation of Our Lady," all large enough to cover
the wall of a room. In this graceful setting the royal pair spent happy
hours "in minstrelsy and song".[10]

Queen Catherine remained at the Castle when her husband
returned to France, and on 6th December, 1421, gave birth to a
prince. There is an old story that when the King heard the news he
said to his chamberlain, "I, Henry, born at Monmouth, shall small

time reign and much get; and Henry born at Windsor shall long reign and all lose."[11]

Bitter truth attended the prophecy. On 3rd August, 1422, King Henry V died in France and was succeeded by the baby son lying in his cradle at Windsor. During his reign the English were driven out of France, and in 1455 there began at home the series of civil conflicts which Sir Walter Scott named the "Wars of the Roses". In this fratricidal struggle, notorious for its savagery, the gentle and pious Henry VI lost his throne, bringing to an end the kings of the Lancastrian line. The powerful figure who emerged from it was Edward Duke of York, great-grandson of King Edward III's fifth son, Edmund of Langley, Duke of York, and a descendant through his grandmother, Anne Mortimer, sister of the little "heirs of March", of Lionel Duke of Clarence. He was recognized as King Edward IV on 4th March, 1461, ten years before the death of his deposed rival. The warring roses represented diversities in their ancestral badge. They stemmed from the golden rose of King Edward I, whose descendants differenced the tincture, the House of Lancaster bearing a red rose as badge, and the House of York a white one.

In the years beforehand, King Henry VI put into practical effect the guiding vision of his life, which prompted him to see in service to Church and State the noblest pursuit open to human endeavour. He was only eighteen when he founded Eton College in 1441, placing it on the Buckinghamshire side of the Thames, where its chapel holds dominion in the valley overlooked by the Castle. It was appropriate that he, who was born on the feast of St. Nicholas, patron saint of children, should care so especially for education and the welfare of the young, but sentiment alone was not the animating factor. He deliberately planned Eton and King's College, Cambridge, to match William of Wykeham's two foundations, Winchester and New College, Oxford.[12]

The full title of Eton College is "The King's College of Our Lady of Eton beside Windsor". It serves as a reminder that from boyhood King Henry had especially reverenced the feast of the Assumption of the Virgin Mary. The three silver lilies which together with a gold fleur-de-lis and lion make up the arms of Eton confirm his devotion, white lilies being the emblem of Our Lady.

From his windows at Windsor he could see the work in progress.

Stone to build the chapel was brought from Caen in Normandy, and floated up the river to a wharf below Windsor Bridge. Meanwhile, a temporary chapel was erected "within the new church above the high altar", and roofed with tiles. A drawing on a leaf of an early fifteenth-century manuscript of Ranulf Higden's *Polychronicon* in Eton College Library shows the King and his young Queen, Margaret of Anjou, whom he married in April 1445, attending a service there. In the background appears the earliest picture of the Castle, a topographical view which is the more important because of its skilled and painstaking delineation.

The school was built on the convenient collegiate plan, with the chapel standing along one side of a court or quadrangle and the communal apartments on the other three sides. Bricks for the scholastic buildings were made at the nearby hamlet called "le slough", on the highway from London to Bath, where they were sometimes burned with thorns and sometimes with coal. The latter cost 7s. a chaldron, which was over a ton. A labourer named William Slotte received 6s. 8d. for digging a path for carriage of bricks along the road between Slough and Eton.

During the remaining years of peace, while the College was gradually taking form, the King found happiness in following its life and work. The earliest scholars of Eton, like the generations that succeeded them, liked to wander in the Castle grounds, and it is recorded by John Blacman, chaplain and later Carthusian monk, Henry's first biographer, that sometimes they met their royal founder. Always "he would advise them concerning the path of virtue, and with his words he would also give them money to attract them, saying: 'Be you good boys, gentle and teachable, and servants of the Lord.' " If, as is more than likely, these lads raced up to "le Doungion", which was the contemporary name for the Round Tower, they ascended steps similar in plan to those which are thronged in summertime today. The covered staircase, though restored in the course of succeeding centuries, survives as it was rebuilt in 1439–40 by King Henry VI.[13]

The usurper of his throne, King Edward IV, "the first English Prince of the Renaissance type", offers a contrasting study in calibre. Formed by nature for social and intellectual pleasures, and the pursuit of outdoor activities, his taste was for kingly display. The regal elegance he introduced was derived from the Court of Charles the Bold (or Rash), Duke of Burgundy, who in 1468 married his sister, Margaret of York. It was the most luxurious in the western world, and since the reign of Charles's father, Philip the Good, had set the pattern for Europe. King Edward had an ardent influence in his beautiful and worldly wife, Elizabeth Woodville, widow of Sir John Grey of Groby and niece, on her mother's side, of the head of an historic French house, Peter of Luxemburg, Count of St. Pol and Brienne, who seceded to Burgundy. Their elaborate etiquette governed Court life for more than a century, though the English monarchy never allowed itself to be enslaved by such extravagant forms as developed in Spain and France.

In September 1470, when briefly deprived of his throne by the Lancastrians, King Edward took refuge at Alkmaar in Holland. With his brother-in-law's assistance, he returned to England in March 1471, having been in the meantime magnificently entertained at The Hague and at Bruges by Louis de Bruges, Seigneur de la Gruthuyse and Prince of Steenhuyse, Lieutenant-General of Holland, Zealand and Friesland. A visit by this nobleman to England in September 1472, when he came on an embassy from Duke Charles, gave the King an opportunity to repay his friend's hospitality. Edward's possession of the crown, strengthened by the birth of a son and the death of King Henry VI, was by this time secure, and the full procedure ordained for state visits was set in motion at Windsor. One of the royal heralds, Bluemantle Pursuivant, wrote an account of it.[14]

After a triumphal journey from Dover to London, the guest rode on with his son and train of attendants to his reunion with the King. The Lord Chamberlain, William Lord Hastings, conducted him from the Castle gate to the royal presence, and then led him to two chambers on the further side of the Quadrangle, which had been imposingly prepared for his initial reception. They were hung with tapestries and furnished with beds of state. After Lord Gruthuyse had supped he was again escorted to the King, who took him to the Queen's chamber. Here a gracious but merry scene presented itself. The Queen and some of her ladies were playing at "morteaux", a game like bowls, while others were trying their skill with the "Closheys of yvery", or nine-pins. In the background the royal minstrels were playing for those who preferred to dance, and the King claimed as partner his eldest daughter, Elizabeth, and trod a happy measure with her. They must have made a delightful picture—the tall, handsome King leading out the fair-haired Princess aged seven.

The formal ceremonies began next morning. The King took his guest to the private chapel to hear mass, which was "melodiously sung". Then he presented him with a gold cup adorned with pearls and surmounted by a great sapphire on the cover. Inside was a large piece of a "unicorn's horn", which was regarded as a protection against poison. After breakfast they rode out for a day's hunting in the Little Park, which the King had enlarged by the purchase in 1466 of the high ground to the east of the Castle. While the company assembled in the Quadrangle, the baby Prince of Wales was brought out and introduced by his father to Lord Gruthuyse. In the Park the King gave his guest his own horse, a hobby, and a crossbow in a velvet-lined case embroidered with the royal arms, together with a set of gilt-headed arrows.

It was late afternoon when the day's sport ended, but the King wanted Lord Gruthuyse to see the royal garden and "Vineyard of Pleasure". The latter was apparently considered an indispensable adjunct to the Castle, since grapes had already grown there for three centuries. It was well tended and produced about thirty tons of wine a year. After sauntering among the vines in the September dusk the King and his friend parted and each went to his own apartments to hear evensong. They met again at a banquet in the Queen's dining-hall. At the table of state sat the King and Queen and Princess Elizabeth, with their distinguished guest, the King's sister, Anne, Duchess of Exeter, the Queen's sister, Katherine, Duchess of Buckingham and her husband, and Elizabeth, Countess Rivers, her sister-in-law. Lower down the table were "divers ladyes and certeyn nobles of the Kinges owen Courte", including Lord Hastings and Lord Berners, Constable of the Castle. Seated at another table was "a great Vue" of ladies, and in an outer room the Queen's gentlemen facing the attendants of the foreign visitor.

Dancing followed until "about ix of the clocke", when the King and Queen, with all the Queen's ladies and gentlewomen flocking in radiant procession after them, led Lord Gruthuyse to "iii chaumbres of Pleasance, all hanged w^t Whyte Sylke and lynnen clothe, and alle the Floures covered w^t Carpettes." In the first there was prepared for the visitor a bed of softest down, with sheets and pillows of the Queen's own choosing, a coverlet of cloth of gold furred with ermine, a golden canopy and silken curtains. The second room held another state bed, and in the third the company discovered two baths draped with tents of white cloth. Here the King and Queen left Lord Gruyhuyse with the Lord Chamberlain, who undressed him and having escorted him to one bath, himself stepped into the other. When they tired of lying in the scented water they were served with green ginger, sugared sweets, syrups and spiced wine. Lord Gruthuyse then retired to his ermine-covered bed and the Lord Chamberlain to the one in the adjoining room.

The ambassador's visit to Windsor ended next day, but the King's favour was not exhausted. On 13th October he created his friend and former protector Earl of Winchester, a title borne in turn by Lord Gruthuyse's son and two grandsons, the last of whom died without male issue in 1572.

Garter ceremonial, which had suffered during the Wars of the Roses, recovered its prestige during King Edward IV's reign. It gave him scope for effect, and he increased the number of its officers to five. The Prelate, the Register and the Usher, it will be remembered, dated from the foundation. In 1415 King Henry V created Garter King of Arms, who ranked first among the royal officers of arms— that is, the kings of arms, heralds and pursuivants who today form the College of Arms. To these four officers King Edward IV added the Chancellor in 1475.

Since the ceremonies lasted for three days, and the officers were attended by many servants, they enjoyed the use of residences in the Castle. The Bishop of Winchester, as Prelate, stayed at Winchester Tower, which takes its name from this ancient association. As a further mark of dignity he was allowed a court livery for himself and his servants, equal to the rank of an earl, whenever he went to Windsor.[15] Garter Tower was allotted to Garter King of Arms, and Salisbury Tower to the Chancellor (who was originally always the Bishop of Salisbury). The Gentleman Usher of the Black Rod had a lodging, now gone, which stood between King Henry III Tower and the Devil's Tower, immediately within the indented wall.

The Knights of the Garter no longer wore mantles made of woollen cloth. A change to blue velvet lined with white silk had been noted as early as the beginning of King Henry VI's reign, and so their apparel brought fresh richness of effect to Garter processions. At the celebration at Windsor in 1476 King Edward IV found a further means of glorifying the spectacle. Instead of walking to and from the chapel, he and the Knights Companions went "all mounted on horseback in their habits of blew".

On the Grand Day, which was Sunday, they breakfasted after mattins with the Dean, and then returned to their stalls in the choir for high mass. At this point a second royal cavalcade approached the chapel. The Queen, Princess Elizabeth and the Duchess of Suffolk, sister of the King, who were Ladies of the Garter, rode with a high-born company, including the fifteen-year-old Cicely, Marchioness of Dorset, wife of the Queen's son by her first marriage, to join the Sovereign and the Knights at mass. The royal ladies wore "a livery of murrey [dark red] embroidered with garters." They did not occupy stalls, but were placed in the rood loft which separated the choir from the nave.[16]

Chaucer's repair of the chapel nearly a century earlier, though thorough, did not secure it from eventual destruction. Already King Edward IV had decided to build the present St. George's Chapel to the west of it. A desire to surpass the achievement of King Henry VI at Eton probably helped to dictate the grandeur of his vision. In the early years of his reign he had come near to suppressing the unfinished College of Eton and annexing its property to the College of St. George's. The bells and ornaments of the chapel were actually removed to the Castle in 1465, but after King Henry's death more generous impulses prevailed and they were returned, and work on the chapel resumed. Henceforth, King Edward found sufficient satisfaction in directing his mind to his own great foundation at Windsor.

The earliest notice of his intention is in letters patent of 19th February, 1473, appointing Richard Beauchamp, Bishop of Salisbury, master and surveyor of the works "both of the chapel within the Castle of Windsor, and of divers other works there, to be newly constructed." On 12th June, 1475, he empowered the Bishop to remove any buildings which stood in the way of the projected chapel.[17] This applied to the Great Hall. Its southern end abutted on the plan of the nave, and part of it at least was demolished. The royal withdrawing-room against the north wall seems to have been allotted to the choir school of St. George's, and much later, probably in the eighteenth century, was embodied in a large house where its medieval features were for many years lost to view.[18] The brick front of this cloistral house, which is immediately opposite the north door of St. George's Chapel, discloses a fragment of the wall of the Great Hall. The well sunk in 1252 continued in use and was later turned into a pump, which is still to be seen on the lawn under the chapel wall.

The plan of the new chapel extended from the arcaded west front of the old one, which became its eastern end. The double doors leading into Henry III's chapel henceforth served as the east entrance, opening into the ambulatory behind the high altar. They were covered with elaborate scroll-work in wrought iron, which being gilded stood out in arresting relief against the scarlet gesso on the woodwork, and this striking scheme, hitherto an exterior effect, now brought vivid beauty to the interior of the new building. In time the finish wore away, but in 1955 the gold and scarlet were renewed, so that the doorway might fittingly rank as the Sovereign's private entrance into the chapel.

King Edward IV's design included the Horseshoe Cloister around the west front. It was erected between 1478 and 1481, when the choir was steadily rising but the nave had still not progressed beyond the foundations. The semi-circle of two-storeyed brick and timber houses provided new homes for the minor canons, who for some reason had left the Canons' Cloister in 1409. They continued to take their meals together in a nearby hall erected for the purpose in 1415.

The houses of the Horseshoe Cloister fill the space between the chapel and the western wall of the Castle, hemming in the Curfew Tower, which can be reached only by the covered alley around their inner curve. While the cloister was taking shape, the tower was being filled with a massively constructed timber belfry and surmounted by a lead-covered bell-cage and dome. In about 1479 the chapel bells were carried there from William of Wykeham's tower on the south side of the Lower Ward. There were eight of them (as there are still), the two largest being named Mary and Jesus, and the others George, Edward, John, Aston, Wyron and the "cope bell".

If the glory of the King's scheme was inspired by a wish to outdo

King Henry VI, it was also attributable to a desire for a burial place where he would be the first to lie, and which he could furnish with such solemn splendours as he thought fit. When he made his will on 20th June, 1475, only eight days after issuing the grant to Bishop Beauchamp, he directed that he was to be laid in the new chapel, "lowe in the grounde", and added instructions which show that he intended his tomb to form a small chapel in the north choir aisle.[19] To enclose it a pair of iron gates flanked by two towers were wrought by the King's celebrated smith, John Tresilian, in about 1482. Overhead a room was built which was intended to serve as his chantry or private memorial chapel.

Like King Henry VI, he did not see his cherished scheme fulfilled. When he died on 9th April, 1483, the choir was ready for use, but the walls of the nave reached only to the level of the window sills, and so remained for twenty years. Work gradually ceased after the King's burial, which took place in accordance with his wishes. He died at Westminster and his long funeral procession travelled by road to Windsor, taking two days to complete the journey. The coffin was attended by every token of majesty, and upon it lay a figure resembling the King, wearing his royal robes and the crown of England, and carrying the orb and sceptre.

The King was buried with sombre pomp in the bay on the north side of the high altar. Tresilian's gates, gloriously gilded, were set across the aisle, and over his tomb was hung his "coat of mail, covered with crimson velvet, and thereon the arms of France and England quarterly, embroidered with pearl and gold, interwoven with divers rubies." The precious trophy remained there until the chapel was plundered by Cromwell's men in 1642.

The gates were spared and were standing in front of the vault when it was accidentally opened in 1789, during the repaving of the choir aisle. The King's coffin was found, and beside it that of his Queen, Elizabeth Woodville, whose burial at 11 o'clock on a summer night in 1492 reveals a humbling contrast with the regality she had once observed. Her body was conveyed by water and carried through the Little Park, and at her own request placed in the grave without "rynging of any belles . . . or solempne dirge or masse". The lofty monument which marks their resting place was erected in 1790. The gates, which are of surpassing delicacy, though no longer gilded, were moved at the same time to their present position behind the monument, on the north side of the high altar.

The King's chantry provided for the appointment of "two select Priests to offer in particular for his Soul", and they were described in the Black Book as "now good old Men, honest, learned, and entirely given up to their Founder, beside whose Tomb they Morning and Evening perform divine Offices", carrying out their duties "in a solemn, leisurely and pious Manner, as if they had nothing to mind but the procuring of their Founder's happiness." Several noble benefactors followed the royal example and endowed chantries in St. George's. One of the historic shrines so established is in the north choir aisle, close to King Edward IV's tomb. It is the Hastings Chapel, and within it lies that same William, first Lord Hastings, who received Louis de la Gruthuyse in 1472. He was a Knight of the Garter and a trusted friend of the King, whom he outlived by only two months. In the troubled weeks following Edward's death Hastings supported the boy King, Edward V, against his uncle, Richard Duke of Gloucester, who had made himself protector of the realm. On 13th June, 1483, he was present in the Council Chamber of the Tower of London when Gloucester entered. The Duke accused Hastings of plotting against his life, and declared that he would not sit down to dinner until his enemy's head was off.

Bishop John Morton, later Archbishop of Canterbury, who was present and was himself arrested, later described the scene to Sir Thomas More. He in turn recorded Morton's story, and his words provide an account of Hastings' swift and violent end. "So was he brought forth into the green beside the chapel within the Tower and his head laid down upon a long log of timber and there stricken off."[20]

The little King and his brother, Richard Duke of York, both of whom vanished so mysteriously in the Tower of London a few months later, made no mark on Windsor history. Nor did their uncle, who became King Richard III, play any memorable part except by his removal of King Henry VI's body from Chertsey to St. George's Chapel. The contemporary account of John Rous, the antiquary of Warwick, says that the King's body was taken out of his grave in the abbey church of Chertsey in August 1484, and honourably received in the new collegiate church of the Castle of Windsor.

It was reinterred in a bay on the south side of the high altar, the stone vaulting above the tomb being painted with the various badges used by King Henry VI, beautifully displayed on a blue ground. At the time of its translation, Rous continues, "that same body was very odoriferous, not indeed from spices employed when it was buried by his enemies and tormentors. And it was in great part uncorrupt, everywhere entire as to the beard and hair, with the face as usual, though somewhat sunken, with a more meagre appearance than ordinary. And there abounded forthwith miracles declaring the King's sanctity, as is sufficiently evident from the written accounts there."

The power of miraculous intervention ascribed to King Henry was prompted not only by the saintliness of his life, but by the pitiful manner of his death. It was generally accepted that he had been murdered, and his posthumous reputation was that of a martyr as well as a model of goodness. Possession of his body was therefore a valuable gain for St. George's Chapel, which drew large revenues from the offerings of pilgrims attracted to the various shrines. The tomb of "Holy King Henry" was venerated by travellers from every part of England, especially Devonshire and Cornwall. They offered tapers and wax images at the grave, where relics of the King were preserved and eagerly sought. A red velvet hat which had been his was supposed to cure any illness in the head when worn for a short time. A chip of his bedstead was also among the articles which together with costly jewels and ornaments covered the tomb. The very sheets in which he had lain when he died in the Tower of London on 21st May, 1471, were obtained for St. George's.

Such were the miracles attributed to the dead King that in 1498 Westminster Abbey tried to obtain his body, but it never left Windsor. After King Henry VIII abolished the adoration of shrines and relics his tomb was gradually forgotten, and in time the painted decorations above it wore away. The vault in which he lay came to light again in 1798, at about the same time as King Edward IV's. An inscribed slab was then laid down to mark the place. On 4th November, 1910, it was reopened and the King's body identified.

So the "red rose of Lancaster" and the "white rose of York" lie together in common ground. Only the breadth of the choir separates the dust of the rival Kings. Now, every year on the eves of 6th

December and 21st May, white lilies for Eton and roses for King's College, Cambridge, are placed during evensong on the grave of King Henry VI. In this way the anniversaries of his birth and death are commemorated. And on 20th June, the date on which King Edward IV made his will, the document is read aloud at the beginning of evensong, and the service ends with a procession to the tomb where he lies with his Queen, Elizabeth Woodville.

6

THE TUDORS

Although the Wars of the Roses did not begin as a dynastic feud, they evolved into a conflict for the succession, and it was only slowly that the genius of the House of Tudor gathered old stresses into maturing union. Henry Tudor, Earl of Richmond, who defeated King Richard III at Bosworth on 22nd August, 1485, and was crowned as King Henry VII on 30th October, assumed his sovereignty by conquest rather than right. His father was the son of a Welsh gentleman, Owen Tudor, and Queen Catherine, widow of King Henry V, and therefore a half-brother of King Henry VI, to whom Henry Tudor was also related on his mother's side. She was a descendant of John of Gaunt, and thus, like Henry VI, whose memory he venerated, he represented Lancastrian stock, but his reign removed the grounds for faction between this and the rival line. In fulfilment of pledges to his Yorkist supporters, and with historical propriety, he took as his Queen the eldest daughter of King Edward IV, that young Elizabeth who had once danced so merrily with her father at Windsor.

In this beautiful and gentle lady, the least self-assertive of Queens, is vested the link between the medieval and the modern sovereigns of England. Daughter, wife and mother of kings, she was also the founder of every succeeding royal house. Through her daughter, Margaret, wife of King James IV of Scotland, she was the great-grandmother of Mary Queen of Scots, whose son, King James VI, became King James I of England and the progenitor of all English monarchs since.

Her marriage to King Henry VII was symbolized by the heraldic blending of the white rose of York and the red rose of Lancaster into the Tudor rose. The new emblem was adopted for the Collar of the Order of the Garter, which King Henry VII introduced. It is a chain formed of twenty-six enamelled roses within garters, linked with gold knots, and is worn over the mantle and secured with white ribbons on the shoulders. From it hangs the George, a beautiful jewel displaying the "Image of St. George on horseback, who, having thrown the Dragon upon his back, encounters him with a tilting spear."

Queen Elizabeth appeared in radiant prominence at the Garter Festival in 1488. It was the first one held by King Henry VII, and was deferred on account of the Easter celebrations, which the King and Queen observed "very solemnly" at the Castle. When the festival took place at the following week-end King Henry and the Knights Companions rode on horseback to the chapel while the Queen, wearing her robes as a Lady of the Garter, drove in a chariot refulgent with cloth of gold and drawn by six horses harnessed with gold. Beside her sat the King's mother, Margaret Countess of Richmond and Derby. The elder lady was newly admitted to the Order, and was the last Lady of the Garter to be appointed until the twentieth century. They were followed by the Queen's sister, Princess Anne, and a retinue of twenty noblewomen robed in crimson velvet and mounted on white palfreys, the saddles of which were made of cloth of gold, and the trappings covered with white roses in compliment to the Yorkist Queen.[1]

The Countess of Richmond was the patron of John Skelton, later tutor to the future King Henry VIII, and it was he who composed the laudatory verses addressed to the Sovereign and Knights Companions on this occasion. Ashmole indicates that poems composed

---

1. Windsor Castle from the west

Topographical views of the Castle were attempted as early as the seventeenth century by John Norden and Wenceslaus Hollar, and with charming results. Photography from the air continues the tradition with spectacular authenticity, presenting both layout and detail in full realism. The three great towers along the west front, built in 1227–30, are perhaps the most compelling illustration today of the Castle's ancient system of defence. The Curfew Tower is at the left-hand corner, Garter in the middle, and the Salisbury Tower on the right.

2

3

for Garter festivals were delivered during the banquet in St. George's Hall, which consisted of two "courses" each comprising many dishes. When the second course was carried in, the King bestowed his largesse, or gift of money, on the officers of arms, and his titles were proclaimed with rhetorical pomp. New Knights then added their largesse, and their titles were recited. It was at the conclusion of this ceremony that Skelton's poem was read. His praises provided an effective sequel, for they began:

> O most famous Noble King! Thy fame doth spring and spreade,
> Henry the Seventh our Soverain in eache Regeon.

Having reminded the assembly that

> This Realme a Seasone stoode in great Jupardie,

he bade England rejoice to see her King so flourish in might, and after drawing graceful attention to the Company—

> O Knightly Ordere clothed in Robes with gartere
> The Queen's grace and thy Mother clothed in the same—

turned for his ringing finale to the patron saint:

> Wherefore now St. George all we pray to thee
> To keep our Soverain in his dignetye.

---

2. The Round Tower from the south-west

A view which emphasizes the "rounded square" formation of the Tower.

3. The East Front and Terrace Garden

The four towers which dominate the east front are (*from left to right*) the Queen's Tower, the Clarence and Chester Towers, and the Prince of Wales's Tower. Along this front are the Private Apartments, the White, Green and Crimson Drawing Rooms and the State Dining Room. Next to the Queen's Tower on the south side is the smaller Augusta Tower, and then come the twin York and Lancaster Towers which flank the King George IV Gateway. The East Terrace Garden, originally laid out by King George IV, is opened to the public on Sunday afternoons in summer, when regimental bands play there. On the right of the garden is the Orangery, now a private swimming pool.

Although the building of the chapel had not progressed, the choir as completed by King Edward IV already made a stately setting for the traditional services. It was still only roofed with oak, but the canopied Garter stalls carved by Robert Ellis and John and Robert Filles in 1478–83 were in use, and some fifty enamelled stall-plates of the earlier Knights had been brought from the old chapel and placed above them. The state sword of the Founder, King Edward III, was another precious relic removed to the new St. George's Chapel, where it still hangs behind the altar. In 1503 building was resumed. The money came by bequest from Sir Reginald Bray, a wealthy statesman who was also a Knight of the Garter and a friend of King Henry VII. In his will, dated 4th August, and proved on 28th November, 1503, Bray first of all desired "my sinfull body to be buried within the church of the College of our lady and seint George within the Castell of Wyndesore in the west ende and south syde of the same church within the chapell there newe made by me for the same entent."[2] The chapel to which he referred was the south transept, which represented the westernmost limit of the building as it stood at the time of Bray's death. He then directed his executors diligently to complete the body, or nave, of the chapel "as well in stone werke, tymbre, ledde, iron, glasse and alle other thinges necessary and requisite for the utter perfourmaunce of the same." His benefaction is commemorated by the incidence of his badge, the hemp-bray (a comblike appliance used by weavers for crushing hemp), among the carved and painted decorations of the chapel. It appears 175 times.

The resumption of the work brought horses toiling once again into the Castle with their burden of oak, and boatloads of stone began arriving at the wharf below Windsor Bridge. Some came from Caen, but most of it was English. The Taynton quarries, which had supplied King Edward III with 35,000 feet of stone, yielded a like amount for the building of St. George's Chapel.[3] The cost was 2d. a foot.

In carrying out Bray's request between 1503 and 1509 his executors added the westernmost bay, which did not form part of the original design. The completed nave was an achievement of superb and daring virtuosity. The builders raised the south and north walls with windows which form sheets of light, creating an effect of unforgettable contrast with the shadowed richness of the choir. At a great height they roofed their nave with oak, adding an outer skin of lead, and about six feet below spanned it with a glorious ceiling of carved stone, weighing thousands of tons. It rests on slender groups of pillars, though the weight was designedly transferred to low flying buttresses on the outside. Heraldic stone beasts such as Tudor dragons set on pinnacles around the roof helped to achieve the delicate balance required.

The vaulting must undoubtedly have been the work of the royal masons, John Hylmer and William Vertue, who, having completed it, contracted with the Sovereign and Knights of the Garter on 5th June, 1506, to vault the choir. The agreement provided not only for the setting up of the vault, but for the building of the flying buttresses, parapets and pedestals which form a continuation of those of the nave. The new vault was to be similar in pattern to that of the nave, but its principal keys or bosses were to be "more pendaunt and holower", and to bear the King's arms, crowned and supported by lions, antelopes, greyhounds and dragons. The lesser keys were to be wrought with roses, portcullises, fleur-de-lis "or any other devyce that shall please the King's grace to have in them." For this work Hylmer and Vertue were to receive £700, and the contract stipulated that it should be completed by Christmas Day 1508. It was not until 1528 that the vaulting of the nave and choir was finally united by the superb section over the organ loft, which displays the arms of Henry VIII and Knights of the Garter then living, and for which Vertue alone was apparently responsible.

To add to the feast of beauty a choir of graceful stone angels to the number of 302 was carved around the walls at clerestory level, and the great west window was filled with stained glass figures of kings, princes, popes and saints, seventy-five in all. Among this imposing assembly is a master mason, probably either Henry Janyns, the architect of the chapel—one of the foremost designers of the fifteenth century—or William Vertue. He stands in the lower corner on the north side of the window, which is said to be the third largest in England. It was a medieval tradition to include the architect's portrait in the building.

The half-finished nave was curtained off with cloth of gold when King Philip of Castile, who had been elected a Knight of the Garter in 1503, was installed on 9th February, 1506. He and his consort, Joanna, daughter of the powerful Spanish sovereigns, Ferdinand of Aragon and Isabella of Castile, were driven by storms into English harbourage while sailing from the Netherlands to Spain, and invited to Windsor. The King preceded his wife, whose younger sister Catherine was the widow of Henry VII's first son, Arthur Prince of Wales, and future wife of his second son, King Henry VIII. On Saturday, 31st January, King Henry rode out, attended by many noblemen and gentlemen "right honourably apparelled" in silks and velvet, to meet his guest at Clewer Green. Minstrels and sackbuts played as they entered the Castle and rode up to the royal apartments. When they "approached near the place where they alighted, the King of Castyll tarryed, and wold have alighted before the King, but the King wold not suffer him, and soo lighted booth at ons." Philip removed his hat, and Henry did likewise. Then both solemnly replaced them in unison.

Side by side they ascended the stairs to the royal apartments. In "the King's Grete Chamber", which was "richly hanged with Cloth of Arras", and decked with gold plate, the knights and gentlemen in King Henry's retinue halted. The rest of the procession moved on into a second room, "also richly hanged", where the barons in attendance took up their station. Bishops and earls followed the two Kings into a third chamber, "hanged with very rich Arras, in the which there was a Cloth of Estate, and as rich a Bed," added the chronicler, "as I have ever seen." At this point they too came to a standstill, leaving King Henry and his guest to enter the fourth room, which was "all hanged with rich Cloth of Gold, the bordure above of Crimson Velvett, and brodered upon [with] the Kinges Armes." The King of Castile entreated his companion not to trouble to return with him to his own lodging, whereupon King Henry gracefully intimated that he wished to place these very rooms at his guest's command, and an elaborate exchange of courtesies and compliments ensued.

On the following Saturday, after a week of solemn ceremonies and varied diversions, the two Kings repaired to the wooden tennis court in the eastern half of the Round Tower ditch. A gallery with gold-cushioned seats had been made ready for them, but the King of Castile grew tired of watching and himself "played with the

Rackets", conceding fifteen points to his opponent, Thomas Grey, 2nd Marquess of Dorset, who played with the hand. The King won the set.

Formalities were resumed on Monday, when articles of "Amity and Peace" were signed. The royal guest's installation as a Knight of the Garter followed. In the chapter house, where the first part of the ceremony took place, delicate wax tapers lit up the shining gold canopy of King Henry's throne, the gold cushions and the cloth of gold covering the table. Here King Philip took the Sacred Oath, which he swore on the "true cross", the most sacred relic in the treasury of St. George's. It was the *Croes Naid*, a jewelled Celtic cross originally in the possession of the Princes of North Wales, which contained a reputed fragment of the cross on which Our Lord died. Edward I received it among his spoils in 1283, at the close of his campaign against the Welsh, and Edward III gave it to the chapel at Windsor in 1352. Half a century after Philip of Castile's visit all but the gold base had disappeared, but when it was laid with proud reverence before him in 1506 it was apparently still rich in rubies, emeralds, sapphires and pearls. After swearing the Oath, King Philip was conducted into the candlelit choir and installed according to the prescribed ritual.[4]

These records of pageantry at Windsor dispute the assessment that Henry VII accumulated money only to satisfy a miserly streak. When he died on 21st April, 1509, "the richest prince in Christendom", he bequeathed to his son an established order of wealth, dominion and pomp. If it was not also replete with security, that was not his fault. Although King Henry VIII was accounted the "flower and very heir" of the strains of York and Lancaster, the Wars of the Roses still poised their threat over the sixteenth century, forcing upon him and his issue the ultimate destiny of the crown. His dynastic responsibility partly explains the faction and sick tyranny of his later years, which were unforeseen when he succeeded to the throne, a youth of seventeen, endowed with regal attributes of mind and body. These alone provided him with a passport to renown, and his varied accomplishments were closely noted and universally admired. When he stayed at Windsor after his accession he "exercised himself daily in shooting, singing, dancing, wrestling, casting of the bar, playing at recorders, flute, virginals, in setting of songs, and making of ballads." Two masses which he composed were often sung in the chapel.[5]

In 1515 the Venetian ambassador Giustiniani added further recommendations. The King, he wrote, "draws the bow with greater strength than any other man in England, and jousts marvellously." He was a tireless huntsman, and to see him play tennis was "the prettiest thing in the world". The tennis court at Windsor, being in the natural amphitheatre of the Round Tower ditch, allowed both players and spectators a full measure of enjoyment. The Court ladies were wont to watch the game from the battlements. Such at least is the implication in a poem by the ill-fated Henry Howard, Earl of Surrey, who was under restraint at Windsor in 1537 after breaking the peace in the King's domain. In his "cruel prison" he recalled former pleasures, which included

> . . . palme-play, where, despoiled for the game,
> With dazed eyes oft we by gleams of love
> Have missed the ball, and got sight of our dame,
> To bait her eyes, which kept the leads above.[6]

At the outset of his reign King Henry VIII enriched the Castle with an important new feature. In 1509–10 he rebuilt the entrance gate in the Lower Ward, setting up the handsome stone gatehouse which bears his name. Its flanking towers accommodated the Colehouse, and the chamber above the archway served as the court room. Through it, ten years later, on Friday, 27th May, 1519, rode the most tremendous cavalcade which ever ushered in a Garter ceremony. Knights elect, Ashmole records, frequently "took their journey from London to their Installation at Windsor, in the nature of a solemn and stately Cavalcade, and this Proceeding on Horseback was generally set forth with exceeding pomp; whether we consider the great number of their honourable Friends, who on gallant Coursers rode along with them, or the multitude of their own Attendants well mounted, the richness of whose Apparel, Jewels, Gold Chains, rich embroideries, and Plumes of Feathers of their Lords Colours, even dazzled the Eyes of the beholders."[7] The cavalcade in 1519 was not the prelude to an installation, but to a Garter festival. It was a royal spectacle, ordered by the King himself, and set out from Richmond on the day before the eve of St. George's feast.

Esquires and gentlemen rode at the head, followed by royal chaplains, messengers and heralds, bishops, the Prelate of the Order, twenty Knights of the Garter, riding two by two, "as they were in degree", dukes, Garter King of Arms, the Sword-bearer and the King. Owing to the "scarcyte and straitnes of Lodging" and the desire to "avoyd and eschew of the corrupt air" (perhaps tainted by an outbreak of plague), a restriction was laid on the strength of each participant's retinue. A duke was permitted sixty horses, an ordinary knight sixteen, "with their Carriages and all". Even though curtailed, the procession was of incalculable length, and all along the route people flocked to see so exceptional and glorious a sight.

As it approached Windsor the procession halted at an inn called "The Catherine's Wheel" at Colnbrook, not far from Slough, where Queen Catherine and her ladies were assembled to greet the King. Here he mounted his courser, which was followed by "nine coursers with nine children of honour upon them." The Queen and her attendants, "having seen the noble Compagnie pass by . . . rode to the [Datchet] Fery, next way to the Castle", and there crossed the river, while the King and his glittering train rode on through Slough and Eton and over Windsor Bridge to the Castle gate. The members of the Order then went to the chapel and put on their mantles to attend prayers.

The ceremonies observed next day, on the eve of the festival, concluded with a regal supper at which two "courses" were served each consisting of fourteen dishes. One of the cook's fancies was "Porpoise in Armour". On the Grand Day the King rode with the Knights Companions to the chapel for mattins, took breakfast at the Deanery, and after holding a chapter returned to the Sovereign's stall until the Grand Procession was ready, "which was ordered as of old tyme accustomed." When mass had been celebrated the Company rode back to the palace, and after the King had "paused a while in his Chamber", proceeded to St. George's Hall for dinner. The royal table was set with "Salt, Spoones and Cupps all of fyne gold, Pearle, and Stones of wonderful great price and valew", and the feast was "very sumptueuse", with "many subtiles". The customary two courses each comprised eighteen dishes, and the "subtleties" included "A George on Horseback" and "Custard planted with Garters". Just before the second course was carried in, the Queen and her ladies entered the gallery at the west end of St. George's

Hall, to watch the procession of dishes and the ceremony of proclaiming the King's titles. Trumpets took up the resounding theme, ceasing when it was the turn of the royal minstrels to provide a background of gentler music for the remainder of the banquet. Next morning the requiem mass was celebrated, as ordained, and with appropriately sombre show, no trumpets being heard that day.[8]

King Henry made the Knights revise their statues, so that he gained the convenient right of "proroguing" St. George's Day from 23rd April to any date which happened to suit him. It was also decreed that any Knight unable to appear at Windsor on the appointed day must wear his Garter robes throughout it, no matter where he was or what he was doing. The decorative but heavy and enveloping raiment must have proved a distinct inconvenience had the absent Knight wished to go about his ordinary affairs.

At the beginning of King Henry's reign the insignia of the Order comprised the Garter, which dated from the foundation, and the Collar and George introduced by his father. He himself added the Lesser George, an oval medallion, usually of gold and enamel, formed by the Garter enclosing the mounted figure of St. George attacking the dragon with drawn sword. The King intended it as a Garter badge for everyday attire, and directed that it be worn on the breast from a light chain of gold or a riband. The colour of the riband remained undefined until 1622, when King James I directed that it should be "of a Blue colour, and no other". It seems to have been usually worn as it is today, crossing the wearer's breast from left to right, so that the Lesser George rests on the wearer's right hip, but this was not made obligatory until 1681.

A Garter procedure which happily was rare took place in the chapel on 8th June, 1521. It was the degradation of a Garter Knight, in this instance Edward Stafford, 3rd Duke of Buckingham, who had been convicted of high treason and beheaded. The proceedings called for the presence of Garter King of Arms and the other officers of arms, who assembled in the choir, one of them being stationed above the offending Knight's stall. On this occasion it was Somerset Herald who mounted to the rood loft. Garter King of Arms read aloud an account of the Duke's disloyalty, and as he spoke the words "Be expelled and put from among the arms," Somerset Herald "violently cast down in the choir, his crest, his banner and his sword."

Then the officers of arms kicked them into the nave, first the sword, then the banner and then the crest, and so continued through the nave to the west door and through the Lower Ward to the drawbridge. Finally they kicked the dishonoured objects into the ditch.[9] There they lay among the Castle refuse, for the ditch had become a domestic appendage, green with bushes but serving as an open sewer and repository for rubbish, with a reputation sinister as well as unsavoury. It was only about half a century earlier that "Thomas Lumeley after Lorde Lumeley slew in the diche of Windesore Castelle Thornton bastard to riche Thorneton." (We owe this story to Leland, who however produces some confusion, for Thomas, son of George, second Baron Lumley, by his wife Elizabeth, daughter of Roger—or "rich"—Thornton, did not succeed to the title since he predeceased his father.)

Henry VIII was still handsome, versatile and accomplished, the affable idol of his people, when in 1522 he and Queen Catherine entertained at Windsor the Queen's nephew, Charles V, Roman Emperor and King of Spain, whose parents, King Philip and Queen Joanna, had come to the Castle in 1506. The two monarchs, unlike in temperament, shared a love of power, and both delighted in physical prowess, though while Henry indulged in exercise demanding great strength, Charles was devoted to riding. It was said that his accession to the Empire, on the death of his grandfather Maximilian I, had deprived Spain of the best light horseman of her army. Thus a delicate compliment was implicit in the "disguising or play of the proud horse" with which Henry entertained his guest. The theme of it was "that there was a proud horse which would not be tamed nor bridled, but amity sent prudence and pollicy which tamed him, and force and puissance bridled him. This horse was meant by the French king, and amity by the King of England and the Emperor." A second masque was mimed by twelve men and twelve women, all in "clothes of gold and silver loose laid on crimson sattin, very rich to behold", but the significance of this is lost.[10]

The breach with Charles V in 1527 provoked a renewal of Henry's design, conceived some years earlier, to divorce Queen Catherine, who had given him only one surviving child, the Princess Mary, and this in turn led to his final decision to break away from papal authority. His former relations with Rome had been productive of pleasant interchanges. Back in 1521 he had sent to Pope Leo X a copy of his *Assertio Septem Sacramentorum*, which he had written against the reformer, Martin Luther, and in return had been granted the title *Fidei Defensor* (Defender of the Faith), which his successors have borne ever since. In 1524 Pope Clement VII sent to Windsor the tribute of a golden rose tree in a golden pot. It stood three feet high, and the uppermost rose was "a fair saphire". As it was carried in state along the roads, people waited eagerly in the hope of seeing the vaunted jewel. These courtesies counted for nothing in the King's later policy. His passion for Anne Boleyn provided the ultimate incentive for his divorce, and from this time events at Windsor reflect his growing despotism.

On Sunday, 1st September, 1532, Anne's ennoblement as Marchioness of Pembroke took place there in the "Chamber of the Salutation", or Presence Chamber. She entered in state, richly clothed, and with her hair flowing loose over her shoulders in the manner permitted only to royal ladies, and during the ceremony was arrayed in a robe of crimson velvet furred with ermine and a gold coronet.[11] In April 1533, when she was known to be pregnant and acknowledgment of her status as Queen became vital, Parliament met and approved the Act in Restraint of Appeals which severed England from the papacy. She was crowned on 1st June and on 7th September gave birth at Greenwich, not to the son on whom Henry had counted, but to the future Queen Elizabeth I.

Before the harshest expedients of King Henry's reign imposed their oppressive necessity, there was one achievement which bespoke domestic peace and pleasure at Windsor. In this same year, 1533, he began building the forerunner of the North Terrace. There was already a path along the edge of the cliff below the royal apartments, for in 1506 the Queen of Castile had "entered by the Lytle Park and so secretly came by the backsyd of the Castell", but it was a rough route, and Henry erected a wooden terrace or "wharf" along it. In the Park, beside the bridge which carried the new promenade across the ditch, was built a great arbour, painted in the Tudor livery colours of green and white and gloriously gilded, for use as a banqueting house. On the terrace itself was set up in 1536 "a marke with bordes and quarters . . . for the Kyng to shott at with his hand-gonne". He continued to enjoy active exercise, and so that he could amuse himself on wet days the carpenters provided him in 1542 with "a payer of New buttes made In ye Kynges Hawyll for ye Kynges Grace to shott att". Another task noted in that year was "makyng of blockes for ye Kynges grace to gett upon hys horse".[12]

The Castle was of necessity implicated in the tart and tortuous policy which produced the Reformation. John Foxe, in his *Actes and Monumentes*, first published in 1563, set down with vigorous realism the effect produced when the King's supremacy passed in Parliament in 1534. The Dean, Dr. Richard Sampson, hurried to Windsor late at night and ordered the College to assemble at eight the next morning. He then denounced papal authority, at which the Canons, who were for the most part conservative, "were all stricken in a dump". One of them voiced an objection, but the Dean interrupted him, "called him old foole and took him up so sharpely, that he was faine to hold his peace." Then the Dean brought a number of papal pardons from where they hung in the chapel, burned them in the fireplace before the eyes of the Canons, "and so departed".

Two years later, during the Catholic rising known as the Pilgrimage of Grace, a local butcher was rash enough to speak openly in favour of the rebels. One October morning, as he was selling his meat, a customer offered less for a sheep than he had paid for it, whereupon the butcher answered, "Nay by God's soul, I had rather the good fellows of the North had it among them, and a score more of the best I have." His words were seconded by a priest who was standing by, and who had already been preaching that the insurgents were "God's people", fighting "God's quarrel". Both were swiftly arrested, condemned and hanged, the butcher "on a new pair of gallows set up at the (draw)bridge and before the Castle gate", the priest on a tree at the foot of Windsor Bridge. The borough accounts contain an entry of 2d. expended on nails for the butcher's gallows, and 1s. paid to the gaolers who watched the prisoners for two nights.[13]

Although there was no question of a return to papal authority, the King took his stand on Catholic doctrine with the Act of Six Articles in 1539, a severe enactment in which Stephen Gardiner, Bishop of Winchester and Prelate of the Order of the Garter, took part. It imposed death by burning on those who in spoken or written words repudiated its orthodoxy, and the persecution of forthright Protestants followed accordingly. Out of this statute arose the proceedings against the Windsor Martyrs in 1544. There were three of them: Robert Testwood, singing-man of St. George's, Henry Filmer, churchwarden of Windsor, and Anthony Pearson, a priest. The story of "these good saints of Windsor" is told in the *Actes and Monumentes* (popularly called the *Book of Martyrs*), and Foxe says he had it from John Marbeck, organist of St. George's Chapel and author of the first English Concordance of the whole Bible. Marbeck only narrowly escaped death himself.

Testwood had earned the particular hatred of the Dean and Canons by his expressed contempt of the shrines and relics from which they drew so considerable an income. It was not until later that King Henry VIII abolished all such adjuncts, and in 1544 St. George's still held some famed examples. Dating from its medieval collection there were the *Croes Naid* and the heart of St. George. The chapel had been further enriched in 1481 by the body of John Schorne, Rector of North Marston some twenty miles north of Windsor, who died in 1314. He is commemorated in the jingle

> Master John Schorne, gentleman born,
> Conjured the devil into a boot,

and old paintings show him carrying a boot with a pert little devil leaning over the top. He was credited with power to make the devil pop in and out, in token of his own ability to drive away toothache and other ills, and the toy known as "Jack in the Box" is said to derive from this trick.[14]

King Edward IV, who brought Master Schorne's bones to Windsor, hoped thus to attract pilgrims away from King Henry VI's tomb at Chertsey. He could not know that Henry's body would soon lie near his own in St. George's, nor that his rival's grave would become even more revered than the good rector's.

All this was an abomination to Testwood, who placed himself in peril by trying to persuade people to stop visiting the shrines. Seeing pilgrims coming in "by plumps, with candles and images of wax in their hands, to offer to good King Henry of Windsor", and placing the King's old hat upon their heads, he exhorted them to cease. Another time, when he came upon worshippers kissing a pretty statue of Our Lady which stood in the chapel, he broke its nose, bidding them note that it was but dust and ashes. "A dear nose" it should prove to Testwood, vowed a passing lawyer as he put the fragments in his purse.

This was part of Testwood's "trouble", as Foxe called it. Marbeck's was of a different order. He was engaged on his "greate worke", the Concordance, when his house in the Castle was entered and searched on 16th March, 1544, and he himself, "among others at Windsore . . . taken in a labirinth and troublesome net of a law called the Statute of vi articles . . . for the copying out of a worke, made by the greate Clerke Master Jhon Calvin written against the same sixe articles."[15] Marbeck was hauled off to the Marshalsea in London, where he remained until he was brought back to Windsor and lodged in the town gaol on 21st July, 1544. Pearson and Filmer, against whom charges of heresy had also been laid, shared his prison, and Testwood, who was ill in bed with gout, was brought out of his house on crutches to join them. Their trial took place on the following Thursday. Farmers belonging to the Dean and Canons had been summoned to form a jury, and the judges included the Bishop of Salisbury, Chancellor of the Order of the Garter, and William Franklain, Dean of Windsor, "a timorous man" who persecuted reformers.

All four were found guilty and sentenced to be burned at the stake on the following day. In the morning word came that they were not to die that day, and so they spent another night together, exchanging "such heavenly talk" that the men guarding them were moved to tears. In the morning the cause of the delay was made clear. A pardon had been obtained for Marbeck. He is among the most famous of the musicians who have served St. George's, and it was believed that Bishop Gardiner, to whom he owed his life, saved him on account of his skill. Gardiner it was who provoked the attack on the "humble society of reformers at Windsor", probably in an attempt to involve the King's sixth wife, Queen Catherine Parr, who was a patroness of the new learning.

The others, as they passed through the town on the morning of Saturday, 28th July, desired the crowds "not to be moved at their afflictions, for it was the happiest thing that ever came to them." The place of execution was the Chapter Garden, anciently the canons' burial ground, below the North Slopes, where a stake had been set up in readiness. No details of it survive, but we can tell what it was like from the payments made when Archbishop Cranmer suffered at Oxford twelve years later. The account for the stake on that occasion reads: "For an hundred of wood-faggots, six shillings; for an hundred-and-half of furze-faggots, three shillings and four-pence; for the carriage of them eightpence; to two labourers, one and fourpence."[16]

Both kinds of firing are shown in a woodcut illustrating the death of the Windsor victims which was made for Foxe's *Book of Martyrs*. It is not found in the 1563 edition, but appears for the first time in the second volume of *Ecclesiastical history contayning the Actes and Monumentes of Martyrs*, which is undated while the first volume bears the date 1570.[17] The picture adds its own grim and vivid evidence to Foxe's narrative, showing with crude realism the flames rising round the three men, while a labourer prepares to heap more sheaves at their feet. One of them is covering his head with straw. This is Anthony Pearson, the priest. Foxe records that he, "pulling the straw unto him, layd a good deale thereof upon the top of his head, saying 'This is God's hat; now am I dressed like a true soldier of Christ'."

The onlookers are supposed to have included the "Vicar of Bray", whose habit of being papist or protestant as occasion demanded gave rise to the proverb, "The Vicar of Bray will be Vicar of Bray still". It was quoted by Dr. Thomas Fuller in his *Worthies of England*, pub-lished in 1662, and the famous song based on it is believed to have been composed in King George I's reign. Fuller declared that the cleric in question was incumbent of Bray in the reigns of King Henry VIII, King Edward VI, Queen Mary I and Queen Eliza-beth I, and that "he had seen some martyrs burned (two miles off) at Windsor, and found this fire too hot for his tender temper." The vicar at the time, Simon Symonds, very likely did see the gruesome spectacle, for he was also a canon of Windsor and a royal chaplain: it was to his beautiful riverside church that the choir had emigrated in 1537, when a minor canon fell ill of the plague. Contemporary references show that he displayed a certain doctrinal flexibility, but since he died in 1551 he does not entirely coincide with Fuller's turncoat vicar.[18]

According to Foxe, the King was hunting in Guildford Park when he saw two of his officers sitting on horseback together, and calling them over, asked how his laws had been carried out at Windsor. They told him so pitiful a tale of the death of these three men that the King, turning away his horse's head to depart from them, said "Alas, poor Innocents."

Although he still hunted and took part in energetic exercise, Henry was beset by ill-health. He had grown so grossly fat that ropes and pulleys were installed in his palaces to haul him up and down stairs, and his temper bore witness to his afflictions. He suffered too from lasting grief at the loss of his third and best-loved Queen, Jane Seymour, who died in 1537 after giving birth to the future King Edward VI. It was Henry's intention that she should share a tomb with him in the choir at Windsor. Her body was therefore carried to St. George's Chapel in "a chair covered with a rich pall; and thereupon the representation of the Queen in her robes of state, with a rich crown of gold upon her head, all in her hair loose, a sceptre of gold in her right hand, and on her fingers rings set with precious stones, and her neck richly adorned with gold and stones, and under the head a rich pillow of cloth of gold tissue. The said chair drawn with six chariot horses trapped with black velvet." At its journey's end her coffin was lowered into a vault in the middle of the choir aisle.[19]

The story of the tomb which King Henry was preparing for himself and Queen Jane begins long before this. In 1494 his father had begun building a lady chapel at the east end of St. George's, on the site of the chapel of King Henry III and incorporating its north wall. He planned to remove the body of King Henry VI from St. George's into the new building, which was also to be a burial place for himself and his descendants. His intentions did not take effect. King Henry VI remained in St. George's Chapel, and King Henry VII himself was buried in the new lady chapel begun in 1503 at Westminster Abbey, where the elaborate groined vaulting, executed by the master masons who worked at St. George's, owes a basic debt to Windsor. His chapel in the Castle stood unfinished until Thomas Wolsey became a canon of Windsor in 1511. Wolsey is believed to have arranged the contract for completing it on 20th December of that year. In 1514 he became Archbishop of York and in 1516 a cardinal. When he was at the peak of his renown the chapel was granted to him as a burial place by King Henry VIII, and in 1524 he commissioned the Florentine artist, Benedetto da Rovezzano, to design his tomb. It included a black marble sarcophagus of Italian design, raised upon a black and white marble base eight feet long, four feet wide and two feet high, on which his effigy, "all gilt and burnished", was to lie upon pieces of copper wrought in the semblance of cloth of gold. At each corner stood a great pillar of copper bearing an angel with a candlestick, and around the tomb were grouped angels and children holding the Cardinal's arms and emblems.[20]

Wolsey died disgraced at Leicester Abbey in 1530 and was buried there. The King, who as early as 1517 had announced that he would be interred at Windsor and nowhere else, then employed Benedetto to convert the tomb into one for himself, loftier and more sumptuous even than Wolsey's ambition had devised. The plan was to raise the sarcophagus and its base on a pedestal five feet high. Around it were to stand eight pillars ten feet tall, each surmounted by an image of an Apostle, and in between them eight candlesticks only a foot less in height. At the east end of the tomb was to be set an altar under a rich canopy, with four kneeling angels on top, supported on four pillars, and at the base sixteen children each holding a candlestick. All the metal work was to be of gilded bronze, and both tomb and altar were

---

4. The Lower Ward from the west

On the left is St. George's Chapel, officially called "The Queen's Free Chapel of St. George" because it is extra-provincial and extra-diocesan, neither archbishop nor bishop having any authority within it. On the right are the houses of the Military Knights, with their Governor's house (Mary Tudor Tower) half way up. Beyond that is the rounded front of King Henry III Tower. The projecting wall at the top of the Military Knights' row marks the site of the wall, ditch and gatehouse which until 1671 separated the Lower Ward from the Middle Ward beyond.

5. The Quadrangle from the south-west

Wyatville's Grand Entrance to the State Apartments stands out on the north side. In the foreground is the Moat Path, with the statue of King Charles II facing the Quadrangle. On the lawn the guard-mounting ceremony takes place when the Court is officially in residence: at other times it is carried out on the Parade Ground at the bottom of the Lower Ward.

to stand within a bronze closure "all in copper carven and curiously intayled."

Eight pillars and four of the great standing candlesticks had been completed by 1536, when, for an undetermined reason, work ceased on the monument, which according to later report had already cost £60,000. Although it remained unfinished, the King did not abandon his intention to rest beneath it. In his will he directed that his body was to be buried in the choir of St. George's Chapel, "midway between the stalles and the high altar", and that "there be made and set, as soon as convenientlie maie be donne after our decease . . . an honourable tombe for our bones to rest in, which is well onward and almost made therefore already, with a fair grate about it, in which we will alsoe the bones of our true and loving wife Queene Jane be put alsoe, and that there be provided . . . a convenyent aulter, honorablie prepared and apparelled with all manner of things requisite and necessarie for dailie masses there to be said perpetually as long as the world shall indure."[21]

The King died in the palace at Whitehall on 28th January, 1547. After his body had been embalmed it was wrapped in rich cloth and velvet, encased in lead and placed in a coffin covered with cloth of gold. For a fortnight it lay in august state. Then it was removed to a chariot over which a canopy of blue velvet embroidered with gold was carried by six barons. Upon the coffin was laid an effigy of the King, wearing the Imperial Crown over "a night Cap of black Sattin, set full of precious Stones, and apparalled with Robes of crimson Velvet, furred with Minever, poudred with Ermine, the Collar of the Garter with the order of St. *George* about the Neck; a crimson Satten Doublet embroidered with Gold, two Bracelets of Gold about the Wrists, set with Stones and Pearl; a fair Armouring Sword by the side, the Sceptre in the right Hand, and the Ball in the left, a pair of scarlet Hose, crimson Velvet Shoes, Gloves on the Hands, and several Diamond Rings on the Fingers."

In this chariot the royal remains were drawn to Windsor by eight

---

6. The Castle from the north

Throughout the centuries the view of Windsor Castle across the river has been the one most favoured by artists. No other presents so completely the long march of towers and pinnacles.

great horses trapped with black, on each of which rode "a Child of Honour, carrying a Banneroll of the King's Arms." The procession, four miles long, set out from Westminster early on 14th February, halted for the night at Syon and about noon on the following day reached Eton College, where the scholars repeated the penitential psalms as it moved slowly past. At the Castle gate the corpse was received by the Dean and Canons and the choir. It was carried into St. George's Chapel and placed on a magnificent hearse, consisting of thirteen great pillars and "having about it the twelve Banners of Descents". The hearse was standing over the vault where Queen Jane was buried, and this was already open, but covered by a grating.

Next day, about four o'clock, the "Communion of the Trinity" began. After an offering of gold had been made to St. George by the chief mourner of the Knights of the Garter, six knights bore the King's effigy to the vestry and four Gentlemen-Ushers removed the pall. The grating being raised, "sixteen strong Yeomen of the Guard took the Coffin and with five strong Linnen Towels, which they had for their Fees, let it down into the Vault (near unto the body of Queen *Jane Seymour*). Then the Lord Chamberlain, the Lord Great Master, Mr. Treasurer, Mr. Comptroller, and the Serjeant Porter, breaking their white Staves upon their Heads in three parts, as did likewise all the Gentlemen-Ushers, threw them into the Grave."²²

The tomb on which King Henry had set his heart was never erected. A century later, when Cromwell's men occupied the Castle, they found it still standing in "Wolsey's Tomb House", as the chapel built by King Henry VII was long known. In 1646, following an order made three years earlier by the House of Commons for the "removal of scandalous monuments and pictures", the whole of the bronze work was sold for £400. It included "a statue of brass", presumably one of King Henry VIII. The marble sarcophagus and its base were spared, and apparently remained undisturbed during King James II's brief reign, when the chapel was being painted and prepared, according to report, for Roman Catholic worship. Nearly another century and a quarter passed. In 1804 King George III ordered a royal burial vault to be excavated in the chalk under the "Tomb House", and this involved the destruction of the old floor. The chapel itself was being repaired and redecorated with the intention of using it as a chapter house for the Order of the Garter. On account of these various alterations the tomb was removed and placed in store.

After Lord Nelson's death at Trafalgar in 1805 a fitting use was at last found for it. In 1808 it was taken to St. Paul's Cathedral and erected over the grave of the great admiral in the crypt. Here, where memorials of martial glory surround it on all sides, Wolsey's sarcophagus and its base may now be found. And if one goes to Belgium and visits the church of St. Bavon in Ghent, one may see there the four great candlesticks which stood around the tomb at Windsor. After the bronze work and sculptures were sold these became the property of Anthony Triest, Bishop of Ghent, who gave them to the church. A pair copied from the originals were later placed in the presbytery of St. Paul's Cathedral, and in 1930 King George V and Queen Mary presented another pair to St. George's Chapel, where they flank the high altar. The rest of the ornamental work vanished completely. Had the tomb ever been set up according to Henry VIII's plan, the choir of St. George's would have been furnished with a chantry similar to that designed by Pietro Torregiano for his parents in Westminster Abbey, where Henry VII "dwelleth more richly dead in the Monument of his Tomb than he did alive."

7

SHAKESPEARE'S WINDSOR

During the short reign of King Edward VI, who succeeded his father at the age of nine and died when he was fifteen, the days became "more gloomy". This joyless child did not care for Windsor. "Methinks I am in prison," he complained, "here be no galleries, nor no gardens to walk in."[1]

Nor did he warm to the traditions of the Order of the Garter, which since the beginning of the Tudor era had ceased to be entirely military and was becoming a brotherhood of civilian as well as soldierly distinction. During his reign no anniversary of St. George was kept at Windsor by a Grand Festival. He set out to secularize the Order, and at a chapter held at Westminster on 17th March, 1552–3, issued a notorious revision of the statutes which, had he lived, would have produced this effect. He died four months later, on 6th July, and was succeeded by his half-sister, Queen Mary I. The only one of King Edward VI's ordinances now likely to attract interest is the first, which decreed that the Order "from hensforth shall be cauled the order of the *Garter*, and nat of saynte *George*, leste the honor which is dew to God the Creator of all things mighte seme to be geven to any creature."[2]

In the records of the Castle a single landmark stands out. Up to this time even the royal apartments still had to depend for their water supply on wells and rain water cisterns. While King Edward VI was on the throne a scheme was put in motion to bring water from Blackmore Park, in the parish of Winkfield five miles away, and the first pipes were laid. The work was resumed after the accession of Queen Mary I, when labourers set about digging a trench through a field called the "Oley pitte" at the back of High Street. It continued through "Gods Archard" adjoining the old Vicarage, through the churchyard and across the Castle ditch to the Rubbish Gate.

On 9th October, 1555, the pipe was brought up into the middle of the Quadrangle, "and there the water plenteously did rise 13 foot high". Over it stood a fountain composed of "a canopy raised upon columns, gorgeously decorated with heraldic ornaments coloured and gilt, and a dragon, one of the supporters of the Tudor arms, casting the water into the basin underneath."³

The religious persecutions which prevailed in Queen Mary's reign did not touch Windsor. There she left happier, more personal memories. Within a year of her birth she had had her own home at Ditton Park, near Datchet, and in 1517 spent Christmas at the Castle. There is a record of 3s. 3d. being paid to the keeper at Datchet Ferry for bringing the baby princess over the Thames. When she was six, and stayed at Ditton Park for Christmas, painters and decorators from Windsor prepared the scenery for pageants, and the Castle clergy went to sing to her.

During the desolate years following her mother's divorce, when she herself was declared illegitimate, she was a stranger to Windsor. It was not until after the execution of Anne Boleyn and her father's marriage to Jane Seymour in 1536 that she was again received at Court. In 1537 she revisited the Castle, where the most touching demonstrations of affection greeted her. Gifts of apples, peaches, cakes, partridges and venison were brought almost daily "for my lady's grace". In August of that year we find her rewarding these faithful friends with her bounty, and distributing alms to the poor of Windsor.⁴

The Castle retains pleasant tokens of her reign. On 24th July, 1554, she married her cousin, King Philip II of Spain, son of the Emperor Charles V, at Winchester, after which they set out in a great cavalcade for Windsor. Their journey ended on 5th August, when they were met at the lower end of Peascod Street by the Mayor and Corporation. Amid fanfares of trumpets the procession wound its way uphill to the Castle and entered St. George's Chapel by the west door. There the Queen invested her husband with the mantle and collar of the Order of the Garter, and he was installed as joint-Sovereign. To commemorate their union she had the royal arms of

England and Spain carved on the square tower half-way up the Lower Ward—that same tower that William of Wykeham had built long before to hold the chapel bells.

This was done in 1557, when it was converted into a residence for the Governor of the Poor Knights, a purpose it still serves. Nearly four hundred years later (in 1952) the name "Mary Tudor Tower" was bestowed upon it. To the Poor Knights themselves the Queen allotted the adjacent houses erected by William of Wykeham for the singing-men, which she rebuilt. Her father had fixed the number of Poor Knights at thirteen, and as there were insufficient houses she added a lower row between Mary Tudor Tower and King Henry VIII Gateway. They were built in Caen stone hacked out of Reading Abbey, which her father had suppressed eighteen years earlier, and interpose a deep honey-coloured frontage between the masses of grey stone at either end.

The Military Knights (as the Poor Knights have been called since 1833) still occupy these houses, but under no such obligation as Queen Elizabeth I laid upon their predecessors in 1559. She decreed that they should wear blue cloth mantles with the cross of St. George on the left shoulder, and that whenever the Sovereign visited Windsor they should stand before their doors in their apparel and bow. Not only to the Queen and her successors were they to pay this respect: the same courtesy was accorded to the Knights of the Garter. The Poor Knights' houses at that time corresponded to monastic cells, for like the clergy they were not permitted to marry.[5]

Queen Elizabeth had personal memories of the Castle as a prison. When she travelled by barge from the Tower of London to Woodstock in 1554 she spent a night in "the Dean of Windsor's house, a place more meet for a priest than a princess". The Castle gave her a more joyous welcome after her accession in November 1558. She spent the first Christmas of her reign there, and availed herself of the festival to make her religious inclinations known. Sir William FitzWilliams, Keeper of Windsor Great Park, who was with the Court, described the occasion in a letter written on 26th December: "On Chrystemas day the quene's majestie repayryd to hyr great closet with hyr nobles and ladyes, as hath ben acustomyd yn such high feasts. And so parseving a bysshope p'paring himself to masse all in the olde ffowrme, she taryd there on'till the gospelle was done;

and when all the people lokyd ffor hyr to have offryde according the olde ffaccon, she with hyr nobles reeturnyd agayn ffrom the closet and the masse onto hir pryvye chambr."[6]

She found the Castle cold, which, as it was quaintly suggested, "may be holpen with good fyres". At the beginning of her reign it must have been very cold indeed, for it was in considerable disrepair. Rabbits in the ditch were undermining the foundations, and in the walls there were holes where pigeons nested, doing much harm to the stonework. Nor could the Queen at first be persuaded to part with money to restore it. In 1573 the Esquires of the Body were still shivering in a room which needed a new ceiling and floor, "for that it is so ruynous and coulde". The Maids of Honour too had their difficulties. Their servants annoyed them by peeping over the partition in their chamber, and they asked to have it raised. Complaints were not confined to the Castle. The royal stables, then situated at Eton, were declared in 1577 to be "in great ruin", while "the bakehouse of our lady the Queen" which "standeth in Pescod streete farre from the Courte" was broken down and the ovens "in sore decaie". There is a very old story that Queen Elizabeth complained of her dinner always being cold, and was told that it was because the meat had to be brought from the bakehouse in Peascod Street. While this is unlikely, there seems no reason to doubt that some baking for the Court was done in the "Royal Oven" there.[7]

The grievances were many and continuous, but they do not give an entirely true picture, for the Queen had by this time begun not only to restore the Castle but to add to it. A few years earlier she had built "Queen Elizabeth's Gate" across Castle Hill, a little above King Henry VIII Gateway. It bore the inscription "Elizabethae Reginae xiiii 1572". At the same time she turned her attention to her father's wooden terrace along the north edge of the cliff. It had rotted, and between 1572 and 1578 was replaced by a stone terrace which crowned the slopes with softening grace and came to be regarded as one of the glories of Europe.

In 1582 the Queen further enhanced the importance of the north front by building a noble picture gallery which linked the royal apartments with the Norman Gateway. Her grandfather had begun the extension in 1497 by adding "to the western part of the upper area, where the Castle shines out most, a new and elegant work of squared stones." The addition was a three-storeyed tower for the convenience of his Queen, who had no private sleeping quarters, and whose requirements were agreeably met by the new building. The whereabouts of the Queen's bedroom in earlier centuries remains a mystery: the poor lady seems to have had to fit one in as best she could. The room called "La Rose" may once have served the purpose, though "ye chamber wch usually is named where K^g Hen:6 ;was borne" is indicated as being on the north front. When King Henry VII built the new tower for his wife she too was apparently sleeping in or near this room, for "the Queenes ould Bedchamber" is later referred to in connection with work done on the North Terrace.[8]

The tower was connected with her apartments by a large closet over which was her jewel house. A vice, or winding stairway, called "The Queen's Privy Stair", in one corner, led upwards to the jewel house and downwards to the terrace. The closet opened into "The Queen's Pallet Chamber", where the gentlewoman in attendance would sleep, and this formed an ante-room to the Queen's Bedchamber, which had at the north-west corner a charming oriel to serve as her "raying chamber" or little dressing-room, and at the south-west corner an "armory" of cupboards. Queen Elizabeth I's gallery led out of the Bedchamber, and since it had windows along both sides, combined the infinite variety of the northern view with the convenience of a southern aspect. Royal consequence was reflected in its elaborate ceiling of moulded plaster, or "frettingwork", and in the great stone chimney carved by Robert Pinckney in 1583. This masterpiece of delicate artistry embodies the Queen's cypher flanked by a rose and a fleur-de-lis, and her badge, derived from her mother, Anne Boleyn, of a crowned falcon on a rosebush.

It was the Queen's intention to have a new tennis court made on the North Terrace, immediately below the tower at the end of her gallery. With this in mind, she had a great curved window inserted, so that she could sit and watch the play, but the idea was abandoned, the old court in the Round Tower moat having already been rebuilt in brick in 1580. The terrace was at this time divided into two parts, the "Dean's tarras walk" at the west end, overlooking the Chapter Garden, and the more extensive "royal terrace" which led, like King Henry VIII's wooden wharf, over a bridge into the Little Park, "wher hir highnes must needes make her walke." A century and a half later there was still to be seen at the entrance to the Park "an agreeable Machine ascrib'd to Queen Elizabeth." It was "a large Seat, with a high Back and Cover for the Head, which turns so easily, the whole being fix'd on an Iron or Brass Pin for that Purpose, that whoever sits in it, may turn it from the Wind, or the Sun, in case either should prove incommodious, and may enjoy, even in a Storm, a perfect Calm." The Queen was said to have invented it because though she "took great Delight in being out in the Air, and even, in the Rain, if not too violent," yet she could not endure "to be russled by the Wind."[9]

The earliest view of the North Terrace appears in an engraving by Marcus Gheeraerts the Elder, who shows the Queen taking part in the Garter procession of 1578, with the north front of the Castle as a background. This was one of the few festivals held by her at Windsor after her decision in 1567 to celebrate them wherever she happened to be on St. George's Day, "which gave an almost fatal blow to the growing honour of this no less famous than ancient Castle." The last cavalcade to the chapel had taken place in 1564, and in Gheeraert's panorama the procession is going on foot. One of the first persons to describe the Terrace was Paul Hentzner, a German traveller who visited Windsor in 1598. He called it "a walk of incredible beauty, three hundred and eighty paces in length", and saw the slopes as green hills rising from the Little Park, where "fields and meadows clad with variety of plants and flowers" presented a scene of endless delight. The landscape he summed up as "a valley extended every way, and chequered with arable lands and pasture, cloathed up and down with groves, and watered with that gentlest of rivers, the Thames."

He concluded that the English kings had been attracted to Windsor by its "deliciousness", and conveyed in happy words the magnitude and grandeur of the Castle. The two great courts, enclosed by impregnable walls and noble buildings, appeared to him to form "a town of proper extent, inexpugnable to any human force". Visitors were permitted to view the royal apartments, where Hentzner saw the Queen's own bed, with its curious coverings of embroidery, and the beds of her parents and grandparents, "all of them eleven feet square, covered with quilts shining with gold and silver." The Queen was not at Windsor during Hentzner's visit, but he had already seen her at Greenwich. He found her "fair, but wrinkled, her eyes small, yet black and pleasant, her nose a little hooked, her lips narrow, and her teeth black." She was sixty-four, and very majestic, and she moved in awesome state.

When Hentzner saw her she was going to prayers. "First went Gentlemen, Barons, Earls, Knights of the Garter, all richly dressed and bare-headed; next came the Chancellor, bearing the Seals in a red-silk Purse, between Two; one of which carried the Royal Sceptre, the other the Sword of State, in a red scabbard, studded with golden Fleurs de Lis, the point upwards." The Queen wore a white silk dress bordered with pearls the size of beans, a golden crown and resplendent jewels, and her long train was carried by a marchioness. Wherever she turned her face, all beholders fell on their knees.

At that period the Yeomen of the Guard were in attendance upon the sovereign day and night, and as Hentzer saw, fulfilled a role of unique responsibility in the royal household. Their station was in the Guard or Watching Chamber at the head of the state staircase, where their weapons stood ready upon the walls. None but privileged visitors (who might be introduced by way of the back stairs) could pass into the further apartments except under the eye of this stalwart phalanx, which controlled the only public route to the royal presence. The Guard Chamber opened into the Presence Chamber, a kind of state ante-room which in Queen Elizabeth I's time was used for the reception of ambassadors and as a ceremonial dining-room. Beyond it was the Audience or Privy Chamber, where the sovereign dined in private, and this in turn led into the Withdrawing-room, through which were the Bedchamber, closets and backstairs.

It was the duty of the Yeomen of the Guard to carry in the royal dinner. On the day Hentzner saw Queen Elizabeth she returned after prayers to her inner chamber to dine privately. He then saw the Yeomen of the Guard, in their scarlet uniforms, with a golden rose on the back, bear into the Audience Chamber "a course of twenty-four dishes, served in plate most of it gilt". The dishes were laid on a table presided over by the Lady Taster. From each one as it was set before her she cut a mouthful of food, which she served to the guard who had carried it in, for fear of poison. When he had eaten, the dish was carried into the Privy Chamber for the Queen.[10] Such was the state observed at Greenwich, and it would have been the same at Windsor.

The Castle was considered her safest refuge in time of plague. She remained there during the winter of 1563, when "the Sickness", as it was called, was raging in London and spread to Reading and Newbury. To deter infected persons from invading Windsor "a newe payre of gallowes was set up in ye markyt-place to hange all such as should come ther from London, so that no person or eny kynde of wares mought come or be browght from London, to, or thrughe, nether by Wyndsore, not so myche as thrughe ye ryver, upon payne of hangynge with out eny judgement, and suche people as reseyved eny wares out of London into Wyndesore were burnyed out of theyr howseys."[11]

Despite preventive care, plague crept through the defences and into the Castle in November 1593, when a page died of it in the Round Tower. The poor boy's death was the more alarming because his mistress, Philadelphia Lady Scrope, was one of the Queen's bedchamber ladies, and in close attendance on her. Carts were ordered to be in readiness for the Court to move, but the Queen stayed on at Windsor, continuing her translation of the Latin author Boethius. The child's skeleton found in 1670 under an inscribed stone in the Round Tower, as John Evelyn records, was perhaps that of the little plague victim.

Less deadly than pestilence, though almost as frightening to most people, was the continued fear of witchcraft. In 1574 the witches of Windsor were suspected of using their arts against the Queen, and the Dean was called upon to question them. The foolish women may have ended up in the stocks outside the Parish Church. This was the fate Sir John Falstaff escaped in Shakespeare's *Merry Wives of Windsor*, when he dressed up as the "Witch of Brentford" and was flung out of Master Ford's house. Once he was safe he began boasting that but for his own quick wit "the knave constable had set me i' the stocks, i' the common stocks, for a witch."

The *Merry Wives* was said to have been written by order of the Queen, who was so eager to see a play showing the old fat knight in love that she commanded it to be finished in fourteen days. The first performance traditionally took place in the Castle, in a fine hall with open-timbered roof which overlooks the Horseshoe Cloister. (It was built in about 1415, and in 1693 became the library of St. George's Chapel, which purpose it still serves.) The Queen was present and was very well pleased with the entertainment. This was towards the end of her reign. Shakespeare later improved on the play, and it was several times acted at the court of King James I.

It is a comedy rich in local associations. Shakespeare was a member of the Royal Household and clearly knew Windsor well. He used familiar names for his principal characters. Those of Ford and Page are found in the sixteenth-century registers of Windsor Parish Church, and Master Fenton, who successfully courted "sweet Anne Page", bore a name well known at Datchet. The action of the play is set in places near the Castle. Frogmore and Datchet Mead would have been known to everyone, from Sovereign to scullion; and when Simple looked "pittie-ward" for Dr. Caius, the audience would have been at no loss. He was referring to the field through which Queen Mary I's water pipes were laid. It was then known as Pits Field, and ancient tradition says that this was because gravel was dug out of it. In King Edward III's reign, when the longbow became the national weapon by royal prescription, butts had been set up there for practice. Shakespeare knew it as a pasture and recreation ground. The cruel sport of bull-baiting was held there, and it was the scene of fairs and games.

The Garter Inn, which stood almost at the corner of High Street and Peascod Street, facing Castle Hill, was another landmark as familiar to Queen Elizabeth herself as to Shakespeare. We know its whereabouts because the town records show that it adjoined the White Hart, and there is still a hotel of this name on the site.

We know too what the Garter Inn looked like. It is shown in a survey prepared early in King James I's reign by the topographer, John Norden, and entitled: "A Description of the Honor of Windesor Namelie of the *Castle, Foreste, Walkes, Parkes, Rayles, Lodges, Townes, Parishes, Hamletts, Howses* of note, *Woodes, Riuers, Rills, Brookes, Bridges, Hills, Highwaies*, And all other thinges memorable, within, or belonging unto the saide *Honor*, And the *Liberties* of the same Liynge within And extending into The Counties of *Barke*, *Surrey*, and *Buckingham*. Taken and performed, by the perambulation uiew and deliniation of *John Norden* In anno 1607." He made two copies, one for the King and the other for his son, Henry Prince of Wales. The former is in the British Museum, the latter in the Royal Library at Windsor. Both consist of double-page illuminations on vellum, charmingly coloured and touched with gold. One of these is a topographical view of the Castle and town, which shows the "White Hart" and the "Garter" side by side, and readily identifiable by sign-posts and cross-beams. The "Garter", which stood nearer the junction of the roads than the "White Hart", had a massive porch and a large open courtyard at the back. Immediately opposite, under Salisbury Tower, Norden shows three shops which the borough records tell us were "new builded by the Castle ditch" in 1523.

Shakespeare used a local legend to provide the climax of his comedy:

> There is an old tale goes that Herne the hunter,
> Sometime a keeper here in Windsor forest,
> Doth all the winter-time, at still midnight,
> Walk round about an oak, with great ragg'd horns;
> . . . . and shakes a chain,
> In a most hideous and dreadful manner.

According to tradition handed down through generations of dwellers in Windsor Forest, Herne was wounded by a stag which he finally killed. He went mad, tied the antlers about his head, and hanged himself on a great oak in the Little Park. A manuscript of King Henry VIII's reign in the British Museum reveals that there was a Richard Horne who had confessed to poaching in His Majesty's forests. The name "Herne" appeared as "Horne" in the original sketch of the play.

The Little Park remained a deer park until 1785. The oak associated with the story stood about half a mile south-east of the Castle, beside an elm avenue named after Queen Elizabeth I, though planted by King William III. A supposedly haunted path led past it to the dell where, in the play, the fairies crouched until they were ready to rush out and tease Falstaff.

In 1796 Herne's Oak was cut down with other dead trees, to the great regret of King George III. Some people then chose to accept another tree as Herne's Oak. It was blown down in 1863, and Queen Victoria planted a new one in its place. This in turn was removed in 1906, when Queen Elizabeth's Avenue was replanted with limes and widened towards the north. The site of the original oak having been located, King Edward VII commanded a commemorative tree to be planted there. This, with the remains of the fairy dell, stands in that part of the park which now forms the private grounds of the Castle.[12]

Herne the Hunter was said to roam also through the wider realm of the Great Park and Forest, and Harrison Ainsworth, in his *Windsor Castle* (first published in 1843), uses the ghostly legend with exciting if fantastic effect.

8

THE ROYAL MARTYR

King James VI of Scotland, who in March 1603 became King James I of England, lost no time in viewing his new palaces. He concluded his tour at Windsor, where he received his Queen a fortnight later.

In the following December thirty-two feet of the north wall against which the canons' houses were built suddenly fell down. The royal officers denied liability, and the Dean and Canons petitioned the King. He in turn referred the matter to the Lord High Treasurer, Thomas Lord Buckhurst, who thought that as the canons had "accompted the said wall to be their owne, and in that right have opened windowes thorough it, and maide sinckes and passages for water and avoydances of their howses thorough the lower parte," they were themselves to blame for its decay. The canons protested that they had only beaten out "a litle wyndowe of twoe foote square", and a commission was then appointed to examine the history of the wall. Another winter passed. In April 1605 the commission concluded that the Crown ought to renew the wall, since it was older than the houses and a "wall of defence framed wth Battlementes".[1]

The canons thus emerged victorious, but their triumph at this point was technical, for it did not speed the repairs. John Norden saw "the breach in the wall" when he was working on his survey of 1607, and it is carefully reproduced in his charming topographical view of the Castle. The wall was rebuilt in the following year.

The protracted dispute had hardly begun when the King's new subjects received evidence of a lack of graciousness in their sovereign. He began by attacking the English gentry in his *Counterblast to Tobacco*, in which he scolded them for spending £300 or

£400 a year on what he called "this precious stink". Although the author was not named when it first appeared in 1604, the work gave vivid assurance of King James's disposition. Windsor did not escape the royal zeal for reform. As hunting was his favourite sport, he was often at the Castle. The townspeople dutifully rang their church bells whenever he arrived, as well as on the anniversary of his accession and Guy Fawkes's Day, but they noted with dismay his revival of old forest laws and restrictions long overlooked.

In Queen Elizabeth's time no one had troubled when folk took their dogs into the Great Park and caught hares, or when the poor loaded themselves with firewood, but King James I would have none of this. Norden's survey probably helped him to enforce his will, for being chiefly devoted to the Parks and Forest, it gave him a clear picture of his very considerable domain. The Forest at that time penetrated westward into Berkshire for some fifteen miles and southward into Surrey as far as Guildford twenty miles away.

Nor did the King ever relent. In 1623 Richard and Jeffry Richbell, who were caught riding in the Great Park at night with "staves and greyhounds", found themselves in gaol—presumably the Colehouse.

---

7. The Burning of the Windsor Martyrs, 1544; from a woodcut in Foxe's *Book of Martyrs* (1570)

The interest of this gruesome woodcut is not confined to the pitiful spectacle in the foreground. It is also one of the earliest views of the Castle, showing the medieval north front which King Charles II demolished. The walk along the top of the slopes is King Henry VIII's wooden terrace, with a bridge leading over the precipitous ditch at the east end to the arbour in the Little Park.

8. The North Front and Queen Anne's Garden; from an engraving by Kip after Hauduroy in *Nouveau Théâtre de la Grande Bretagne*, 1724

The picture shows the north front as it appeared from 1675 until King George III began the changes finally effected by Wyatville. The bastion thrown out by King Charles II in front of his Star Building is still a feature of the North Terrace, which Queen Elizabeth I built to replace her father's timber walk (shown on Plate 7). Whether Queen Anne's Garden in "Maestricht" ever reached the perfection and symmetry shown here is uncertain, but the engraving records the transformation at which she aimed.

The condemning of Anthony Perſon, Marbecke, Teſtwood, and Filmer, with the burning of the ſayd Perſon, Teſtwood, and Filmer, vnder the Caſtle of Windſore, here liuely deſcribed. Read pag. 1319. Marbecke ſaued by the Kynges Pardon.

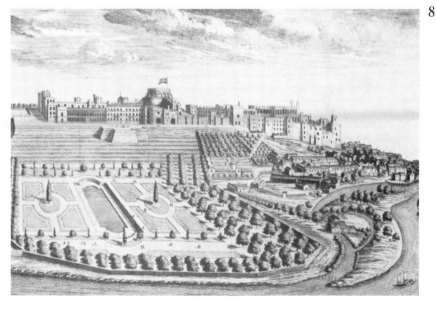

9

Then, one day towards the end of his reign, he was hunting when the Vicar of Windsor approached him, with the Mayor and four aldermen. They presented a petition on behalf of the vicar, who claimed that he had not enough to live on, but the King waved it aside and attacked the Mayor on quite another matter. "Am I ill neighbour to you?" he demanded. "Why then do you vex me by permitting your poor to cut down and carry away my woods out of my parks and grounds?" The offenders, he said, must be whipped.

Such repressive measures were not calculated to endear him to his subjects, and although he brought the Garter festival back to Windsor, his reign was not in local minds a memorable one, nor he a well-loved King. He lacked even the redeeming Stuart charm so hauntingly portrayed in Van Dyck's portraits of his second son, King Charles I. Windsor was the first English home of this tragic monarch, who arrived there from Scotland in 1604, when he was three years old, and it was destined to be his last. The shadow of the scaffold began to enfold him in August 1642, when the great Civil War began. After the indecisive battle of Edgehill on 23rd October the King marched towards London. Immediately Colonel John Venn broke away from the opposing army and on the 28th took possession of Windsor Castle in the name of the Parliament.

The King's nephew, Prince Rupert, Count Palatine, followed and on 7th November his artillery pounded the Castle for seven hours, but without effect. It remained the headquarters of the Parliamentary army throughout the war. Venn became Governor of

---

9. The Garter Banquet in St. George's Hall; from the engraving by Hollar in Ashmole's *Order of the Garter* (1672)

Hollar illustrated the proceedings at the point when the Second Course was being carried in. The dishes are borne by a double row of Gentlemen Pensioners on the right. The Treasurer of the Household and the Controller of the Household lead the procession, and the Cofferer and the Master of the Household bring up the rear. King Charles II is seated alone at the royal table, with his attendant nobles around him. Along the north wall the Knights of the Garter dine at a sumptuously laden table, each with his own server before him. Between them and the Pensioners are stationed the Officers of Arms with Garter at their head, facing the King. Below the windows on the south side of the hall are ranged the "Court Cubbords, that Serve the Knights Tables". Hollar's skill was equally successful in delineating the original appearance of St. George's Hall.

the Castle, while the Earl of Essex, who commanded the whole army, made the Round Tower the centre of operations.

On 11th January, 1643, the first batch of royalist prisoners was sent from London to Windsor, and herded in the towers and gate-houses. One was Sir Edmund Fortescue, of Devonshire. He was lodged in the room over the Norman Gateway, where his name and arms are carved in the stone wall, together with the words "Prisoner in this Chamber" and the date 12th January. Among those with him was Sir Francis Dodington, who also carved his name and arms. Both managed to escape during the following summer. This was not a common occurrence, for the prisons were grimly secure. The chambers over the gatehouses were connected with the ground floor by a vice, or spiral staircase narrowly enclosed within stone walls, and sentries and porters were stationed at the foot. The towers too had winding turret staircases barred by doors for which padlocks and staples were ordered. Their inner flank being thus made safe, no other special precautions were necessary. The outer walls provided no means of exit, since they were still not pierced with windows as they are today.

Six roughly scratched coats of arms on the ground floor of the Curfew Tower show that prisoners were confined there too. Winchester Tower was in use, and such was the pressure on accommodation that the Poor Knights had to crowd others into their houses. Thomas Knyvett, a Norfolk gentleman, who was thus uncomfortably detained, wrote to his wife in April 1643, "We had but two rooms for 7 of us on the first night, and one bed for us all."[2]

These were gentlemen of quality, for whom the Castle was chiefly reserved, but there were also a number of "Poor Prisoners"—sometimes as many as 165—who "lay upon straw in the common prison." The term probably indicates the Colehouse and the rough chalk dungeons under the Norman Gateway. The vaulted basement of the Curfew Tower was another likely place. Although the Curfew Tower was within the territory of the Dean and Canons, they were in no position to dispute its use by the Parliament. The Dean, Dr. Christopher Wren, had already been ejected from his house in 1642, and the canons from theirs, and the cloisters taken over by the soldiery.

Colonel Venn was succeeded as Governor in 1645 by Colonel

Christopher Whichcott. He was in charge of the Castle when the famous three-day prayer meeting was held there in April 1648, at which the religious enthusiast, William Goffe, preached to Oliver Cromwell and his fellow officers on the text, "Turn you at my reproof." Rallied by Goffe's impassioned words, they decided that it was their duty "to call Charles Stuart, that man of blood, to an account for the blood he had shed, and mischief he had done." It was to Whichcott that Cromwell wrote later that year, on 22nd December, bidding him prepare to receive the King as his prisoner. The notice was short. On the very next afternoon King Charles rode into the Castle under heavy guard. Rain was falling, and as he entered he saw kneeling in the wet gloom James Duke of Hamilton, once his Master of the Horse. During the war they had disagreed and been reconciled, and now, in forlorn finality, Hamilton kissed the King's hand and called him "my dear Master". Then the guards closed in and the King had to ride on.[3]

We may be sure that Colonel Whichcott observed Cromwell's order to lodge the King in the safest portions of the royal apartments, but he was allowed to choose the arrangement of his suite. This done, he asked the Governor what other prisoners he had in the Castle besides the Duke of Hamilton. Whichcott singled out for mention Captain Browne Bushell and Sir John Owen, the Welsh royalist leader. Both were among the King's most devoted supporters. Browne Bushell, "the great Sea Agent against the Parliament", was in the room over the Norman Gateway, where like his predecessors, Fortescue and Dodington, he left his name and arms carved on the stone wall. When the King had heard their names he turned and leaned his arm on his chair, gazing sadly into the fire.

In the whole of English history there can have been no sorrier Christmas. Puritan rule had banned the immemorial pleasures and observances of the season, and so it was an already dismal picture that was underlined by the King's plight. Only his own fortitude gave dignity to it. The issue of *Perfect Occurrences* for 29th December, 1648, reported: "The King, though the cook disappointed him of mince pies and plum porridge, yet he resolved to keep Christmas; and accordingly put on his best clothes, and himself is chaplain to the gentlemen that attend him, reading and expounding the scriptures to them."

On 26th December the Lord General Fairfax gave the King's tailor a pass to bring him three new suits. Two were made of cloth richly trimmed with gold and silver lace, the other of black satin with a velvet-lined cloak. The report in *Perfect Occurrences* continued: "The King is pretty merry and spends much time reading of sermon books, and sometimes Shakespeare, and Ben Jonson's plays." He had with him during this desolate time his precious second folio copy of Shakespeare's plays, in which he wrote on the fly-leaf the words *Dum spiro spero* (While I breathe, I hope). Before his death he gave it to Sir Thomas Herbert, who attended him to the end, and after further wanderings it finally returned to Windsor Castle, where it rests in the Royal Library.

He went out very little: only on the Terrace sometimes. Perhaps, looking down on the river, he was reminded of August evenings long before. In their golden glow he had gone with a choice company to swim between Windsor Bridge and the weir, a stretch of the river which for centuries was a favourite royal bathing place.

On 19th January, 1648–9, he was moved to St. James's Palace in London. His trial took place next day, and on the 30th he was beheaded at Whitehall. There is preserved in the Royal Library at Windsor the "second shirt" for which he asked on the morning of his execution. "Let me have on a shirt more than usual," he is reported to have said, explaining that if he were to shiver in the bitter cold the crowd might think he was afraid. "I fear not death," he added, "Death is not terrible to me. I bless my God I am prepared." This historic shirt is made of finest Holland, pale buff in colour, wrought with drawn-thread work of unsurpassed intricacy and beauty, and adorned with little pink and blue bows.

After his execution the King's body was carried back into the palace at Whitehall. It was then embalmed, placed in a plain lead coffin under a black velvet pall and taken to St. James's, where it remained for a week. Meanwhile the Parliament decided that it should be taken privately to Windsor and buried in St. George's Chapel at a cost not exceeding £500. The arrangements for the funeral were entrusted to one of King Charles's most devoted courtiers, James Stuart, Duke of Richmond.

On 7th February the body was removed to Windsor in a black-draped carriage driven by the King's coachman, Mr. Murray. Sir

Thomas Herbert and Captain John Joiner, who had once been the royal cook, accompanied it, together with other servants who followed in four coaches hung with black. All wore mourning liveries. Two troops of horse escorted the melancholy little procession.

On reaching the Castle the King's body was carried into the Deanery. There it was laid, according to tradition, on a long oak table which stands to this day in the Dean's study. Later it was taken to the royal apartments and placed in the King's own bedchamber. Sir Thomas Herbert's accounts show that he paid £3 for thirty-six torches to light the way.[4]

Permission to attend the King's funeral had been granted to the Duke of Richmond, the Marquess of Hertford and the Earls of Southampton and Lindsey, who had been officers of his bedchamber. On the following afternoon they arrived at St. George's Chapel with Dr. Juxon, Bishop of London. They found that Colonel Whichcott had already had a shallow grave prepared on the south side of the high altar. This did not meet with their wishes, and they refused to lay their dead master anywhere but in a vault. An aged Poor Knight directed them to the middle of the choir, where he had been told King Henry VIII lay buried, and in the winter twilight the four lords began tapping the floor. They were at length rewarded by hearing a hollow sound. A stone was taken up and in the darkness below they made out a large leaden coffin with a smaller one on the left. The large coffin was that of King Henry VIII, the lesser one that of Queen Jane. There was just room for a third, and so the little company agreed on this vault as the resting-place of the King. All that remained was to decide on the inscription for his coffin. The Duke of Richmond commanded a workman to engrave the words "King Charles 1648" on a lead panel, and this was soldered by the Castle plumber on to the coffin.

Next day the King's body was taken from the bedchamber into St. George's Hall, and from there carried by soldiers through the Castle grounds to St. George's Chapel, the four lords supporting the black velvet pall. Despite the bitter cold, the sky was serene and clear as the melancholy train set out, but almost immediately it darkened and snow began to fall. The phenomenon evoked memories of King Charles's coronation, when against all custom he had worn a suit of white velvet: white was anciently regarded as unlucky for a king or queen of England, and in the superstitious view the "White King's" choice was ominous of misfortune. The snowstorm supplied an awesome finale to the tragedy of his reign. Before the procession reached its journey's end the flakes were swirling sharply around it, and when the coffin was carried into the chapel the black pall was covered with snow. "Thus went the White King to his grave."[5]

Colonel Whichcott had "positively and roughly" refused to allow the Bishop of London to read the burial service. "It was not lawful," he stated. "The Common Prayer book was put down, and he would not suffer it to be used in that garrison where he commanded." All entreaties proved vain, and the Bishop of London stood weeping beside the vault as the King's coffin was lowered.

No entry recording the burial was made in the register of St. George's Chapel, but in that of Windsor Parish Church the vicar wrote: "Feby.9. King Charles in the Castle." The Castle is outside any parish or diocese, and the vicar's action has never been satisfactorily explained. It has been suggested that a burial service for the King may have been held at the Parish Church at dead of night.

Soon afterwards a story began to go about that "the body of King Charles the First was privately put into the sand at Whitehall and the coffin that was carried to Windsor was filled with rubbish." Few people seem to have believed this, and the vault was confidently pointed out to visitors as the King's burial place. Fifty years after his death it was opened to admit a tiny coffin, in which lay a stillborn son of whom the Princess of Denmark (later Queen Anne) was delivered at Windsor on 15th September, 1698, but since it was marked by no memorial its whereabouts presently faded from mind.

There is a sequel to the story for which it is necessary to by-pass a century and a half, reaching the year 1813. King George III was living at Windsor, blind and bereft of reason, and the role of sovereign was being carried out by the Prince Regent, later King George IV. In St. George's Chapel workmen were making the subterranean tunnel to the royal vault which is entered beneath a slab at the foot of the altar steps. One of them accidentally made a hole in the foundations which revealed a small arched vault containing four coffins, and when the discovery was reported to the Prince Regent he ordered an investigation.

On 1st April, 1813, the vault was opened in the presence of the

Prince himself, his brother, Ernest August Duke of Cumberland, the Dean of Windsor and Sir Henry Halford, a royal physician and close friend of the Prince Regent. It was found to be 9 feet long, 7 feet wide and less than 5 feet high. Within the vault were found the coffins of King Henry VIII and Queen Jane, "one very large, of an antique form, and the other little," the infant's coffin draped with crimson and beneath it, still covered with the black velvet pall, the lead coffin bearing the name of King Charles I.

A square opening was cut in the upper part of the lid, disclosing an inner wooden coffin, very much decayed. An account written by Sir Henry Halford describes how the King's body came to view, carefully wrapped in waxed grave-clothes.[6] Only the head was inspected, and the cloth was removed without difficulty. "At length, the whole face was disengaged from its covering . . . the left eye, in the first moment of exposure, was open and full, though it vanished almost immediately . . . the pointed beard, so characteristic of the reign of King Charles, was perfect. The shape of the face was a long oval."

Its resemblance to coins and busts, and especially to Van Dyck's portraits, was immediately apparent. As Sir Henry continued his examination, the head was found to be loose and "without any difficulty was taken up and held to view. It was quite wet, and gave a greenish tinge to paper and to linen, which touched it." Sir Henry believed that the liquid in which it lay was the King's blood. "The hair," he went on, "was thick at the back part of the head and in appearance nearly black. A portion of it, which has since been cleaned and dried, is of a beautiful dark brown colour. That of the beard was of a redder brown."

When he inspected the neck he found that "the fourth cervical vertebra was cut through, transversely, leaving the surfaces of the divided portions perfectly smooth and even, an appearance which could have been produced only by a heavy blow, inflicted with a very sharp instrument." This evidence, he concluded, "furnished the last proof wanting to identify King Charles the First."

The portion of the beard which was later cleaned and dried was retained by Sir Henry Halford, who took away with it the severed vertebra and an eye tooth. The relics were laid in a casket and deposited at Wistow Hall, his home in Leicestershire. The house already held memories of King Charles I. Sir Henry's ancestor, Sir

Richard Halford, had been a devoted royalist, and the King spent a night there before the fatal battle of Naseby in 1645. After his defeat he and Prince Rupert made their escape, and during their flight changed horses at Wistow seventeen miles away. So great was their haste that the saddles were not taken from the backs of the horses they had been riding, but were left at Wistow, together with the King's sword.

The Windsor relics remained for seventy-five years in Leicestershire. In 1888, long after Sir Henry's death, his grandson decided that they ought to be returned to royal custody. Accordingly he took them to London and himself handed them to the Prince of Wales, later King Edward VII, who in turn sent them to the Dean of Windsor. The Dean had a lead case made, bearing an inscription which recorded the history of the relics, and in this they were laid. A note in the Prince's own handwriting was enclosed with them.

On 13th December, 1888, after five o'clock evensong, the vault was reopened. There was no difficulty in locating it, for on the Prince Regent's orders an inscribed slab had been placed over it in 1818. At half past seven the Prince of Wales arrived. Candles were held around the vault, and going down on his hands and knees he himself lowered the lead casket by means of a handkerchief until it rested on the coffin of King Charles I.[7]

To return to that sad February of 1649, we find other human tragedies in the background. The Duke of Hamilton had escaped on the day of the King's execution—though it was not long before he shared his master's fate—and Sir John Owen was on trial in London, but there still remained in the Castle other prisoners of the royal persuasion. Did they peer through their windows to catch sight of the King's coffin as the snowflakes fell? Did the giant porter at the Norman Gateway put out a hand to touch it when it passed his door? This man is said to have been named Daniel Curtis, and was reputedly 7½ feet tall. Daniel became a religious maniac, and by 1678 was in the new Bethlem Hospital for lunatics in Moorfields, London, where sightseers found him an object of especial interest because his bed was covered with Bibles and "his breeches filled with them", while in the middle of the room stood a "Church Bible" given him by King Charles II when he visited the asylum.[8] His height is traditionally indicated by a circle about five inches across, carved high up on the twelfth-century wall extending westward from the Norman Gateway. He served as the model for the fettered figure of "Acute Madness", which, with its companion, "Melancholy Madness", was made in Purbeck stone by Caius Gabriel Cibber in 1680 for the gate of Bethlem: they were preserved when the hospital was moved south of the Thames, and today, in the London Guildhall Museum, one may still look upon the ravaged face of Daniel. "The statue [Cibber] did for Bedlam Gate," noted the seventeenth-century antiquary, George Vertue, "he modeld from Olivers porter, and it was very like him."

The Castle continued to serve as the headquarters of the Parliamentary army throughout the Commonwealth. Every night the countryside was reminded of its authority when the curfew-bell sounded at nine o'clock. It narrowly escaped destruction in 1652, when the House of Commons contemplated selling it,[9] but this threat having passed, was maintained according to the claims of security and convenience, and no wilful harm apparently inflicted. When John Evelyn passed through Windsor two years later he found the royal apartments "Melancholy & of antient magnificence", but made no mention of any damage. Despite sad times, the Castle still set its ancient spell on the beholder. Evelyn's words reveal its continued dignity at this time, when it had lost its King and was awaiting the coming of his successor. "The keepe (or mount)," he wrote, "hath besides its incomparable Prospect, a very profound Well, & the Terrace towards Eaton, with the Park, meandring *Thames*, swete Meadows yeilds one of the most delightful prospects in the World."

Even in St. George's Chapel, where he reverently sought out the burial place of "our blessed *Martyr K. Charles*", there was no evidence of gross misuse. Elsewhere the Puritans smashed stained glass and defaced carvings, leaving a trail of ruin. At Windsor they had plundered the altar plate and King Edward IV's coat of mail on 23rd October, 1642, five days before Colonel Venn took command, and in the following year he himself removed the rich hangings, the vestments and the brass lectern, font and candelabra, but the chapel itself received little harm. Throughout the Commonwealth, its legion of stone angels continued their tranquil communion undisturbed, and no hand defaced the pre-Reformation saints and popes in the great west window. The forbearance of the occupying troops conformed with orders issued to Colonel Venn by the House of Lords on 23rd April, 1643, "to take care that there be no disturbances made in the Chapel at Windsor; and that the evidences, registers, monuments there, and all things that belong to the Order of the Garter may be preserved without any defacings."

Although he had disestablished the Dean and Canons and other members of the College, Cromwell dealt more kindly with the Poor Knights. In 1654 he issued orders for the continuance and maintenance of the foundation, and directed that every two years the Poor Knights were to have "a gown of broad cloth of a sad grey colour," with the Commonwealth arms embroidered on the left shoulder. At his funeral eighteen Poor Knights were present, for the original thirteen were augmented during the Commonwealth. The additional five were established in accordance with the wills of Sir Peter le Maire and his brother-in-law, Sir Francis Crane, and lived in "a fair pile" completed in about 1658 between Salisbury and Garter Towers, and known as "Crane's Buildings". The institution was commonly described later as the Lower Foundation, to distinguish it from the Royal Foundation, into which it was absorbed in 1919.[10]

The last Governor during the Commonwealth was Bulstrode Whitelock, a distinguished lawyer who recorded the traditions and duties of his office for his successors. Two patents were issued to the holder. One appointed him Governor and Captain of the Castle at 10s. a day, the other named him Constable of the Castle and Keeper of the Forest and Parks. At that time the title Constable was more generally used. It was "a great Command", though productive of very little profit. As Keeper of the Forest, Whitelock's salary was £20 a year and "Tenn Load of wood for fuell."[11]

A definition of the Governor's authority based on Whitelock's manuscript was included by Joseph Pote, an Eton bookseller, in his *History and Antiquities of Windsor Castle*, published in 1749. Describing the topography of the Upper Ward, Pote says: "The *Keep*, or *Round Tower*, is the Lodging of the *Constable* or *Governor* . . . who has the intire government of this Castle, and is an Officer of great antiquity, honour and power . . . his office is partly Military, and partly Civil; as a military Officer, he is obliged to defend this Castle against all Enemies, whether foreign or domestick, has the charge of prisoners brought hither; and is answerable for them, and for all that is in the Castle to the King."[12]

In his civil capacity the Governor was judge of the Castle court for "tryell of Suites of any value" arising within the honour of Windsor. As Keeper of the Forest he had care of the "Vert and Venison" and held the power to punish and imprison in the Colehouse, or "Cole-hole", as Pote colloquially called it, all those who killed game without a licence or cut down any trees.

The Forest, which Whitelock stated to be 120 miles in compass, suffered during the Commonwealth and long afterwards from the activities of a swarm of "squatters" or commoners, a picturesque and wily race. It is related that if a squatter could build himself "a hut of turf and have a fire lighted and a *pot boiled* in the rudest chimney, the hut became established as a house, and was wholly unassailable except by the regular processes of the law, which the Forest officials frequently declined to institute." If the pot had not boiled they might proceed without ceremony to pull the place down.[13]

Both the Great and Little Parks were sold after King Charles I's death. The latter was bought back for the Protector, and with the Castle immediately reverted to the Crown at the Restoration. The Great Park, which had been parcelled out, was gradually recovered, and "the honour of Windsor" presently resumed its royal aspect.[14]

9

"THE MOST ROMANTIC CASTLE IN
THE WORLD"

Care was cast aside in May 1660, when the Commonwealth came to an end and Charles II was proclaimed King. Nowhere were the rejoicings heartier than in Windsor. A former Mayor named Matthew Day captured for us some of the happiness of the proclamation ceremony in the royal borough and Castle:

> King Charles the Second was proclaimed King of England, Scotland, Frawnce and Ireland, uppon the 12th of May 1660 at the Rownd Market howse in New Windsor; at which tyme the troupe of the county horse was in the Towne, and Mr. Gallant, an Innkeeper, being mayor [this was William Galland, host of the "Three Tuns"] was there attended with his Company in their gownes, who had a Trumpeter sounding a trumpet before them; and from thence went to Windsor bridge, and from thence went to the Castle Gate and ther with the troupe of horse and trumpet did likewise proclaime the King. And was desired by the officers that were in ye Castle to come into the Castle and there to proclame King Charles the Second in the Castle, wch was also there proclaimed with great Ioye.[1]

Released from Puritan constraint, the Castle resumed its ancient role as a king's home. Pepys went there on 26th February, 1666, and after being shown where King Charles I was buried, and King Henry VIII and "my Lady Seymour", visited the royal apartments. The "neatness and contrivance of the house and gates" satisfied his sense of propriety and stirred him to the heart. "It is the most romantique castle that is in the world," he wrote that night in his diary, and added, "But, Lord! the prospect that is in the balcone in the Queen's lodgings, and the terrace and walk, are strange things to consider, being the best in the world, sure."

After so long a lapse of royal maintenance, the Castle was beginning to look in parts "exceeding ragged and ruinous". The words are Evelyn's, and they were written on 28th August, 1670, two years after the appointment of the King's cousin, Prince Rupert, to the office of Constable and Governor. The Prince had already begun to "trim up the keep, or high round Tower", which was his official residence. It was at this time that the name "The Round Tower" first became familiar. It is found in the surveyor's and storekeeper's records as well as Evelyn's journal.

Prince Rupert had done more than "trim up" the keep, as Evelyn found when he climbed the "huge steepe stayres" leading to it. There were more than a hundred of them, and they were said to have been so constructed (when rebuilt in 1439–40) that horses could easily mount them.[2] The Prince had found a novel decoration for the stone walls on either side. They were hung with armour, weapons and drums, "all new & bright, & set with much study, as to represent, Pillasters, Cornishes, Architraves, Freezes, by so disposing the bandalliers, holsters & Drums, so as to represent festoones, & that without any Confusion, Trophy like." So Evelyn described the mural effect, which he thought very unusual and handsome. In the great hall of the Round Tower he found the walls similarly adorned with "a furniture of Armes, which was very singular; by so disposing the Pikes, Muskets, Pistols, Bandilers, Drumms, Back, brest & head pieces as was very extraordinary." The soldier-Prince displayed contrasting tastes in his bedchamber and private rooms. Here the walls were hung with tapestries wrought in gold and silver, illustrating classical mythology. "Curious & effeminate Pictures," was Evelyn's comment, "so extreamly different from the other, which presented but Warr & horror, as was very Surprizing & divertissant."

The tall figure of the Prince roaming the fields at dusk, with his big black dog beside him, soon became familiar, though he told his sister with grim amusement that he believed people thought him a wizard and always felt slightly uneasy. If he was an unconventional Governor, he was also a popular and heroic one. When Shakespeare's Garter Inn was burned down on 18th July, 1681, the flames threatened to consume half the little cluttered, inflammable town.

They continued spreading until Rupert descended from his tower and took command, and then, it was gratefully reported, the fire was "happily stopped by the great pains of the Prince".[3]

He was one of the first Fellows of the Royal Society, of which the King was also a member, and had a forge and a laboratory in the Castle where he shut himself up for hours to carry out experiments, not disdaining even "the most sooty and unpleasant labour of the meanest mechanic." The King and his attendants liked to stroll in and watch him. If their chatter annoyed the Prince he would coolly throw something on the fire which produced fearful fumes. The visitors would then rush out half-choked, vowing in mock fury never again to enter "that alchemist's hell". Horse-play of a deadlier kind cut short the King's visit to Windsor in February 1677. He had gone there intending to stay a week, but one night

> ... some of his Courtiers fell to their cups and drunke away all reason, at last they began to despise art to(o), and brake into Prince Rupert's Laboratory, and dashed his still, and other chymicall instruments in pieces. His Majesty went to bed about 12 aclock, but about two or three aclock one of Henry Killigrew's men was stabbed in the company in the next chamber to the King. .... The Duke [of Buckingham] ran speedily to His Majesty's bed, drew the curtain, and said, "Sir, will you lye in bed till you have your throat cut?" whereupon His Majesty got up at three aclock in the night and came immediately away to Whitehall.[4]

Not to be outdone by Prince Rupert, the King had his own laboratory at Windsor, and took a serious interest in scientific experiments, but the chief outlet for his tastes was the range of woods and water-meadows. The sparkling freshness of summer mornings called him out early to enjoy a game of tennis, which Prince Rupert also played expertly, and there was no lack of attractions during the rest of the day. Swimming below Windsor Bridge, fishing at Datchet, hunting the stag, shooting, or watching horse-races on Datchet Mead, which dipped its grassy verge in the Thames a mile south-east of the Castle: these were King Charles II's habitual pastimes. Sociable evenings, with cards or dancing or a play in St. George's Hall, brought the idyllic days to an end. Music, both of strings and voices, was an everyday pleasure, and one may imagine how sweet it sounded, floating out from the candlelit rooms and dying away among the trees of the Little Park.

Light-hearted diversion was the keynote of life at Windsor, where entertainment sometimes took a novel form. On an August night in 1674 Pepys and Evelyn were present at an action illustrating one of the allied victories of the Third Dutch War, which brought Charles II and his cousin Louis XIV into bitter conflict with Charles's nephew, the young Prince of Orange, later William III of England. The spectacle was the siege and capture of Maastricht, reputedly the oldest town in Holland and according to Louis XIV, to whose army it had fallen on 29th June, 1673, the most strongly fortified in Europe. This proud fortress, older by many centuries than Windsor, was modelled for the King's pleasure under the windows of the royal apartments. The setting was that part of the Little Park which lay between the North Slopes and the Thames, where in Evelyn's words, "works were thrown up to show the King a representation of the Citty of Maestricht, newly taken by the French".

His account shows how realistically the mock feat of arms was staged against the simulated fortress. "Bastions, bulwarks, ramparts, palisadoes, graffs, hornworks, counter-scarps, &c. were constructed. It was attack'd by ye Duke of Monmouth (newly come from the real siege) and ye Duke of York, with a little army, to shew their skill in tactics. On Saturday night they made their approches. . . ." Everyone found it very exciting, for great guns were fired, mines sprung and prisoners taken, and being night, it made "a formidable show". For nearly two hundred years afterwards, this northern reach of the Little Park was called "Maestricht" in commemoration of the event.

While the King was well pleased with the country amenities of Windsor, he found himself increasingly disturbed by the antique properties of the royal apartments. He had learned modish tastes during his exile in France and Holland, and the superb palace which Louis XIV was completing at Versailles served as a starting-point of unrest. Here at Windsor he himself was lord of "the most romantique castle that is in the world", and yet it fell far short of the baroque splendour which seemed to him the only fit setting for sovereignty. He began toying with the Castle in 1671, when the old middle gatehouse was removed: by this time it served no purpose apart from providing "Nichols the gunner" with a home. The cross-ditch seems to have been already filled in, except for a remnant on the north side, which was peaceably occupied by the Deanery and its forecourt. The removal of the gatehouse proved to be the forerunner of more arbitrary changes. In 1675–78 the north front of the royal apartments was completely rebuilt. The picturesque, if irregular, walls and towers gave place to a plain, four-storeyed front. The western half, where the King had his Withdrawing-room and Bed-chamber, formed a projecting block called the Star Building because it bore carved in the centre a gilded Garter Star twelve feet in dia-meter. This was the latest emblem to form part of the insignia of the Order of the Garter: it had been introduced by King Charles I in 1629.

Tall, round-headed Italianate windows lit the principal floor. They were introduced not only on this north front, but around the Upper Ward and even on King Henry III Tower (where a pair may still be seen). Around the basement there was a series of circular windows like portholes. The effect, elegant in itself, was strikingly out of character in a battlemented Gothic castle.

The interior, though equally incongruous, presented a display of beauty so arresting that criticism falters and is rendered impermis-sible. The Italian artist, Antonio Verrio, painted the ceilings and many of the walls, and his work glowed with colour. Rene Coussin,

---

10. King Henry VIII Gateway from Castle Hill, *c.* 1770; from the coloured drawing by Paul Sandby in the Royal Library, Windsor Castle

The main entrance into the Castle as it appeared in the eighteenth century. The tall old houses which then adjoined it are depicted by Sandby with such sweetness that one forgets the squalor that pervaded the ditch behind them. The one nearest the Castle gate was probably the bookshop which King George III frequented. Salisbury Tower, wearing a pretty if incongruous crown, shared in the collective effect of domestic well-being. Today only the front of the gateway itself remains unaltered in appearance.

11. King Henry VIII Gateway and the Colehouse from the Lower Ward, *c.* 1770; from the coloured drawing by Paul Sandby in the Royal Library, Windsor Castle

A prisoner angles for alms through the barred window of his cell. At the foot of the wall a placard plays on the feelings of visitors with the words "Pray Remember the Poor Confin'd Debtors".

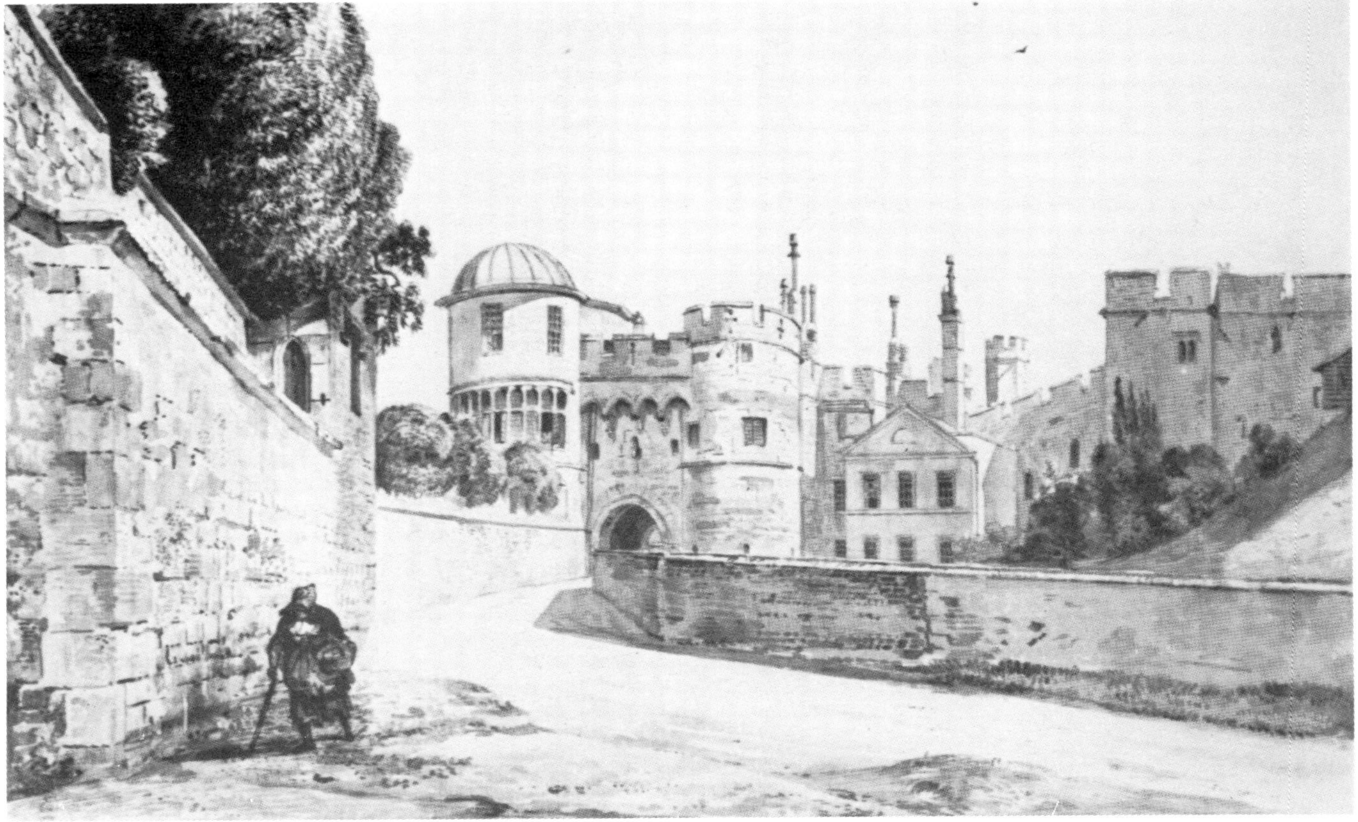

who gilded the Garter Star, applied leaves of gold beyond number to heighten the effect of Verrio's glorious scenes. Grinling Gibbons carved exquisite cascades of fruit and flowers in limewood.

A new "Eating Room" flanked by two music recesses was built for the King on the north side of the Queen's herb garden, and here the ceiling was painted with a sunlit "Banquet of the Gods". In this lovely dining-room the King kept one of his many pets, "the Bird called Cockatoo". On the south side of the herb garden, which was renamed Brick Court, a small chapel was built for his Portuguese queen, Catherine of Braganza. On the ceiling of her Presence Chamber next door Verrio painted the Queen herself, surrounded by Virtues, and in her Audience Chamber she could look up and see herself seated in a triumphal chariot drawn by swans.

Verrio's richest work was achieved in St. George's Hall and the chapel at its western end. Over the altar he painted the scene of the Last Supper, and by a clever device, showed Our Lord and the Apostles seated under a dome, through which the real organ of the chapel was visible. The north wall he filled with "The Miracles of our blessed Saviour". Verrio was fond of including in his frescoes portraits of himself and his friends (and sometimes, with less flattering intent, his enemies), and in the scene of the Miracles, it was said, "among the Spectators, is Verrio himself, in a full black Wig, who looks directly at you, whilst all the rest appear very attentive to the Subject of the Picture."[5] He painted himself again in a black hood and scarlet cloak among the characters of Shakespeare's *Merry Wives of Windsor*, which he introduced into "The Triumph of the Black

---

12. The West Approach to the Norman Gateway, *c.* 1770; from the coloured drawing by Paul Sandby in the Royal Library, Windsor Castle

The drum tower on the left of the gateway reveals Queen Elizabeth I's "Window for watching the Tennis Play", erected at the end of her Gallery when she was planning to have a tennis court on the North Terrace. Although the project was not carried out, the window would have afforded her a superb view across the river. The house built in about 1760 for the Lieutenant Governor (now part of the residence of the Constable and Governor) may be seen in the Moat Garden, below the tower on the right. Inside the passage of the gateway a door on the left opened into the "Porter's Residence".

Prince" on the north wall of St. George's Hall. The Prince was shown seated in a triumphal car, receiving King John of France and King David of Scotland, while a host of slaves and captives bore him along, and the Countess of Salisbury wove a garland for him.[6]

With the completion of the chapel and St. George's Hall in 1682–1683 the great works in the royal apartments came to an end. The traditional pattern had been preserved, the King's and Queen's suites being each approached through its own Guard Chamber and state staircase, to which the Grand Entrance (Edward III's *La Spicerie*) gave access. For the King a domed staircase had been built across the east side of Horn Court. By this name the King's former cloister and herb garden was henceforth known, on account of a large pair of stag's horns which hung there. It was paved with Purbeck stone, and the north and south walls were decorated by Verrio and Coussin, as were the walls and ceiling of the staircase. On the west side a gallery paved with black and white marble led from the King's Audience, or Privy, Chamber to the chapel at the end of St. George's Hall. All his private rooms faced north, while the Queen for the most part enjoyed the sunnier view which looked southwards over the Quadrangle. She had in effect the best of both aspects, since her drawing-room was at the western extremity of the Star Building, looking north like her adjacent Bedchamber.

Immediately below the King's apartments a remodelled suite of rooms accommodated his mistress, the Duchess of Portsmouth, and her son by him, Charles Lennox, Duke of Richmond.[7] The convenience of the arrangement is revealed by the proximity of the old backstairs, now gone, which were guarded by the King's confidant, Will Chiffinch, closet-keeper and page of the bedchamber. A contemporary poet sketches the scene:

> in the twilight of the day
> As England's monarch in his closet lay,
> and Chiffinch stepp'd to fetch the female prey.

At the same time as the royal apartments were being redecorated, work was also being done on the east and south fronts. As a preliminary the Norman ditch had been filled in as far as the Rubbish Gate in 1676. Long-standing references to "crack't towers" indicate a measure of urgency. Between 1677 and 1680 the towers which

King Henry II had originally built and to which King Edward III gave extra depth were repaired, and the one known as the "Watch Tower" at the south-east corner entirely rebuilt.

The rooms along these two fronts were panelled, painted and decorated with carvings to fit them for royal occupation. They became the apartments of King Charles II's brother, the Duke of York, later King James II, and his second wife, Mary of Modena. Communication from the King's and Queen's block was by way of a room over the Kitchen Gatehouse, at the north-east angle of the Upper Ward. It was dignified with the name of "The Duke of York's Guard Chamber". Both the Duke and his Duchess had a formal suite of rooms, comprising Presence and Audience Chambers, Drawing Room and Bedchamber. For "the lady Anne" (later Queen Anne), the Duke's younger daughter by his first wife, the "ruinous tower" at the north-east corner was taken down and "rebuilt larger than now it is."[8] After the Duke's accession his apartments were nominally set apart for the use of a Prince of Wales, and "The Duke of York's Guard Chamber" became "The Prince of Wales's Guard Chamber".

With such palatial splendours accruing to his dignity, King Charles II was unwilling to leave the Dean and Canons in virtual possession of part of the North Terrace. In 1676 he issued a Warrant stating that as he had thought fit to enlarge it by "taking in the Colledgate walke belonginge to the Deane and Cannons of ouer Royall Chappell," they and their successors should have "ffree use of ouer said Tarrace walke with full liberty to enter in with their own Keys". The members of the Chapter thus exchanged their portion for the privilege of entering the North Terrace by a gate immediately below Winchester Tower.[9]

In front of the Star Building the King widened the Terrace in 1678, so that at this point it opens out into a broad bastion. At the east end he caused to be placed the sundial which still stands there on a stone base carved by Grinling Gibbons. It was the work of a craftsman named Henry Wynne, who received £20 for making the "large brasse horizontal dyall placed at ye end of ye north terrace & for a journey to Windsor to place it upon ye Pedestal". The innovation became equally a focus of interest for sightseers and a trap for the unwary. In the earliest guide-book to the Castle, Bickham's

Deliciae Britannicae, or the Curiosities of Hampton-Court and Windsor-Castle, published in 1742, there is an instructive reference to Wynne's "curious Sun-Dial . . . whereon all the Points of the Compass are particularly delineated, at which Place a Centinel always stands, and when any unguarded Spectator claps his Hand upon it he claims, by Dint of Custom, Sixpence as a Forfeit."[10]

The ditch being already filled in as far as the Rubbish Gate, a continuation of the Terrace was built along the east front and part of the south. Again we are indebted to Evelyn for a view of what was being done. In June 1683 he recorded: There was now the *Terraces* almost brought round the old *Castle* [he meant the Upper Ward, which writers sometimes called "the castle"]: The Grass made cleane, even, & curiously turf't, also the *Avenues* to the New-Park, & other Walkes planted with *Elmes* & limes, and a pretty Canale, & receptacle for fowle." Under the new East Terrace a bowling green was laid out.

The "new park" was an extension of the Great Park which brought it up to the boundary of the Little Park, though they still did not meet because a hiatus was imposed by the road leading into Park Street from Frogmore. It was the last lap of the highway from Staines, which traversed the ancient circuitous route between the Saxon palace at Old Windsor and the Castle. The land for the "new park" was surveyed in 1680, following the appointment on 12th May of four commissioners empowered to treat with the various owners. The royal warrant which gave them their authority revealed that the King was "disposed to have an avenue 240 feet broad made in a direct line between our Castle of Windsor and our Great Park there." Possession of the land was obtained by the Crown for £1242 4s. 9d., and planting of the "Great Avenue" or "Long Walk" began in 1684.[11] It stretched not only through the "new park" but penetrated deep into the older portion of the Great Park as far as Snow (or Snowdon) Hill three miles distant from the Castle. Celia Fiennes, an intrepid gentlewoman who toured England on horseback and came to Windsor in 1698, described it as a "fine walk or rather road planted with trees, of a huge length into the Forest which King Charles made for his going out in the divertion of shooteing."[12]

Today the Long Walk creates a seemingly endless vista from the middle of the south front. The effect was not fully accomplished when it was first planted because there remained between the avenue and the Castle, not only the Frogmore road, but a little complex of territory where buildings cut across the view. A continuation of Castle Hill skirted the South Terrace, entering the Little Park through a gateway made in 1635, and continuing until it reached "Mother Dodd's Hill" at the end of the slopes, where it dropped down into the Lower Park and ended at Datchet Ferry. On its way to the Little Park it passed a red-brick house standing opposite the Rubbish Gate, in front of the royal "garden plott", and then a long, mysterious-looking building which everything points to as an amalgam of the Cockpit, Chocolate House and Playhouse mentioned in contemporary accounts. This public pathway and its various adjacent features constituted a barrier which remained uninvaded for another 150 years.

No less famous than the planning of the Long Walk, Evelyn considered, was the "exalting of so huge a quantity of Excellent Water, to the enormous height of the Castle, for the use of the whole house, by an extraordinary invention & force of Sir *Samuell Morland.*" Sir Samuel's engine, worked by a water mill called Underore Mill, which was leased and later bought from the Corporation of Windsor, forced water from the Thames up to a reservoir in the middle of the Quadrangle. The machine had caused a sensation when it was first demonstrated two years earlier. On 16th July, 1681, four men had pumped sixty barrelsful of water into a cistern placed on the North Terrace, the King himself timing the operation with his "minute-watch". A fortnight later, on 30th July, eight men forced up a stream which rose into the air to a height of sixty feet above the Terrace.

On this occasion red wine was mixed with the water to make it more clearly visible. The performance was watched by the King and Queen, the Prince of Orange and about 1,000 other people, including many foreign ambassadors. All agreed that it was the boldest and most remarkable experiment every carried out with water in any part of the world.[13] Morland perfected his invention by September 1682, when it replaced Queen Mary I's system. His pumping-station was the forerunner of the modern Castle waterworks on the same spot, and permitted the installation of "a Marble Batheing Cistern" for the Queen, into which water was led by copper pipes. Marble cisterns were also being placed in the royal "stool rooms" at the time of King

Charles II's death, but whether water-closets were ever attached to them is uncertain. The wardrobe accounts continue to talk about "close-stools" with realistic frequency. Those used by royalty were covered with red velvet fringed with gold, and had red leather covers for travelling. It is clear that they embodied only primitive convenience, for the wardrobe accounts also record the intermittent issue of pewter close-stool pans and lengths of serge "to the necessary woman to carry them in".

Over Morland's new reservoir was placed the fine equestrian statue of the King which now stands at the western end of the Quadrangle. Evelyn, who fortunately missed nothing, had seen it in July 1680, when he described it as "the King on Horseback lately cast in Coper, & set upon a rich Pedestal of white Marble, the worke of Mr. *Gibbons*, &c., at the expense of *Toby Rustat a Page of the Back Stayres*, who by his wonderful frugality had arrived at a grate Estate in Money, & did many works of Charity; as well as this of gratitude to his Master, which cost him £1000." Tobias Rustat was yeomen of the robes to the King from 1660 to 1685. The statue which so grandly commemorates both sovereign and servant was the work of a German sculptor, Josiah Ibach.

The structural alterations in the Castle were carried out for the King by an architect named Hugh May, who was appointed controller of the works in 1673 and remained in office until his death on 21st February, 1684. He was buried in the church of Mid-Lavant near Chichester, where his coffin-plate recorded that he was "sole Architect in Contriving and Governing the Works in the Great Alterations" at Windsor.[14] One of the last items mentioned during his lifetime was the erection in 1680 of a new guardroom which Bickham said was "capable of receiving Three Hundred Men". It made the distal end of a range of red-brick buildings extending, like a long arm, from the south side of Winchester Tower, and had a steeply pitched roof with dormer windows. The inner end was an office, later converted into a tavern called "The Royal Standard", and this adjoined a three-storeyed house standing next to the tower.[15]

The soldiers rehoused in the guardroom had been living in improvised quarters in the eastern part of the moat, where the tennis courts used to be, and some may have continued to do so, for the "ill state of the barracks in the Round Tower ditch" called for attention as late as 1717.[16] King Charles had released the site of the tennis court in 1675, shortly before building a covered court on the south side of Castle Hill, on part of the old royal vineyard. Although his successors used it little, if at all, it remained there until about 1800.

May's successor was Sir Christopher Wren, already famous as the architect of St. Paul's Cathedral. Wren's father had become Dean of Windsor in 1635, when he himself was two years old, and retained the appointment until he died in 1659. The Castle had therefore been Wren's home, but closely though his name is linked with it, his contribution to its fame was slight. No structural addition can with certainty be assigned to him. The guardroom seems to have been completed during May's tenure, but Wren perhaps added the three-storeyed house linking it with Winchester Tower, which is the only remaining portion. If he did, it is now so altered that he himself would hardly recognize it.

He did not disdain to bend his mind to the trivialities that remained. When Henry Angell, Gentleman Porter of the Outer Gate, represented the comfortless conditions of the Colehouse in 1686 to Henry Howard, seventh Duke of Norfolk and Governor of the Castle, the Duke in turn passed the complaint to Wren. It was a sorry picture, "the roof and glass windows of the prison being very much out of repair and there being many poor prisoners now in Custody, and the Rain and weather being very injurious to them."[17] Wren saw that the repairs were done. Some years later we come across him considering the erection of a shop by Mrs. Elizabeth Edwards, whose husband, by reason of debt, was "withdrawn". She had been turned out of her home in the town, and had many children to support. In this plight, Mrs. Edwards, who was a sempstress, appealed to King William III for leave to erect a shed "on the right hand within the gate going into the Lower yard of Windsor Castle." Wren thought it would be no inconvenience, and on 14th March, 1699, Mrs. Edwards received sanction for her shed, which remained inside the Castle gate until 1719.[18]

Yet Wren nursed revolutionary schemes for the glorification of Windsor, and a glance at them adds colour to the changing trends of taste. Already in 1678 he had designed for King Charles II, who planned to remove his father's body from the vault in St. George's Chapel, a domed mausoleum 150 feet high, richly adorned with coloured marbles and gilt-brass. It was intended to replace "Wolsey's Tomb House", but the scheme never progressed beyond the completion of Wren's plan, which is preserved in the library of All Souls' College, Oxford. In later years he was to produce for King William III a design to transform the entire Castle in the Italian style, but this proved equally barren. He was left with the Colehouse, Mrs. Edward's shack and the recurrent problem of the ditch, where at this time there was "a small piece of void ground, formerly a garden, but at present a Common Nuisance, abused by the laying of Carrion and making Dunghills and emptying Jakes's upon it, which makes it very noisome to Their Majesties' Court and all persons passing y^t way."[19] To improve the ditch Mr. Philip Lovegrove, a Windsor gardener, was allowed to plant a new garden in 1699. It extended from the drawbridge past the backs of the Military Knights' Houses to Mary Tudor Tower, and included a vineyard.[20]

St. George's Chapel benefited in a more positive way from Wren's attentions, though here too his dreams of stylish novelty bore no fruit. In 1681 the Dean and Canons invited him to make a survey of the fabric, which was showing signs of decay, and he found that the roof in particular stood in need of repair. "It contains a vast deal of excellent Timber," he reported, "& it is a fault there is soe much, the Scantlings being too great & heavy. . . . However I cannot advise a new roofe by reason of the damage that may be done accidentally to the Vault." Choked gutters and holes in the lead, through which rain leaked in, called from him the opinion that once a quarter the roof should be inspected, "for drips," he sensibly observed, "happen sodainly, & one shilling seasonably expended prevents great charges."[21]

So great had been the neglect that many of the Royal Beasts—the heraldic stone animals which surmounted the pinnacles and lent both grace and a measure of stability to the flying buttresses—lay broken in the gutters. Among his timely suggestions for the conservation of the chapel Wren advised: "I could wish the Beasts might be taken of(f), and if in liew Pine-apples were added to coape the Pinnacle from weather, it would be a decent ornament, & the charge not soe considerable, as the advantage it would give the Fabrick." The pineapple was a fashionable novelty at the time. Rose, the royal gardener, had succeeded in growing one, and a painting in the royal collection shows him presenting it to the King on bended knee. In the back-ground is a house said to be Dorney Court, which stands a mile or two north-west of Windsor, on the Buckinghamshire side of the Thames. It was there that Rose is reputed to have grown the pine-apple, which was thought to be the first ever raised in England. The date of his achievement is unknown, but the story further asserts that the culture was made from suckers of a King-pine served at a banquet at Whitehall in August 1668. Evelyn both saw and tasted the fruit, for the King gave him a slice from his own plate.[22]

The broken beasts were removed as Wren advised, but no pine-apples took their place. Two and a half centuries passed before radical restoration brought the pinnacles again under review, and during that time they stood unadorned.

10

GARTER PAGEANTRY

Elias Ashmole, a noted lawyer and antiquary who was also Windsor Herald, prepared his monumental record of the Order of the Garter during the years immediately following the Restoration.

He began collecting his materials in 1658. In the following year he visited Windsor, taking with him the celebrated Bohemian etcher, Wenceslaus Hollar, who had taught the King to draw and paint when he was Prince of Wales. Between then and 1663 Hollar made a number of skilful views and drawings of different parts of the Castle, most of which were used by Ashmole to illustrate his book.[1] It was published in 1672 under the title *The Institutions, Laws and Ceremonies of the Most Noble Order of the Garter*. Hollar also provided choice engravings which show the Garter costume and ceremonial maintained by King Charles II, who swiftly redeemed and abundantly glorified the Order after its eclipse during the interregnum.

We are thus equally indebted to Ashmole and to Hollar. To the former for much of our knowledge of the early history of the Order. To the latter for valuable views of the Castle before King Charles II's alterations, as well as illustrations of Garter display at its most spectacular.

Ashmole listed the number of people on whom the ceremonial depended in his own time. Besides the officers of the Order and the officers of arms, there were thirteen noblemen, not themselves Knights of the Garter, who held special appointments. One carried the King's sword of state before him in the procession. Three others bore his train. The rest played their part at the Grand Feast. There was the Sewer, whose responsibility it was to make all the arrangements for the banquet and to supervise the seating. Another lord was the Carver, another the Cup Bearer. The remaining six were concerned in the ceremony before and after the banquet, when the King washed. At the time Ashmole was writing, the thirteen noblemen were all earls.[2]

To such a peak of glory had the Order attained that a Garter procession was a parade of jewelled grandeur beyond compare. It set out from the King's Audience Chamber, descended the great domed staircase to Horn Court and passed through the Grand Entrance to the Quadrangle, continuing under the Norman Gateway and through the Middle and Lower Wards. At its head walked the Poor Knights, in pairs, followed by the Heralds. The latter created a conspicuously vivid effect, for the royal arms which covered their blue tabards were embroidered in gold and pearls. The Knights of the Garter came next, two by two, in order of their appointment, the most senior walking last, and then the Officers of the Order in crimson robes, and the Sword Bearer immediately before the King. The three Lords followed, carrying the King's train, and the royal bodyguard of the Yeomen of the Guard brought up the rear. On the Grand Day the King walked under a canopy of cloth of gold carried by twelve Gentlemen of the Privy Chamber.[3]

He enhanced the finery of the apparel by ordaining in 1661 that the Knights should wear under their robes a doublet and puffed breeches of cloth of silver, and white silk stockings. Their surcoats and hoods were of crimson velvet, which offered a rich contrast to the deep blue of their mantles. Their caps were high-crowned ones of black velvet adorned with curling plumes of white ostrich feathers with a tuft of black heron feathers in the centre, and bound about with a band thickset with diamonds. As they walked, the radiance of a thousand jewels was released, for all the insignia of the Order was rich with gems. The George, says Ashmole, was "garnished with diamonds and other precious stones at the pleasure of the Knight of the Garter who owns it," and the Lesser George was often encircled with diamonds. The blue velvet Garter was fastened with a jewelled buckle, and the motto of the Order was sometimes outlined with precious stones. The Garter worn by King Charles II had the motto formed around it in rose diamonds.

The heavy mantles of blue velvet lined with white silk also lent themselves to adornment. They were fastened with cordons or loose strings of blue silk and gold, and the Garter encircling the cross of St. George on the left breast was embroidered with "Oriental pearls". The insignia was completed by the Garter Star, or "Glory", added by King Charles I in 1629.

Robes were ordered for everyone who took part in the ceremonies. The canons wore mantles of dark red taffeta with the cross of St. George worked in gold and silk on the right shoulder. The minor canons and the gentlemen of the choir had copes of cloth of gold. All the mantles fell in full, stiff folds to the ground, and hundreds of yards of costly material went into their making. The Prelate's and Chancellor's robes each took eighteen yards of purple velvet, and ten of white taffeta for lining. The Register, Garter King of Arms and Black Rod wore crimson satin robes for which similar lengths were allowed, together with the same amount of white taffeta.

The pageantry was heightened by the gold altar-plate set out in the chapel, the velvet canopy over the Sovereign's stall and the velvet cushions. The choir of the King's chapel at Whitehall joined that of St. George's for the occasion, and the rites were made the more impressive by their singing, and by the organ and the "Instrumental loud Musick" introduced by Captain Cook, Master of the Children of the King's Chapel. Ashmole relates that during the Grand Procession, which after the Reformation took place during the revised service, maintaining the effect of dividing it into two, a hymn of thanksgiving was sung which had been composed in 1665 by the Dean, Dr. Brune Ryves, and set to music by Captain Cook. Clergy and choir joined in the Grand Procession, which if weather permitted was an outdoor one. The route varied. In the later years of King James I's reign, when he was unable to walk in the procession and had to be carried in a gout chair, it left the chapel by one door and quickly re-entered by another, but usually it went through the west door and proceeded around "the bounds of the church yard"—by which Ashmole meant the Lower Ward—to the Castle gate. Then it continued past the Poor Knights' houses and back to the chapel through the Dean's Cloister. During the second part of the service the traditional offerings of gold and silver were made.[4]

The return of the Sovereign and Garter Knights to the royal

apartments was proclaimed by trumpets, which preceded the Poor Knights and sounded all the way to the King's great staircase. There they ceased, and the drums and fifes began to beat and play. These in turn gave place to wind instruments playing in the gallery of St. George's Hall as the King entered.

The furnishings in the banqueting hall were of gold and silk, and gold plate gleamed on a table set along the south side. Hollar depicts the scene in a finely detailed drawing, and Ashmole describes the elaborate layout and ceremonial. The King's table was set across the east end of St. George's Hall, on a dais reached by three steps, and was 12 feet long and 3½ feet wide. On the top step a strong rail was placed across the room to "keep off the crowd from the Sovereign's table". The Knights dined at a table set along the north side. According to custom, they wore their robes, high-crowned caps and jewels throughout the banquet.

When the King reached his throne, water for washing was brought up with three reverences by the noblemen appointed for this service. Four presented the Great Basin. A fifth carried the Ewer, from which he poured out fragrant rose water. The last handed the Surnap, or towel.

Grace was said, and the first course carried in. Towards the end of it the nobleman who served as Cup-Bearer handed a gilt cup filled with wine to the King. The Knights Companions uncovered, the King drank their health, and they in turn pledged the King.

When the second course was brought in, Garter King of Arms, attended by all the officers of arms, advanced to the dais, cried "Largesse" three times and proclaimed the Sovereign's titles in Latin, French and English. In response to the call for the royal largesse £10 in gold was placed in Garter's hat for distribution among the officers of arms.

The party then retired backwards and all together cried "Largesse" three times more. The style of newly installed Knights Companions was next proclaimed in the same manner, each in turn, but in English only and with one cry of "Largesse" before and after.

When the banquet ended the King washed again with the same ceremony as before. Then he rose and passed through the lines of Knights and spectators to his Presence Chamber.[5]

Ashmole recorded some of the Garter menus, which included such delicacies as "Peacock in Pride", peacock pie, lamprey pie, roast lobsters and "Eggs of Portugal". Here is the one for the royal table at Windsor on St. George's Day 1671.[6] The number of dishes was less than in former times, but it is clear that culinary standards were maintained:

FIRST COURSE

1 *Wild Boar* Pye	2 *Salmon*
3 Chine of *Beef*	4 Haggest *Puddings*
5 *Beatilia* Pye with Patties	6 Gamon *Bacon* with 12 tame Pigeons
7 *Ducklings* boiled 12	8 *Chickens* boiled 12
9 Chine *Mutton* and *Veal* 4	10 *Pikes* rosted 2
11 *Buck* baked	12 *Green Geese* 6
13 *Carpes* great	14 *Chicken* Pye frosted

15   *Sallet* [Salad]
16   *Sweet-breads*
17   Almond *Pudding*
18   *Petty Patties*
19   Hasht *Sallet* with 4 *capons*
20   *Chicks* marrionated

SECOND COURSE

1 *Pullets* soused 16	2 *Tongue* Pye
3 *Rabbets* rosted 12	4 *Cream* Tarts
5 *Pheasants* with eggs 6	6 *Crabs* Buttered 6
7 *Quails* 24	8 *Pigeons* tame 12
9 *Lobsters* 6	10 *Chicks* fat 12
11 Gamon *Bacon* with 2 *Tongues*	12 *Ruffs* 12
13 *Tarts* sorts	14 *Ducklings* 12

15   *Sallets* of Pickles
16   *Eggs* of Portugal
17   *Jelly*
18   Luke *Olives*
19   *Pease*
20   *Prawnes*

Besides the main courses, there were red and white strawberries, China oranges, ice cream and seventy pounds of sweets.

A festival planned on such a scale, and lasting for three days, was a drain on the royal purse. This is probably one reason why it was not held regularly, and not always at Windsor, but sometimes in London. A multitude of people had to be present, apart from those leading figures already mentioned. So many were necessary to the King's state and comfort that the Upper Ward was crowded, and the Knights Companions had to stay in the canons' houses. Ashmole gives a list of the members of the Royal Household required at Windsor for a Garter festival:

The Lord Chamberlain and servants
Mr. Vice Chamberlain
The Groom of the Stole
Gentlemen of the Bedchamber
Bedchamber-men
Privy Purse
Secretaries of State
Secretaries of State, Scotland
Gentlemen-Ushers of the Privy Chamber
12 Gentlemen of the Privy Chamber in Waiting
4 Gentlemen-Ushers daily waiters
2 Carvers
2 Cup-bearers
2 Sewers
2 Quarter-Waiters, Gentlemen-Ushers
2 Pages of the Presence [Chamber]
2 Chaplains
2 Esquires of the Body
2 Physicians
2 Apothecaries
2 Chyryrgeons [surgeons]
4 Serjeants at Arms
Mistress Seamstress and Laundress to His Majesty
8 Sewers of the Chamber
4 Grooms of the Chamber
Pages of the Backstairs
14 Lords to attend His Majesty
Captain of the Guards
Officers of the Guard
Officers of the Robes
Yeomen of the Guard
2 Grooms of the Privy Chamber
3 Masters of the Tents
Groom-Porter
Master of the Ceremonies
Marshal of the Ceremonies
Aid of the Ceremonies
Removing Wardrobe
Jewel House
Gentlemen of the Chapel

Musicians
5 Messengers
Yeomen of the Bows and Guns
16 Trumpeters
Captain Cook, and the Children of the Chapel
Serjeant-Trumpeter
Drum-Major, 4 Drummers and a Fife

The same procedure and state were observed when the festival was held at Whitehall, where the ceremonies on 22nd, 23rd and 24th April in the year 1667 were colourfully described by Evelyn.[7] Much of what he saw displeased him. The feast was disorderly, and he felt that insufficient regard was displayed for the solemnity of the occasion. He opened his mind on the subject to Pepys when they took a long walk together on 26th April:

> Evelyn did tell me [wrote Pepys] of the ridiculous humour of our King and Knights of the Garter the other day, who, whereas heretofore their robes were only to be worn during their ceremonies and services, these, as proud of their coats, did wear them all day till night, and then rode into the [Hyde] Parke with them on. Nay, and he tells me he did see my Lord Oxford and the Duke of Monmouth in a hackney-coach with two footmen in the Parke, with their robes on; which is a most scandalous thing.

Evelyn was among the last people to have an opportunity of witnessing the protracted ritual. Even while Ashmole was recording its stupendous conventions at Windsor a few years later, it was already doomed, and after 1674 the three-day festival was abandoned. From that time the ceremonies took a more compact form. Another procedure of the Order which did not long survive was the prescribed form of degradation. The last Garter Knight whose sword and banner were kicked out of St. George's Chapel was the "generous, princely and brave" James Butler, 2nd Duke of Ormonde. He was condemned for his Jacobite sympathies in King George I's reign, and the ignoble ceremony took place on 12th July, 1716.[8]

11

THE LATER STUARTS

When King Charles II died in 1685 Verrio had begun painting the interior of "Wolsey's Tomb House". He completed the work for King James II, whose reported intention of holding Roman Catholic services there was perhaps never realized, since Wolsey's sarcophagus was not removed. Rumour was enough to cause unrest, and James heightened the alarm when at the healing of the King's evil at Windsor in 1686 he "began to make use of the Latin service and his owne preists, and discharged the Dean of the Chappell and the Chaplains from attendinge any more in that office."[1] The Tomb House was said to have been damaged by the crowd that assembled on 3rd July, 1687, to watch the arrival of the Papal Nuncio and his train of thirty-six coaches, each drawn by six horses. After King James's brief reign Verrio's work was left to regale the eyes of casual visitors, and as no effort was made to preserve it, it gradually decayed. The ceiling, said to have been among his finest achievements, showed the King in Garter robes, treading down a hydra, while at the eastern end Fame held in her right hand an oval of King Charles I, and in her left a similar representation of King Charles II.[2]

King William III and Queen Mary II, for their part, preferred Hampton Court to Windsor, but maintained the royal apartments in seemly style. Celia Fiennes, when she visited Windsor in 1698 (four years after Queen Mary's death), pronounced it "the finest pallace the King has". In the Queen's Bedchamber she saw a bed hung with Indian embroidery on white silk, the gift of the East India Company, and surmounted with great plumes of white feathers, and noted at the foot a low screen of cedar wood and brass wires. This, she explained, was "instead of the rails use[d] to be quite round the kings and queens beds to keep off companyes coming near them." The King's Drawing Room revealed to her shrewd and appreciative gaze a throne of green velvet richly embroidered with silver and gold, under a canopy "newly made to give audience to the French ambassador to show ye grandeur and magnificence of the British monarch." The canopy was so rich and curled up, and in some places so full, as to look altogether glorious, and Miss Fiennes, although she had a Nonconformist conscience to grapple with, could not but admire it wholeheartedly. "Some of these Foolerys," she conceded, "are requisite sometymes to create admiration and keep up the state of a kingdom and nation."

Adjoining the King's large Bedchamber of State she noted "the King's constant bed chamber." Her observation is a reminder that he slept in the latter, and used the former for political purposes. It was the custom in Stuart reigns, certainly in King Charles II's, for the most secret affairs of state to be conducted in the great Bedchamber, in a space between the bed and the wall.

Like most other visitors throughout the centuries, Miss Fiennes climbed the hundred or more stone steps to the mount and continued up the flight leading to the leads of the Round Tower. It was less high than it is now, but even then the view from the battlements was said to embrace twelve counties—Berkshire, Buckinghamshire, Bedfordshire, Essex, Hampshire, Hertfordshire, Kent, Middlesex, Oxfordshire, Surrey, Sussex and Wiltshire.[3] She noted too that around its walls grew black and white maidenhair fern, a herb much used for coughs. Leaving Windsor by the riverside path to Datchet Ferry, she enjoyed the full beauty of the northern front of the Castle. It looked "very noble, ye walls round, with ye battlements, and gilt balls, and other adornments." The route was a pleasant one, wandering along the river bank beside a brick wall which King William III was building around the Little Park. He had enlarged the Park by taking in Datchet Mead and other riverside fields, and although deer still roamed there he entertained visions of elaborate developments below the north front of the Castle.

They made part of his plan to complete King Charles II's work and Italianize both Upper and Lower Wards, the aim being to introduce "improvements in a similar style, and on an equal scale of grandeur with Hampton Court". It was in this same year, 1698, that Sir Christopher Wren produced his romantic design for the King. It was impassioned, beautiful, and insubstantial. The Round Tower, that massy keep, was to be approached by an immense double flight of steps. The Horseshoe Cloister he intended to remove, leaving St. George's Chapel open to view from the town. Below the North Terrace there was to be a lower terrace, leading down to "Maestricht", which would no longer conduct the eye over a homely plain, but through a vista of formal gardens with an ornamental canal and fountains extending to the river.[4]

For this part of his project the King sought the co-operation of André le Nôtre, who had created the canal at Versailles thirty years earlier, and traditionally remodelled the parks at Greenwich and St. James's Palace for King Charles II. The old man was eighty-five, and had retired in 1693, but he acquiesced. William Bentinck, Earl of Portland, Ranger of the Great and Little Parks and Superintendent of the Royal Gardens, acted as intermediary. A letter from him to the King from Paris, dated 7th March, 1698, brought the welcome intelligence: "M. le Nostre will make me a plan for the gardens contemplated at Windsor."[5] The plan presently arrived, but we hear no more. Wren's ambition was too costly, and so the dream faded, and the Castle was spared its elegant, outlandish motley.

The idea of the gardens was not lost on the King's sister-in-law, the Princess of Denmark, who tried to put it into effect when she succeeded to the throne in 1702. She was deeply attached to Windsor, partly because of her fondness for stag hunting, and after her marriage in 1683 continued to have a home in the Castle. As well as "the lady Anne's tower" she was given the use of the "Prince of Wales's apartments" adjoining it along the east front, where her father had lived as Duke of York. The registers of St. George's Chapel record that "Princess Anna Sophia ye Daughter of Prince George and Anne of Denmarke was Born here in Windsore (in ye Prince of Wales his Lodgeing in ye Chamber over ye Staires yt goes downe into ye Tarrace Walke) ye Twelfth day of May one Thousand six Hundred & eighty six."

After the death of Nell Gwyn in the following year Anne and her husband took as their private home Burford House, built by (or for) that lady on part of the old royal vineyard. It was the property of

Charles Beauclerk, 1st Duke of St. Albans, her son by King Charles II. When he came of age in 1691 and required his house, Princess Anne bought from Sidney Godolphin, 1st Lord (later Earl) Godolphin, the red-brick villa which stood opposite the Rubbish Gate. It was small, but sunny and attractive, with an entrance flanked by hexagonal towers. Following the death of Queen Mary II in 1695, King William allowed Anne the use of the Queen's apartments, perhaps because Wren's abortive scheme included an entrance in the middle of the south front (where it was eventually placed for King George IV), and this would have meant the removal of her house. As it turned out, she kept it for the rest of her life, and found her greatest happiness within its friendly walls.

In the autumn of 1695 she brought her son, William Duke of Gloucester, to Windsor for the first time. Out of a catalogue of short-lived infants and miscarriages, this boy alone reached an age approaching maturity, and in him was vested all hope of a Protestant succession for the House of Stuart. When he first saw Windsor he was six years old, and sickly, but his enthusiasm was for warfare, and all his play consisted of planned battles. The Castle enthralled him. Theodore Randue, Keeper of the Palace, wanted him to look at the pictures in the royal apartments, but he had eyes only for Verrio's romanticized but splendid "Triumph of the Black Prince" on the north wall of St. George's Hall. "This will be a good place to fight my battles in," he exclaimed excitedly. Next day some friends from Eton College joined him, and after attending a review in St. George's Hall, and inspecting Gloucester's array of pikes, muskets and drums, the little company broke up into two forces. One side defended the staircase and gallery, which represented a fortress. The mock stronghold was attacked by the Prince, who fought so vigorously that he received bruises on his neck and shoulder.[6]

On 6th January, 1696, he was appointed a Knight of the Garter. King William III chose his seventh birthday, Friday, 24th July, for his investiture and installation in St. George's Chapel, and a great concourse of nobility and gentry assembled for the event. Young as he was, the Prince conducted himself with graceful assurance. His devoted Welsh attendant, Jenkin Lewis, noted with pride his dignity as he walked in the procession returning to the palace. He appeared for a short time at the banquet, and later walked out in the park in his Garter robes for all the world to see.

In the year 1700 he spent his eleventh birthday at Windsor. It was celebrated in the usual joyous manner, with cannon, bell-ringing, bonfires, fireworks and illuminations, and a great banquet in St. George's Hall. This was on Wednesday, 24th July. Next morning the Prince complained of headache and sore throat. By Saturday evening he was very ill. He became delirious, and after a terrible week-end died late on the Monday night. Windsor was still not the accepted royal burial place, and so the body of the young Prince was borne to Westminster Abbey where so many of his ancestors lay. The funeral procession was to have gone by water, but as there was no moon it was judged safer to travel by road. His mother, now childless, shut herself up at Windsor with her grief.[7]

The death of this frail but heroic little prince, who suffered from hydrocephalus, prepared the way for the accession of the Elector of Hanover, the eldest Protestant descendant of King Charles I, in 1714. Meanwhile, William's mother's brilliant reign was still to come. One incident which dramatically reflects its eventful glory took place in the Castle. She was sitting in the oriel in the Queen's Bedchamber when news reached her of the Duke of Marlborough's victory over the French at Blenheim on 2nd August, 1704. The letter which the messenger, Colonel Daniel Parke, handed to her was not addressed to the Queen herself, but to Marlborough's wife, Duchess Sarah. In it he asked her to let the Queen know of his victory.[8]

In return for the manor of Woodstock, where he built Blenheim Palace, the Duke and his successors were to render "to the Crown for ever at the Castle of Windsor on the 2nd of August yearly one standard or colours with three Flower de Luces painted thereupon."[9] For about a century these flags bearing the royal lilies of France were placed in the oriel, which was known as the Blenheim Tower. Today the current banner of white satin, painted with three golden fleur-de-lis and edged with gold fringe, hangs above the Duke's bust in the Queen's Guard Chamber. It has for company the Tricolour flag of modern France which the Duke of Wellington renders annually on 18th June, the anniversary of the battle of Waterloo in 1815, as quit-rent for Stratfield Saye. These are the only two instances of such a grant being made to a British general.

The Queen constantly resided at Windsor in the summer, and
replenished the royal apartments tastefully. At the beginning of her
reign Verrio was painting her state staircase and her private oratory
on the south side of Brick Court, so bringing them into harmony
with the rest of the rich Caroline interior. In 1704 we find her
packing her sister's "India embroidered bed" and its feathers off to
Hampton Court, and setting up a new one of Spitalfields velvet, "the
Ground whereof is White, embossed with a great Variety of blue and
scarlet Flowers". At the same time, green mohair curtains lined with
green taffeta were ordered for Queen Elizabeth's Gallery, and a
crimson taffeta canopy for use at receptions.[10] She entertained the
newly proclaimed King of Spain, Charles VI, at Windsor in January
1704, and received him magnificently, Evelyn said; but her heart was
not in the Castle and its glories, if we may judge by Dean Swift's
experience on one occasion. "There was a drawing-room today," he
wrote to the faithful Stella, "but so few company that the Queen
sent for us into her bed-chamber, where we made our bows, and
stood about twenty of us round the room while she looked at us with
a fan in her mouth and once a minute said about three words to
some that were nearest to her; and then she was told dinner was
ready, and went out." She reserved her favour for the little retreat
opposite the Rubbish Gate. Pote relates in his *History and Antiquities
of Windsor Castle* that she would "daily withdraw from the royal
Lodgings, and the state and splendour of a great and victorious
Court, to enjoy a happy retirement in this House and Gardens."

Although we do not often light upon her in a regal role, her
domestic minutiae offer satisfying compensation. In 1705 she orders
crimson Genoa damask chairs and curtains for the drawing-room of
her "Little House", and a year later, "6 dozen yards of double gold
Purle for a bed torn by the dogs". "Four pairs of white satin down
pillows and two small white satin bolsters of fine down" add a
queenly note. A crimson cover for her gout chair follows, and when
in 1708 she decides on a new bed for the Little House, this too is of
rich crimson damask.[11] One by one the details add up to human
intimacy. She comes closest to reality when she creates "Queen
Anne's Well" in the woods at Chalvey, near Slough, placing over it a
stone engraved with her cypher. The Queen had weak eyes, and this
local water, which fed the once-famed watercress beds of Chalvey,

was particularly prescribed for eye complaints.[12] It was borne to the Castle, not only for her, but years later for Queen Charlotte, in buckets slung across the back of a donkey.

If the Queen does not personally conduct us into her "little retreate out of ye Palace," Celia Fiennes acts as a ready guide. She went all over it when she revisited Windsor in about 1708. Her description indicates that the drawing-room, where she saw the cosy crimson furnishings and some tapestries which struck her as "fresh and lively", was at the back of the house. It faced west, and opened on to a lawn which led to the old royal "garden plott" on the south. Here, in a formal division of the grounds, she found "lawrells fillery cyprus yews, heads and pirramids, and mirtles", then "squares and figures, and all sorts of flowers", and then a cut hedge and an orchard adjoining the gardens of Burford House. Details of the interior add still greater relish to our enjoyment of the past. Miss Fiennes, though unconventionally endowed, had her share of feminine curiosity. She penetrated as far as "a little place wth a seate of Easement of Marble wth sluces of water to wash all down." The revolutionary plumbing which King Charles II was introducing into the Castle when he died was evidently intended to serve models similar to this, but had they ever been installed one feels that Miss Celia Fiennes would have found them.

The Cockpit, Playhouse and Chocolate House next door had gone by this time. They were demolished in 1706, and the site bought by the Crown, since "if built on it would be a great annoyance to the Queen's Little House and Garden". Henry Wise, the royal gardener, added the land to the Little Park. His accounts for work done there show that he made "into Slopes and Levills the Ground where the Cockpit, Chocolate and other old Houses stood." By 1713 men were mowing "the Peice of Ground where the Cockpitt stood that is sown with Hay Seed", and about the same time there is a final reference to "weeding the various Slopes on the . . . South Side of the Castle where the Cockpitt stood."[13]

Pedestrians and horsemen continued to frequent the road leading past the Queen's house, and she herself had to cross it to reach the Castle, but royalty was conditioned to lack of privacy, and there is no evidence that she resented being in the public eye. On the contrary, she displayed neighbourly feeling to such effect that she built a bridge free of tolls to replace Datchet Ferry, and laid out a carriage road to it round the wall of the Little Park on the Frogmore side. The building of the bridge in 1706 coincided with a little *contretemps* in public relations. Some members of the Corporation were heard to proclaim that the Corporation was not two pence the better for the Queen's coming to Windsor, an observation unexplained in the records but possibly inspired by the threatened decline in the tolls of Windsor Bridge.[14] The matter was discreetly glossed over. Humble apologies followed, and it is tempting to see a practical measure of atoning grace in the erection a year later of the Queen's statue in the niche on the north side of the Town Hall. It shows her in royal robes, holding the orb and sceptre, and beneath it is carved an inscription composed by Mr. William Peisley, Recorder of Windsor, who more than once gave the Corporation the benefit of his classical scholarship:

> Arte tua, Sculptor, non est imitabilis Anna;
> Annae vis similem sculpere? Sculpe Deam.

The translation commonly recorded reads thus:

> Carver, forbear! Thy art no Anne can shew.
> Would'st thou shew Anna? Set a goddess to our view.

Sir Christopher Wren presented the posthumous statue of her husband, Prince George of Denmark, in Roman military habit, which was placed in the corresponding niche on the south side in 1713.[15]

Throughout her reign Henry Wise and Michael Studholme, Surveyor of Her Majesty's Roads, were kept busy on exploitation of the Great and Little Parks. The Queen's passion for hunting had put her in complete command of the topography of the Great Park and Forest, for though by June 1696 she had grown too bulky to ride she refused to be baulked and took to a narrow, one-seated vehicle called a calash. Dean Swift described it as "a chaise with one horse, which she drives herself, and drives furiously, like Jehu." In August 1702 she was out in it almost every day,[16] and as late as 1711 Swift was commending her as "a mighty hunter, like Nimrod". To facilitate her progress roads were laid out which made wide detours through the Great Park: they are shown on a plan of the Park made by Wise, and marked as "The Queen's Chaize Ridings".[17] Drains "to carry water from the Queen's chair (or chaise) roads" had to be cut in 1710.

Her flair for country planning found permanent expression in "a new riding now making in the Great Park" in 1704.[18] It was the charming avenue which begins at Queen Anne's Gate, where King's Road enters the Park, and pursues its grassy way until it loses itself in green depths three miles to the south-west. On Wise's plan it is called "The Queen's Walk". Today it bears the likelier name of "Queen Anne's Ride". King Charles II's Great Avenue also derived pleasing benefit from the joint vision of Queen Anne, Studholme and Wise. In May 1710 the Treasury referred to Sir Christopher Wren an estimate presented by Studholme "for gravelling a new road to be made from the Avenue Gate next to Windsor town end to the top of Snowden Hill",[19] and by the end of June the three-mile drive was partly formed. The name Long Walk appears to have originated at this period, for it was in use eight years later.

Next to hunting, the Queen favoured horse-racing. She had continued King Charles II's custom of holding races on Datchet Mead, but in the summer of 1711 (so the story goes), while driving over Ascot Common, noticed its greater possibilities and put her idea into immediate effect. The inaugural meeting was announced in the *London Gazette* on 12th July, 1711:

> Her Majesty's Plate of 100 guineas will be run for round the new heat on Ascot Common, near Windsor, on Tuesday 7 August next by any horse, mare or gelding no more than six years old the grass before as must be certified by the hand of the breeder, carrying 12 st. to be entered the last day of July at Mr. Hancock's, at Fern Hill, near the starting post.

The event was postponed until Saturday, 11th August. Meanwhile, the Court was in a mood of pleasurable excitement, and Dean Swift, writing on the eve, anticipated "a famous horse-race tomorrow". The course on which this first Ascot meeting was held was not the present one, but a low-lying swampy bottom later covered by a plantation. The modern race-course was first formed by William Duke of Cumberland, son of King George II, who became Ranger of the Great Park in 1746 and lived at the Great Lodge, later

Cumberland Lodge, near Snow Hill.[20] No sensational interest attached to Queen Anne's introductory meeting, apart from the appearance of a maid of honour, Mary Forester, later Lady Downing, "dressed like a man", as Swift recorded. It is said to have been the first time that the riding habit as now worn by women was seen at a public assembly.

Queen Anne's Ride and Ascot Races are this sovereign's abiding memorials at Windsor. The gardens with the canal and terraces which she laid out, in pursuance of the scheme entertained by King William III, did not prosper, although we find Wise and Studholme painfully applying themselves for several years to the work "which Her Majesty has commanded to be done in the ground usually called Mastrike." Wise himself planned the gardens, and recorded details show that despite the natural difficulties of creating a pleasance in a water-meadow he achieved a measure of fruition. By 1708 the canal had been made and enlarged, and the terraces partly formed and turfed.[21] Then the Queen seems to have lost heart. Before the construction of the Thames locks, floods spread out like a sea to the foot of the North Slopes, and she may have seen her hopes washed away. (It was a common belief that the tide reached Windsor. Even after it was arrested by the building of Teddington Lock in 1811, people continued to think so, but it is unlikely to have risen so far at any period of history.)[22] Long after her death cattle were grazing round the ragged, shrinking vestige of the canal. Eventually it disappeared entirely, but there is still a patch in what is now the Home Park Public, beside the Datchet Road, which is called "Queen Anne's Lake" because in time of flood an isolated pool wells up there. According to tradition, the rising waters make their first appearance at this spot, which is also the last from which they drain away.[23]

Datchet Bridge too belongs, like her gardens, to an erased topography, but it had a pleasantly documented existence while it lasted. On 25th March, 1706, Lord Treasurer Godolphin was empowered by Royal Warrant to issue his warrant to Edward Wilcox, Surveyor General of Woods, South of Trent, to fell sufficient non-navy timber in Windsor Forest for building a bridge over the Thames "for the better convenience of our passage to and from our Castle at Windsor."[24] The Queen's innovation maintained an age-old route. Datchet Ferry, which the bridge replaced and by which many royal passengers had come and gone, was mentioned as early as 1249, when "a great oak" to make a boat was delivered from Windsor Forest to the keeper, John le Passur'. The Crown bought the ferry from Colonel Andrew Wheeler, who held it by inheritance, in 1700, and discontinued tolls when the bridge was built.

Revenues in Maidenhead as well as in Windsor were affected, and both corporations petitioned the Queen, but to no avail. The public continued to enjoy unrestricted use of her bridge, and in 1708 she added to her bounty by building the road which branched round to it from Frogmore. The new highway hugged William III's wall, which intermittently displayed his cypher and the date 1699 in dark glazed bricks, and represented a minor triumph of road building. The surveyor's report stated: "The soil is so boggy, of the nature of quicksand, as will require a great quantity of gravel with wood &c. to support it or otherwise will be swallowed up for want of a firm footing."[25] It was a devious route, being nearly a mile long, but offered smoother transit than the shelving and sometimes waterlogged river path which Celia Fiennes had taken in 1698. Pedestrians and horsemen still used the track across the Little Park.

By 1770 the bridge had decayed, and King George III replaced it with one of nine wooden arches on brick and stone piers. In 1795 the rustic timbers were again found to be dangerous and removed, but the King declined to accept further responsibility, pointing out that it was now the business of the two county authorities to maintain the bridge. Neither took action, and for fifteen years the piers stood in the water like giant stepping-stones. Meanwhile, the ferry came into use again. A design for an iron bridge with a 270-foot span, still preserved in the British Museum, was submitted to the King in 1799 by John Stickney, who had received a patent from the American Government, but without success. At last the two county authorities built another wooden bridge on the original piers. It was opened by Queen Charlotte on 4th December, 1811, and no doubt the onlookers celebrated in the "Angel and Crown", a picturesque and ramshackle inn invitingly situated at the Windsor end of the bridge.

By 1836 this bridge too was falling down, and the ferry boat was called back into service a second time. Berkshire suggested building an iron bridge, but Buckinghamshire held out for wood, and by-passing argument, constructed its own half accordingly. The enraged

Berkshire magistrates, vindictively inclined, prepared to cut down the old oak joists of the central arch in order to leave the Buckinghamshire half unsupported. They were restrained by a High Court order and had to limit their revenge to building their own half in iron. The finished hybrid, half wood and half iron, with a clumsy join in the middle, made part of the local scene until 1851, when it was replaced by the Victoria Bridge above and the Albert Bridge below. It is believed to be the only main Thames bridge which has completely disappeared.[26]

12

"THIS SWEET RETREAT"

The House of Hanover did not immediately add to Windsor's renown. Neither King George I nor King George II, who succeeded his father in 1727, lived there often, though the latter was careful to maintain the conventions of the Order of the Garter. G. F. Beltz, in his *Memorials of the Order*, published in 1841, records that "the first memorable act of King George II, as Sovereign of the Order, was the assumption of his royal stall in St. George's Chapel which was performed with considerable pomp, and in strict conformity to precedent, on Michaelmas Day 1728." He added that since Ashmole had neglected to describe the ceremony proper to such occasions, he would supply the deficiency by outlining the procedure.

The King went in a chair to the chapel, where he was received by the Poor Knights, clergy, officers of arms and Knights of the Garter, all in their habits. After he had put on his mantle, collar and cap in the chapter house, the procession passed into the choir and the Sovereign entered his stall. The Duke of St. Albans, who had carried the sword of state before the King, took up his station in front of the stall, and held the sword erect throughout the ensuing service. It began with the ceremony of offering at the altar the achievements of the late Sovereign, first the banner, then the sword, and then the helm and crest. Divine service followed, and at the offertory sentence, "Let your light so shine before men . . .", the officers of the Order spread a carpet upon the altar steps, over which Black Rod laid a rich carpet of cloth of gold and a cushion for the King to kneel on when he made his offering of gold and silver. These were removed as the King returned to his stall, and then the Knights of the Garter proceeded to the altar steps and made their offerings. The sermon and benediction followed. Queen Caroline attended the service, with William Augustus, Duke of Cumberland (the future "Butcher of Culloden", then aged seven), Anne Princess Royal and the Princesses Caroline, Mary and Louisa.

Although Windsor was not a favourite home, the rigid habits of King George II, who thought that "having done a thing today was an unanswerable reason for doing it tomorrow," assured it, at least in the earlier years of his reign, of a place in the royal formalities. The old monarchical custom of dining in public was followed at the Castle. In Pyne's *Royal Residences* (1819) we are told that "his Majesty King George II, for the gratification of his subjects who made excursions to Windsor, had the royal board spread on stated days, when as many visitors as the appointed space could conveniently admit, were permitted to see their sovereign at his meal." Because of this, King Charles II's "Eating Room" became known in the eighteenth century as "The King's Public Dining Room".

As the Sovereign's visits to Windsor declined, the Constable and Governor ceased to feel any residential obligation, and his duties devolved on a Deputy Constable and Lieutenant Governor who lived in the house at the foot of the Round Tower steps. The keep, being no longer occupied, was available in 1745 for use as a state prison. The important person secured there was the French Marshal Belleisle, described by Horace Walpole as "England's most determined enemy", who had been captured by Hanoverian dragoons while on a mission from King Louis XV to the King of Prussia. He refused to give his *parole* in the usual way, and was for a short time "kept magnificently close" in the Round Tower at a cost of more than £100 a day. The Government found this so expensive that he was allowed to rent the mansion called Great Frogmore, half a mile to the south-east of the Castle, but his stay was not long. After the battle of Fontenoy on 11th May, 1745, an exchange was made, and the Marshal returned home boasting that he could conquer England with an army of scullions. He was the last state prisoner ever held at Windsor.

The life of the absentee Governor was occasionally disturbed by problems which had nothing to do with military maintenance. In December 1752 the Lieutenant Governor, Colonel John Olivier, a Protestant refugee from France, referred to his superior a question which establishes an early link between Windsor Castle and America. The Governor at the time was George Brudenell, 4th Earl of Cardigan and later Duke of Montagu. The agent of Thomas and Richard Penn, he learned from Olivier, proposed to visit Windsor on New Year's Day to present two beaver skins by which the Penns held the province of Pennsylvania. The agent believed that they should be tendered at Windsor, like the two Indian arrows by which Lord Baltimore held the province of Maryland. The arrows had been faithfully delivered every year on Easter Sunday, as required by the terms of King Charles I's original grant of the province in 1632 "from the Crown as of the Castle of Windsor", but Colonel Olivier had never before been offered beaver skins from Pennsylvania. What action, he inquired of Lord Cardigan, was he to take?

He was evidently instructed to accept the beaver skins, for they shortly figured in a second memorandum. "I most humbly beg your Lordship's commands," wrote the Lieutenant Governor, "how I am to dispose of them, for they are undressed."[1] The answer to this is not recorded.

For half a century royal favour was withheld from the Castle. Elderly ladies with Court connections were given apartments along the south and east sides of the Upper Ward, and in some of the towers. In the keep, Prince Rupert's tapestries were fading, and his trophies had lost their brightness, while a trickle of criticism points to the shabbiness of the royal apartments. Mrs. Lybbe Powys relates in 1766: "There is but little worthy one's observation. The furniture is old and dirty, most of the best pictures removed to the Queen's [Buckingham] Palace, and the whole kept so very unneat, that it hurts one to see almost the only place in England worthy to be styled our King's Palace so totally neglected."[2]

The unkempt appearance of the royal apartments is the more remarkable because by this time a "State Housekeeper" held sway there. Until the eighteenth century men had always held the appointment of Keeper of the Palace in the royal residences. The ladies who succeeded them in these coveted posts were of gentle, and often noble, birth, and enjoyed a salary of £320 a year (out of which they paid £60 to a working deputy), a pleasant apartment, princely perquisites of furniture and linen, an allowance for wine, a seat in the royal chapel, and every social advantage. The first at Windsor was

Anne Marriott, a maiden lady who was reputed to have been painted by Verrio as a fury. She was appointed in 1724. Eighteenth-century custom accorded the prefix "Mrs." to unmarried gentlewomen, and so she was always known as Mrs. Marriott. Everyone thought her house the prettiest in the world, for it made part of the Norman Gateway and included the "Prisoners' Room", where the western windows showed her the Thames flowing through its water-meadows towards Windsor.

When Mrs. Marriott died in 1750 the infamous maid of honour, Elizabeth Chudleigh, later a bigamous peeress, prevailed on King George II to appoint her mother to the post. It was during Mrs. Chudleigh's tenure that the royal apartments suffered their most marked neglect, and one must conclude that she was not at her happiest in a domestic sphere. Horace Walpole tells a story which suggests that her mettle equipped her to control the fortress rather than the palace. Once, when her husband was Governor of Chelsea Hospital, Mrs. Chudleigh was returning home at night when three footpads stopped her carriage. Each thrust a pistol at her breast. She coolly pushed her head through the window and screamed "Fire!" whereupon the pensioners in attendance shot them dead.[3]

Mrs. Chudleigh was not the only defaulter. Broken stonework affronted the gaze of visitors, and tokens of disregarded neglect in St. George's Chapel drew scathing censure. Seventeen four-pounders were still mounted on the gallery of the Round Tower, but there was no firing, as in Stuart reigns, whenever royal personages arrived and departed. A new Lieutenant Governor in 1782 was shocked to find that ammunition had not been held within the gunner's memory. The lack of majesty was the more marked because the pleasures of touring were becoming more popularly exploited, and no traveller failed to visit Windsor. The earliest guide-book, Bickham's *Deliciae Britannicae, or the Curiosities of Hampton-Court and Windsor-Castle*, published in 1742, was followed by a succession of locally produced handbooks for the use of visitors. Between 1755 and 1784 Joseph Pote produced seven editions of *Les Délices de Windesore, or a Description of Windsor Castle and the Country Adjacent*, a readable and successful little primer. It was based on his *History and Antiquities of Windsor Castle*, in which he strove loyally to minimize the sins of omission: the Castle, he pointed out, had "many Towers and strong

Batteries for its defence," though at the time of writing its strength was "considerably abated, by the currency of many years, and the excellency of our national Constitution, whereby Fortresses and Strong Holds are not frequent in this Kingdom, and a happy unity between The Prince and Subject is the great security of both."

Charles Knight, a Windsor bookseller, brought out his first guide-book in 1783 and continued issuing further editions until 1825. The scope of these little faded manuals penetrated far beyond their original purpose. The series covers the most important period in the development of the Castle, and documents its transition from neglected and archaic pomp to modern significance.

The seed of its regeneration was sown as early as 1761, when King George III married the seventeen-year-old Princess Charlotte of Mecklenburg-Strelitz. According to her biographer, Dr. John Watkins, she no sooner set eyes on Windsor than she lost her heart to it, and "from the first moment she saw the place, expressed a desire to reside there." So she did, though not until she had become the mother of a large family (she had fifteen children in all). She cherished her desire until in 1776 Queen Anne's "small neat house on Castle Hill" became vacant, and while the King was considering what to do with it, Queen Charlotte asked him to give it to her.[4] The fulfilment of her wish shortly led to the adoption of Windsor as the summer residence of the royal family. The house was not big enough to accommodate all the Princes and Princesses, with their train of nurses, rockers, laundresses, sempstresses, necessary women, governesses and tutors, and the King employed Sir William Chambers, the royal architect, to enlarge it. He made it into a plain but comfortable mansion which was known as Queen's Lodge.

This made a home for the King and Queen, their eldest daughters and the children still in the nursery. For the remaining Princesses and their attendants the King bought Burford House from the third Duke of Albans in 1777, and renamed it Lower Lodge.[5] Alternative accommodation having been found for the elderly ladies and other tenants inhabiting the south and east fronts of the Castle, the King allotted their apartments to the four eldest Princes and their gentlemen. By the summer of 1778 the whole family were happily housed at Windsor. Queen Charlotte was enchanted and christened it "this sweet retreat".

Although the King was not living in the Castle, his presence neces-
sitated an immediate smartening in the tone of administration and
behaviour. Previously there was only a non-commissioned officer's
guard on duty, but this was now increased to a subaltern's guard.
The Duke of Montagu also realized that repressive action must be
brought to bear on the local public, who were accustomed to doing
as they liked in the Castle. It was only four years earlier that he had
had to rebuke a certain Thomas Moore for digging four loads of
chalk from the cliff and emptying his "necessary house" therein.[6]
"General Orders" issued in 1781 included these regulations:

> The sentries at the King's Gate and Governor's door, are not to
> permit any servants or boys to gallop about the court. No higglers to be
> allowed to bring any meat, fish or greens to sell in the court yard of the
> palace, nor are any articles to be cried for sale in any part of the palace.
> No beggars or disorderly persons women in red cloaks or pattens are
> to be allowed to walk upon the Terrace at any time.[7]

Everyone who held an official appointment was ordered to take up
residence. As the Round Tower was once again being occupied by
the Governor, we find a passing interest in a device erected at the
mouth of the Norman well in 1784. It was an engine, installed under
the direction of a Mr. Gray, "for raising water upwards of 370 feet
by the simple contrivance of a rope; the ends of which, being spliced
together, it is fixed to a wheel and gudgeon in the water and to a
windlass at the top of the well; the windlass being turned with a
moderate degree of velocity, the water adheres to the ascending part
of the rope until it arrives at the top; it is then thrown off, and col-
lected, by means of a semi-circular cap, that encloses the inner wheel
of the windlass; this cap having a spout on one side of it, the water is
conducted into any vessel that may be placed to receive it."[8]

The building of Queen's Lodge coincided with the destruction of
some of the most interesting of the original defences of the Castle. In
about 1779 the moat of the Round Tower was levelled on its eastern
side, where the tennis court and later the barracks had been. At the
same time the remaining part of the ditch on the south front was
filled in as far as King Henry VIII Gateway. The garden and vineyard which had flourished there since 1699 disappeared, and the
drawbridge was finally dispensed with. It was last called into service

in 1765, when a parliamentary election threatened to cause trouble, and the Governor ordered the master gunner to keep it raised day and night. The sum of medieval features sacrificed at this period was completed by the demolition, in about 1785, of King Henry III's indented wall on the south front and Black Rod's residence within it.[9]

No architectural changes were as yet undertaken in the Upper Ward, but the King and Queen renovated some of the royal apartments to make them more fit both for use and show. Queen Charlotte, for her part, bought for the Queen's Bedchamber in 1778 a domed and exquisitely carved gilt bed hung with white satin embroidered with flowers.[10] It was said to have cost £14,000, but it is doubtful if she ever slept in it. Queen Anne's bed of Spitalfields velvet was put in the King's State Bedchamber, and later in the King's Public Dining Room, which became the State Bedchamber until the end of George III's reign. This confusing arrangement he refused to alter, and nothing would induce him to part with Queen Anne's bed. He would not "displace the venerable relic", he declared, "for the most splendid bed in the universe."[11] The real State Bedchamber he turned into the Council Chamber, which at least maintained its political tradition.

In St. George's Hall the King continued the medieval custom, already noted at Garter banquets, of having the royal table placed across the room on a dais, while other tables were placed lengthwise down the hall. Mrs. Charlotte Papendiek, whose husband was a musician in Queen Charlotte's chamber band, described in her journal the dazzling sight of the supper tables in 1789, when the King's recovery from his first attack of insanity was celebrated by a ball. A new service of gold plate was used for the first time, the salvers and cups being ornamented with serpents "twisted round, and made in shining and mat gold, which raised the scales in relief, and made the reptiles look fearfully real. The two mouths met at the top, and from them the beverage was poured." The ornamental dishes included "temples in barley sugar four feet high." Mrs. Papendiek was privileged to watch the scene from the musicians' gallery, which was held aloft by gigantic figures of negro slaves.[12]

The King also fitted up a music room on the east front, where the royal family and their friends listened to concerts on Sunday evenings. At seven o'clock they descended to the terrace and walked through the waiting crowds, while regimental bands played. The King wore the Windsor Uniform of dark blue with red facings which he introduced when he first took up residence at Windsor in 1778. The Princesses accompanied their parents, who walked arm in arm, stopping to talk to anyone they knew. Miss Lucy Kennedy, an old lady who lived for many years in King Henry III Tower, recorded that all the nobility and gentry of the neighbourhood were to be seen on the Terrace. Farmers, tradespeople and servants usually gathered happily in the Long Walk, where another band played, but they too could join the throng on the Terrace if they wished. Provided people behaved respectably, there were no social distinctions.

The magic of these Georgian occasions shines out in letters and diaries. Fanny Burney, who became Assistant Keeper of the Robes to Queen Charlotte in 1786, draws a happy word-picture of Princess Amelia sweetly parading on the Terrace to celebrate her third birthday. She was dressed in "a robe coat covered with muslin", and carried a fan. Miss Burney's father, Dr. Burney, was equally struck by the sight of so many people, all so happy that they seemed to be in Elysium. The scene was one of universal cheerfulness, gaiety, and good humour, "such as the subjects of no other monarch, I believe, on earth enjoy at present." Dorothy Wordsworth's enthusiasm, too, was boundless when she was taken to see the King and Queen in October 1792. "When I first set foot upon the Terrace," she wrote to a friend, "I fancied myself treading upon fairy-ground." Her awed delight was complete when the King actually stopped to play with her young cousins.

Dorothy was staying with her uncle, Canon William Cookson, and found herself equally enchanted with the society in which she lived. The canons were still in their cloister behind St. George's Chapel, but life was very different from the routine of King Edward III's reign. When the clergy were permitted to marry after the Reformation, their lodgings had to be adapted to meet the needs of wives and children. Rooms and staircases were altered or added according to requirements. The result was that by the end of the eighteenth century the Canons' Cloister was enclosed by picturesque, rambling houses, no two alike. Dorothy Wordsworth told her friend, "We compose, as it were, one large family in the Cloisters, for we can visit each other's houses in all weathers without hat or cloak, for they are surrounded by a covered passage. You have been at York, and you probably saw the cloisters there which will give you some idea of the sort of gloom which we inhabit."[13]

It was to the ecclesiastical foundation, which, as we know, stood in need of beneficence, that the King directed his first care, for he was a man of simple but earnest piety and held the Order of the Garter in great reverence. Every morning prayers were held in the private chapel, and every Sunday the royal family attended mattins at "the Cathedral," as St. George's was called to distinguish it from the other, which was also dedicated to St. George. According to the original arrangement, the choir stalls provided alternate seating for the Knights of the Garter and the Canons: there was no provision for the royal family as a domestic unit. To meet the need of a pew the King converted the "Queen's Closet" overlooking the altar on the north side. It was the room which had been intended to serve as the chantry chapel of King Edward IV, and King Henry VIII had inserted a beautiful oak oriel to enable Catherine of Aragon to watch Garter ceremonies. Within this oriel the royal family sat in a semicircle behind curtains of Garter blue velvet. The King shared the new "Royal Closet" in preference to sitting in the Sovereign's stall. This he left for the Dean, who then, as now, used it at all times when it was not required by the Sovereign. The services in "the Cathedral" were very long, lasting up to $2\frac{1}{2}$ hours, but the King and Queen were regular in their attendance.[14]

The King's next, and prime, concern was the restoration of the choir, to which he devoted £16,000. Some of the stalls needed repair, and this was done by a Windsor architect named Henry Emlyn, who began his career as a wood-carver. His work was so skilful that it cannot always be distinguished with certainty from the old. The additions known to have been made by him include four new Garter stalls, two on either side, at the east end towards the high altar. They were made necessary by the King's decree in 1786 that sons of the Sovereign should be Knights of the Garter, even though it meant exceeding the original number of twenty-five. George Prince of Wales and the Dukes of York and Clarence were already members of the Order. His four younger sons, the Dukes of Kent, Cumberland, Sussex and Cambridge, were appointed on 2nd June, 1786.

Emlyn also added the lower rank of stalls, which he decorated with carved pictures after the style of the medieval craftsmen. How fully those old wood-carvers entered into their work is illustrated by its richness and variety. Many of the subjects they chose are Biblical or historical, and the carvings on the seats include scenes full of merry humour. One of them shows Satan pushing three monks in a wheel-barrow into hell. Emlyn did not merely imitate this earlier work. He carved topical scenes, such as the attempted assassination of King George III by Margaret Nicholson on 2nd August, 1786.

In 1789 the rood loft or gallery was replaced by the present organ loft of Coade's artificial stone. The least happy feature of King George III's restoration was the removal of the original stone tracery of the east window. This was done to allow the insertion of a painted glass representation of the Resurrection, designed by the American-born artist, Benjamin West. It only survived for seventy years, and few people seem to have admired it. Horace Walpole commented that Our Lord appeared to be scrambling to Heaven in a fright, as if in dread of being again buried alive.

The nave also needed repair, for it was said to be shabby and neglected, with a floor which would disgrace a barn. In view of the King's generosity in restoring the choir, the Dean and Canons felt compelled to spend £6,000 on setting the nave to rights, and so the whole chapel displayed fresh elegance.

There was no concurrent improvement in manners. The son of Charles Knight the publisher, another Charles, who was born in the shadow of the Castle in 1791, noted practices which the royal family in their velvet-hung eyrie probably never saw. As an old man he published his *Passages of a Working Life* (1864), and from this we learn of the misdemeanours of the choir boys at the beginning of the nineteenth century. They shared with the vergers the privilege of pocketing candle-ends and selling them, in the same way as servants in the royal palaces did (no wonder the expenditure on wax lights for Windsor Castle was stated in the House of Commons in 1812 to be £10,000 a year). As a result greed triumphed over decorum, and the moment a service ended there was a scramble to blow out the lights. Even on a dark winter evening the offenders spared no thought for the congregation, who had perforce to grope their way out as best they could. Another ancient and not altogether seemly habit was the demand for "spur money". Any stranger appearing in the chapel in spurs was set upon by the choirboys, who exacted a fine. The practice was traditional in some cathedrals, and at Windsor it continued until men ceased to travel on horseback.[15]

13

THE KING AS COUNTRY SQUIRE

It must be concluded that Dr. John Watkins was right when he attributed the choice of Windsor as the royal residence to the spell it had fastened on Queen Charlotte in 1761. Purely practical considerations might not have led the King to spend £70,000, which was the sum he mentioned to a friend, on the conversion of Queen Anne's house into a family home. "Sweet retreat" though it was, it offered no privacy. Magnificent walks and rides there were in plenty round the neighbourhood, but no gardens where the King and Queen might walk in seclusion from six to eight on summer evenings, as they had been wont to do at Richmond and Kew. Only a strip of lawn protected by railings separated the front of Queen's (sometimes called Upper) Lodge from the public footpath to Datchet Bridge, and the garden linking it with Lower Lodge was "more of a passage to both than a retreat into the fresh air; moreover every window looked in it." That was Mrs. Papendiek's estimation.[1] Houses stretched along Castle Hill up to Queen's Lodge, and down St. Albans Street, on the site of the modern Royal Mews; and on the other side of St. Albans Street was the town gaol. It was said that whenever the King rode past, prisoners crowded to the windows calling "God bless Your Majesty. We wish Your Majesty would let us out." On account of the annoyance the King built a new gaol, designed by James Wyatt, at the bottom of George Street, opposite the present Western Region railway station.[2]

If the King and Queen regretted the loss of gardens, as Mrs. Papendiek says they did, they bore with the inconvenience and found recompense in social integration. To play the part of a country gentleman exactly suited the King's taste. He rose at six, took a route called the "Cat's Path" to call up his family and attendants, and set off across the Little Park to visit the royal dairy. His interest was practical and well-informed: he was not called "Farmer George" without reason. A scheme in which he took particular interest was the drainage and cultivation of the Great Park, where he founded the Norfolk and Flemish Farms. They were named after the systems adopted there, which were similar to those practised respectively in Norfolk and Flanders.

Charles Knight, who remembered the King as "a quiet, good-humoured gentleman" immediately identifiable by the long blue coat which betokened the Windsor Uniform, evokes a pleasing picture of his excursions in the Park at an hour when only he and the local lads were afoot there. Many a time, Knight records in *Passages of a Working Life*, "had he bidden us good morning when we were hunting for mushrooms in the early dew and he was returning from his dairy to his eight o'clock breakfast. Everyone knew that most respectable and amiable of country squires, and His Majesty knew everyone." As often as not these boys, who looked on the Park as their own, would see the King again as the day wore on. Its green spaces were a glory for kite-flying and cricket, and he liked to wander out and stand watching them at their play.

With such recollections as these, Knight establishes an authoritative survey of the contemporary scene. Royalty, as he put it, "lived in a glass house", and the King's movements were open to common view. Every Wednesday he went to St. James's Palace for a council or a levee. Knight remembered that as his light travelling carriage passed down Castle Hill, Mr. Robert Blunt, the royal saddler, would stand bowing at his door in a cocked hat. The boy saw this because his own home was near the saddler's, which backed on to the Castle ditch, below Salisbury Tower. The three shops shown by Norden in 1607 had been added to until the ditch was lined with a crust of tightly packed houses, which stretched from the Castle gate along Thames Street and down Lower Thames Street to the Hundred Steps.

When the royal carriages clattered past the houses very little room was left on either side, for they extended thirty feet from the Castle ditch. Thames Street was thus only half the width it is today. Some of these houses were built of brick, but most were of lath and plaster. Though very pretty with their tall, sashed windows and high-pitched roofs, they were inflammable, insanitary and malodorous. The ditch behind them still served in places as a drain, and Charles Knight attributed an attack of typhoid fever in his childhood to an open sewer from the Castle creeping at the back of his father's house. His recollection illustrates one of the uglier aspects of life in Georgian Windsor. He remembered, too, his terror when a murderous mob attacked the baker's next door. They were not evil-doers, but ignorant, hungry people too poor to afford the high price of bread.

Knight's early home was probably the house nearest King Henry VIII Gateway. It was his birthplace and his father's first bookshop, and was well known to the King, who liked to bustle in and out of the shops. He often sat quietly reading at the counter, and there is a famous story about one of his visits. The bookseller told this to his son, and he in turn recorded it in his memoirs. It happened soon after Thomas Paine's revolutionary book, *The Rights of Man*, was published on 13th March, 1791. A copy was received by the elder Knight one evening. Next morning, before he had even opened the shutters, he heard the King's voice in the shop calling "Knight, Knight", and hurried down to find the King already seated at the counter. He had picked up Paine's book and was quietly reading it. Half an hour later he left without a word. The Government later tried to suppress the book, but the King never voiced any displeasure at finding it in Knight's shop, nor did his visits cease.

At the sitting-room window young Charles stationed himself early on 1st January, 1801, to watch the sunrise. As the sky reddened beyond the Round Tower he saw the new Royal Standard flying over it for the first time. Gone were the French lilies which King Edward III had adopted. King George III had given up the title "King of France", and for the first time the arms of England were seen quartered only with those of Scotland and Ireland. Soon afterwards father and son moved to the opposite side of Castle Hill (the boy had been left motherless when he was little more than a baby), and there set up a new home and a new bookshop. In a cottage round the corner in Market Street they printed and published the first issue of the *Windsor and Eton Express* on 1st August, 1812. Their newspaper still provides a weekly record of events in the Castle and royal borough.

The elder Knight's guide-books tell how the presence of the royal family stimulated trade. The old markets held in and around the Town Hall for the sale of corn, butter, apples and chairs dwindled as smart shops opened. The Queen's milliner, Mrs. Caley, settled almost next door to Mr. Blunt and the royal surgeon-apothecary, John O'Reilly. Her business prospered, and in 1823 she moved to elegant new premises opposite the Guildhall. The shops vied with each other for royal patronage, so that soon the choice of goods for sale was as varied as in London. The Queen and Princesses, though more formal than the King, also walked in the town and were gracious and friendly.

Nowhere was the sociable atmosphere more convivial than in the Theatre Royal, where, Knight declared, "her majesty's apothecary in the lower boxes might almost have felt her pulse across the pit." This cosy little place was opened in 1793 in High Street, a few yards south of the Parish Church. Through Charles Knight's eyes we can still see its rather shabby scarlet and gold, looking gay enough when the candles were lit and roses and satin playbills graced the royal box. At seven o'clock the King and Queen and their family entered, six fiddlers played the National Anthem, and the dingy green baize curtain swung up on a cramped little stage. The King loved comedies, and laughed so heartily that young Knight sometimes fancied that the walls shook. During the interval, coffee was served to the royal party. In the gallery the audience partook of the Queen's, or Windsor, Ale produced at the brewery which for centuries adjoined the Chapter Garden.

It is to Knight, too, that we turn for an authentic picture of the Castle at this period. The Duke of Montagu's regulations in 1782 may or may not have had the desired effect: certainly the town boys paid little heed, or else they were very kindly indulged. Twenty years later Charles and his friends were having an hilarious time. Looking back in old age he recalled: "The deserted courts of the Upper Quadrangle often re-echoed on moonlit winter nights with our whoowhoop. The rooks and a few antique dowagers, who each had their domiciles in some lone turret of that spacious square, were the only personages who were disturbed by our revelry. In the magnificent playground of the Terrace, away we went along the narrow wall, and even the awful height of the north side could not abate the rash courage of *follow my leader.*"

He remembered, too, dancing with other youngsters in the moat garden below the Round Tower, which King George III had fortunately spared. On the opposite side of the road King Charles II's guardroom was still in use. Running home from his play, the boy would pass the lighted windows of "The Royal Standard" and hear the soldiers making merry within. As he went down the hill he could see the grated windows of the Colehouse in King Henry VIII Gateway, but there was no longer a prison there. It had been condemned in the *Gentleman's Magazine* in 1790 as "a disgrace, not only to the sight, but to the feelings." A year later it ceased to exist, and in 1805 the court room and prison were converted into apartments for the officers on duty in the Castle. The drawbridge, as we already know, had disappeared before Knight was born.

Little had been done in the Upper Ward at the time he played there, though the most important alteration in the history of the Castle had already begun. It was the restoration of the Gothic style, undertaken for King George III by James Wyatt, surveyor from 1796 until his death in 1813. Wyatt contrived a new grand staircase, approached from the Grand Entrance in the Quadrangle through a plaster-vaulted corridor, and he began to replace King Charles II's round-headed windows with Gothic insertions. Young Knight remembered watching the masons at work on the Star Building, and the Queen's Ballroom and Audience and Presence Chambers; but Wyatt got no further. The Napoleonic wars left little money for architectural pursuits.

They imposed no other restrictive effect on the local scene. If anything, they rendered the general atmosphere still more exciting. Charles Knight sums up the background of contemporary life in Windsor as "a continual din of Royalty going to and fro—of bell-ringing for birthdays—of gun-firing for victories—of reviews in the Park—of the relief of the guard, with all the pomp of military music —of the chapel bell tolling twice a day—of crowding to the Terrace on Sunday evenings—of periodical holidays, such as Ascot races—of rare festivities, such as a fête at Frogmore." His last reference is a reminder that the back-to-nature movement which had its origin in

France penetrated the royal purlieus at Windsor. Little Frogmore, the farmhouse where Shakespeare's Anne Page went a-feasting in *The Merry Wives of Windsor*, had been acquired by Queen Charlotte in 1790. Two years later she bought the remainder of the lease by which the adjoining estate of Great Frogmore was held under the Crown. Its pleasant mansion, rebuilt in the Dutch style during the reign of William and Mary, and fronting on formal gardens, was the one which Marshal Bellisle rented in 1745.

Queen Charlotte united the two properties, pulled down the house at Little Frogmore and commissioned the Reverend Christopher Alderson, rector of Eckington, in Derbyshire, whom she characterized as "a man of great natural taste, but not of the world", to lay out the thirty acres of her new domain. Her Vice-Chamberlain, Major William Price, brother of Uvedale Price, the writer on "the picturesque", designed the winding lake which bejewels the lawns with its circuit, while Wyatt enlarged the Dutch house to make a cream-coloured, colonnaded mansion with a bow-fronted wing at either end. The Queen appointed as housekeeper Miss Elizabeth Emilia Pohl, daughter of a royal milliner, and in her enchanting home was able to indulge her personal tastes to the extent of installing a printing press, from which issued some elegant little books of poems and meditations.[3]

Frogmore was her rural retreat as truly as the Little Trianon at Versailles had been Queen Marie Antoinette's. A cascade, a grotto and a real little working mill were among the delights of the Trianon. Queen Charlotte had similar attractions at Frogmore. Before she bought it, so Mrs. Papendiek records, her country villa was the lodge occupied by Mr. Jeremiah Gaskoin, keeper of the Little Park, which stood at the end of Mother Dodd's Hill, beside the public path to Datchet Bridge. Here she and the Princesses enjoyed new milk, eggs and home-cured bacon on summer mornings.[4] At Frogmore they had their own farm to produce these delicacies. A corn-mill worked merrily, and dotted about the grounds were a barn, a hermitage, a "Gothic Ruin" designed by Wyatt, and other "follies" which imposed the satisfying, if counterfeit, impress of rustic antiquity.

Queen Marie Antoinette liked to hold fêtes in the Trianon grounds. So did Queen Charlotte at Frogmore, but hers were more sociable events. Bound by the strict Court etiquette of France, Marie

Antoinette planned festivities only for royal and noble guests. Queen Charlotte entertained all ranks of society. When she invited the townspeople to her "little paradise", as she called Frogmore, she presented them with a round of country amusements. The local beauties dressed up and pretended to rake hay in white kid gloves, and there was a fair with stalls and acrobats. Finally, everyone danced the night away to the music of violins in the Thatched Barn, while coloured lamps glimmered among the trees and across the lake.

With such excitements the kindly Queen enlivened an unsophisticated age. They have only a faded glow today, but one other of the festivities devised by her stands out with historical aptness. In 1800 she introduced local children to the joys of a Christmas tree, though she did not have a fir tree according to the usual German fashion. The party took place at Queen's Lodge on Christmas Day, and proved so memorable that Dr. John Watkins took occasion to describe it in his biography of Queen Charlotte:

> Sixty poor families had a substantial dinner given them, and in the evening the children of the principal families in the neighbourhood were invited to an entertainment at the Lodge. Here, among other amusing objects for the gratification of the juvenile visitors, in the middle of the room stood an immense tub with a yew-tree placed in it, from the branches of which hung bunches of sweetmeats, almonds, and raisins, in papers, fruits, and toys, most tastefully arranged, and the whole illuminated by small wax candles. After the company had walked round and admired the tree, each child obtained a portion of the sweets which it bore, together with a toy, and then all returned home quite delighted.

Queen Charlotte may have chosen a yew because it was the custom in her native Mecklenburg to erect yew boughs laden with coloured lights. These were allowed to burn out so that the twigs and needles snapped as the flames reached them.

14

ROYAL HOUSEWARMING

The peak of this memorable period was reached in 1804, when Napoleon planned his threatened invasion of England. An excited patriotism took possession of the little town, which woke on Sundays to the sound of martial music and parading troops. The Royal Horse Guards (the Blues) and the King's own favourite Stafford Militia were drawn up in the Quadrangle. Presently the King himself would appear, dressed in the regimentals of a captain of the Blues, with cocked hat and heavy jack-boots, and review the troops on his way to mattins.

He would stop again in the Lower Ward to inspect the Windsor Volunteers drawn up near the Moat Garden wall. All the local tradesmen who held commissions in this company were personally known to him, and could be sure of affable nods. By the time the royal family left the chapel, local crowds had been joined by people pouring out of London in their chaises. Some expressed disappointment because the King was not wearing his crown, but all were ready to cheer. In the afternoon everyone flocked to the Terrace to be ready for the promenade of the royal family. Once, during this period of national crisis, Charles Knight saw the Prime Minister, the great Mr. Pitt himself, standing unrecognized among the throng, while people wondered aloud whether he would carry a gold stick before the King.

Towards the end of 1804 the King and Queen left the Lodge and moved into the Castle. They did not live in the royal apartments, but broke with tradition by choosing rooms never before occupied by the Sovereign or his consort. The King had a ground-floor suite overlooking the North Terrace. The Queen lived on the first floor of the

Watch Tower across the Quadrangle, which King Charles II had rebuilt. Henceforth it was to be "the Queen's tower". The Princesses had rooms near their mother's. The eldest unmarried daughter, Princess Augusta, occupied the small neighbouring tower on the south front, which still bears her name.

The King and Queen travelled from London and went straight to

---

13. St. George's Chapel: the West Front

The ceremonial entrance, approached from the Lower Ward by the gateway into the Horseshoe Cloister. Before the marble steps were built in 1870 at a cost of £950 the west door had long been unused: John Carter, writing in the *Gentleman's Magazine* for 1805, commented: "The west front, which is beyond dispute a very fine elevation, seems to be entirely disregarded; or else, why is the door in the centre suffered to remain for ever shut?" The statues in the niches above the west window are those of the Virgin and Child, St. Edward the Confessor and St. George and the Dragon (the chapel being dedicated to Our Lady, St. Edward and St. George), and were made in 1799 at Eleanor Coade's factory at Lambeth. The secret of making Coade stone, which outlasts natural stone, is now lost. The cross on the north side of the steps was erected by Canon Hugh Pearson in 1879 to mark the catacombs, where nearly fifty people were interred during the nineteenth century. The last to be buried there was "Old John the Bell-ringer" in 1892. His real name was John Ellaway. Besides being keeper of the Curfew Tower he cut the chapel grass, and when he lay dying begged that his scythe should be buried with him, a request which was carried out.

14. The Tomb of the Founder, King Edward IV, in the North Choir Aisle

This tomb is the "new monument" devised from "antient materials" by Henry Emlyn in 1790, after the burial vault of King Edward IV and his Queen, Elizabeth Woodville, had been accidentally opened in the previous year. How far the King's original tomb had been completed according to his directions is uncertain. A view published by Sandford in 1707 shows the arch with its lining of touchstone and a black slab of the same material which still covers the grave, the slab forming a base for the iron gates which at a yet earlier period, it is believed, stood across the choir aisle. Emlyn moved the gates to their present position on the other side of the tomb, facing the presbytery, and filled the arch with his new monument, which incorporates a black slab bearing the name Edward IIII in letters of solid brass. When the vault was uncovered, a year earlier, on 13th March, 1789, the King's skeleton was brought to light, showing him to have been a man of 6 feet 4 inches in height, with chestnut hair, portions of which were carried away by visitors.

16

15

their new apartments on the evening of 4th November, 1804. Immediately the Queen's spirits sank. The Castle was not to her liking. "I will briefly tell you," she wrote four days later to her friend, Countess Harcourt, "that I have changed from a very comfortable and warm habitation to the coldest house, rooms and passages that ever existed.[1]

The King had no grievance. He was satisfied with his cheerless rooms, where he rose as usual at six o'clock to light his own fire, and made do with carpetless floors.

However simply he might choose to live in private he upheld the grand traditions of the Castle. To celebrate its reinstatement as a

---

15. St. George's Chapel: the Nave, looking west

The traditional elements of lierne vaulting and side aisles make St. George's Chapel "one of the last great church designs to be carried out before the Reformation", and everything in it is "light, clear and harmonious". The great west window, after escaping puritan destruction, suffered at the hands of unskilled repairers in the eighteenth century, and only prompt action on the part of the Dean and Canons saved it from demolition by King George III. Thomas Willement, who restored it in 1842, found ten of the ancient lights in a storeroom, and these he put back, adding six new ones of his own to complete the window. It was dismantled in 1940, just before a bomb fell which could have caused irreparable damage. When it was replaced in 1945 the opportunity was taken to rearrange some of the ancient glass—which is predominant—in accordance with the original concept. In the last bay but one on the north, almost immediately below the window, is the tomb of King George V and Queen Mary.

16. St. George's Chapel: the Choir, looking east

The choir presents an assemblage of colour and rich detail, heightened by the golden gleam of the armorial plates at the backs of the Garter stalls. In this photograph may be seen the intricate carving of the woodwork, and the splendour of the Garter banners overhead. In the bay to the south of the high altar stands the tomb of King Edward VII and Queen Alexandra; high on the north side, overlooking it, is the carved oak oriel of the Royal Closet. The black and white marble paving of the choir was the gift of Dr. William Child, organist of St. George's Chapel from 1632 until his death in 1697. Below the chancel step is the barely discernible entrance to the Royal Vault, and in the middle of the aisle the slab marking the burial place of King Charles I, King Henry VIII and Queen Jane Seymour.

royal house he gave a great house-warming on 25th February, 1805. Trumpeters in blue and gold played the National Anthem as each member of the royal family ascended the grand staircase, and after a performance of Handel's "Esther", the guests danced on a floor "painted with the most fanciful and appropriate devices, by an eminent Artist, instead of being chalked." The ladies surpassed themselves in stylishness. "Ostrich feathers, to the number of eight or nine, were universally worn; and diamonds in profusion. Taste was stretched to the utmost limit to invent new dresses. The draperies were principally of white satin, ornamented with gold, silver and diamonds. The velvet dresses were richly embroidered and clasped down the front." At supper in the King's Guard Chamber the royal family ate off gold plate, and the guests off silver. The "beautiful damask table cloths with the royal arms wove into them" attracted favourable attention, because they had been "spun by the Royal hands of the lovely Princesses."[2]

In continuation of the festivities the King held an installation of Knights of the Garter on St. George's Day, 1805. It was the first since 1771, when George Prince of Wales and his seven-year-old brother, Prince Frederick, Bishop of Osnaburg, later Duke of York, were installed. During the intervening years a number of Knights had died and the vacancies had been filled by Knights elect who were permitted to wear the Garter and Riband, but not the Star. By 1801 there was a considerable reckoning of Knights awaiting installation, including the five younger sons of the King, though to them the restriction on the wearing of the Star did not apply. The King, therefore, granted them "installation by dispensation", by which means they were authorized to exercise all the rights and privileges belonging to the Knights of the Order, as fully as if they had been installed. This only applied to Knights elected before 1801. By the end of January 1805 there were seven new ones, and it was they who were installed in St. George's Chapel on the sunny morning of 23rd April. They were the 5th Duke of Rutland, the 6th Duke of Beaufort, the first Marquess of Abercorn, the 3rd Earl of Hardwicke, Viceroy of Ireland, the 10th Earl of Pembroke, the 9th Earl of Winchelsea and the 5th Earl of Chesterfield. Only six were present, the Earl of Hardwicke being installed by proxy.[3]

The occasion roused the neighbourhood to the highest pitch of excitement, and imposed a more than passing historic interest because, as it proved, this was the last ceremony of the kind for a century and a half. The Order, far from languishing, was presently augmented by the creation of certain categories of extra Knights— foreign kings and princes, and lineal descendants of King George I —but there was seldom any public ceremonial. Chapter meetings for elections and investitures were usually held in London, and for a long time after 1805 installation by dispensation was the accepted formula.[4]

The procession set out from the King's Guard Chamber at eleven o'clock and passed through St. George's Hall and the private chapel to the grand staircase, and then through the Quadrangle and under the Norman Gateway to the south door of the chapel. In front went trumpeters in their state dress, playing "the installation and jubilee marches, alternately relieved by the drums and fifes." There was one change in the customary marshalling of the procession, for it was led by the Naval Knights of Windsor, followed by the Poor Knights (who did not become the Military Knights until 1833). They were making their first and last appearance at a Garter installation. Although founded by Samuel Travers, Surveyor-General to King William III and Queen Anne, who died in 1725, none had been appointed until 1795. This was because Travers's will was for seventy years the subject of legal dispute. By the time another Garter installation took place they had been long forgotten, for they were disbanded in 1892. They did not live in the Castle, like the Military Knights, but in a house built for them in 1800 with a colonnaded front overlooking the Chapter Garden.[5]

After the Naval and Poor Knights and the Officers of Arms came the Knights elect in their under-habit of silver jacket and puffed breeches, with white silk stockings and kid shoes adorned with silver roses, and carrying their high-crowned caps and feathers in their hands. The Knights Companions followed in the full apparel of the Order, wearing over their silver costumes the crimson velvet surcoat and outer mantle of blue velvet lined with white silk, the crimson velvet hood fastened over their shoulders and their caps and feathers on their heads. Knights of the blood royal went last, the Prince of Wales going in solitary pomp immediately before the Officers of the Order. The King, preceded by the Sword of State, walked under a canopy, his train borne by two marquesses and one other official. Gentlemen Pensioners (now called Gentlemen at Arms) marched on either side, and officers of state followed. The Queen, with the Princesses Elizabeth, Mary, Sophia and Amelia, the Princess of Wales, the Duchess of York, and ladies in waiting, accompanied the procession, attended by Yeomen of the Guard. In the chapel they occupied a gallery set up on the north side of the high altar and covered with a crimson velvet canopy fringed with gold.

After entering St. George's the procession walked around the nave and up the choir aisle to the chapter house, where the Knights elect were invested with their crimson surcoats and swords. They remained there while the Sovereign and Knights Companions proceeded into the choir and entered their stalls. The achievements of four Knights lately deceased were presented at the altar, and then the ceremony of installing the new Knights began. The service lasted a very long time, as each Knight had to be separately escorted from the chapter house and installed with elaborate ritual. After the administration of the Oath, he was conducted to his stall and arrayed in his mantle, hood and collar, to the accompaniment of the prescribed exhortations which reminded him in solemn words of their significance. Finally, his plumed black velvet cap was placed upon his head.

The form of service included the immemorial presentation of gold and silver. At this point the Yeoman of the Wardrobe appeared with the requisite gold carpet and cushion which he laid on the altar steps for the use of the King, who removed his cap and feathers, knelt down and made his offering. After the Prince of Wales had followed his father, the rest of the Company proceeded in pairs to the altar rail. It was past five o'clock when the service ended and the procession returned from the chapel to St. George's Hall, where the banquet had been prepared.

This, too, was carried out with all the picturesque ceremony described by Ashmole. The table at which the King and the Knights of the blood royal dined was set on a dais across the east end of the hall, under a new music gallery richly carved and gilt, and the King sat in a canopied throne of crimson velvet embroidered with gold. The gallery at the west end of the hall, which was supported by caryatids, was reserved for the Queen and the Princesses. Other privileged spectators watched the scene from an enclosure erected along the south side of the hall and hung with scarlet cloth.

As in King Charles II's reign, a gilt cup was handed to the King at the end of the first course, and he drank to the Knights, who then pledged the King. The second course was brought into the hall with processional honours and an appropriate escort, thus:

Four Sergeants at Arms, with their maces, 2 and 2
Comptroller and Treasurer of the Household, together, with their
white staves
The Sewer
Gentlemen Pensioners, bearing the dishes
Two Clerks of the Green Cloth
The Clerk Comptroller   A Clerk of the Kitchen

Garter King of Arms proclaimed the Sovereign's titles and those of the newly installed Knights, with cries of "Largesse" before and after. The Great Basin was presented, and the King washed. Grace was said. The King left the hall, and the great archaic scene was dissolved, never to return.

Dinner was served to the Queen and Princesses, and the many distinguished guests, in other apartments. Two tables in the Queen's Presence Chamber commemorated Britain's sea triumphs in the Napoleonic wars. Trafalgar, and the death of Nelson in final victory, were six months away, and so the subject was one which could be exploited without any alloy of sadness. The decorations were "emblematical and allegorical devices of the four Naval Victories; namely, Lord Nelson's Battle of the Nile, Lord Howe's First of June, Lord Duncan's Camperdown and Earl St. Vincent's off St. Vincent, with excellent likenesses of the four Admirals." In another room the long table was set with "lofty colonnades in white and gold, enriched with Stars and Georges, and an equestrian statue of His Majesty in the centre, under a beautiful cupola."

Outside in the Quadrangle stood nine long tables, on which was placed all the food left over from the feasts, including part of a baron of beef weighing 162 pounds which the King had caused to be roasted. It was too heavy for a jack, and had to be turned by a man, and a silver dish was specially made to hold it. At dusk the Castle gates were thrown open, and waiting crowds, stimulated by talk of the baron of beef and other appetizers, rushed in to snatch up the rich remains.[6]

There was one more outstandingly joyful occasion in King George III's reign, the second longest in English history. His jubilee on 25th October, 1809, was the signal for celebrations throughout the land, but none of his subjects felt more closely allied to him in loyalty and affection than the Bachelors of Windsor. They, too, were celebrating their jubilee. The society had been founded in 1760 to safeguard public rights on Pits Field, or Bachelors' Acre, as it had come to be called. Because butts for the practice of archery were set up in King Edward III's reign, a tradition persisted that he had given it to the young men of Windsor for their recreation. The Bachelors were all men of standing in the town, and to celebrate their King's jubilee they organized a great festival on the Acre. An ox and two sheep were roasted whole, and a gigantic plum pudding boiled.

The King, being blind, did not go down to the Acre, but Queen Charlotte went with the Dukes of York, Clarence, Kent and Cumberland, and the Princesses Augusta, Elizabeth and Sophia. The roasting had begun at midnight, and the ox was ready for carving by the time the royal party appeared at one o'clock in the afternoon. They were welcomed by fifty Bachelors "in their evening dress of blue coats, white breeches and silk stockings." The first slices of beef, mutton and plum pudding were handed on silver plates to the royal guests, who "all tasted and appeared highly pleased with the novelty."[7]

All that day, Windsor was filled with the sound of trumpets, bells and drums, the cavalry paraded, there were feasts and fireworks and illuminations, and the rejoicings ended with a water pageant at Frogmore. A temple had been erected on the island in the lake, in the centre of which was a "large transparency of the Eye of Providence fixed, as it were, upon a beautiful portrait of His Majesty." On the water appeared "two triumphal cars, drawn by two sea-horses each, one occupied by Neptune, and preceded by the other with a band of music."[8]

As night fell on this golden autumn day, so the gladness of the King's reign too began to fade. A year later he was stricken by the death of Princess Amelia, that adored youngest daughter whom Fanny Burney had seen walking as a child on the Terrace. She died on 2nd November, 1810, at Augusta Lodge in St. Albans Street, a house which the King had given to her sister, Princess Augusta. According to the custom then prevailing, her funeral took place in the evening, and the route to St. George's Chapel was lined with soldiers holding torches. She was the first to be buried in the royal vault which her father had had made under "Wolsey's Tomb House."

Soon afterwards the King became lastingly insane as well as blind. For another ten years he lingered in his cold northern rooms, a sad and isolated figure. Sometimes, in his clearer moments, he recognized the soldiers' tread as they passed along the Terrace. Then he would make his way to the window and draw back the curtain. The command "Eyes Right" would be given, and the King would raise his hand in return.

There is a story that after his death on 29th January, 1820, the Ensign, glancing up from force of habit, saw the figure of the King at the window. So clear was the impression he received that he gave the customary order—and saw the King acknowledge it. That Ensign was Sir William Knollys, who became Comptroller to King Edward VII as Prince of Wales. He told the story to the future King George V, who in turn often repeated it.[9]

King George III was the first Sovereign to die at Windsor. His body lay in state in the King's Audience Chamber, and on 16th February, 1820, at about nine o'clock at night, was borne to St. George's Chapel. To convey it a raised track 1,065 feet long, 15 feet high and 19 feet wide, was erected through the grounds. On this the "magnificent coffin and its velvet canopy was impelled forwards, upon the machine constructed to supersede the necessity of carrying so great a weight."[10] The men who accompanied it were hidden by the pall, and thus the coffin appeared to be gliding along the track without human aid. In the late winter evening, with torches lighting the way, the scene produced an almost unearthly effect. The King was buried in the royal vault with Queen Charlotte and four of their children. Besides Princess Amelia, Edward Duke of Kent, father of the future Queen Victoria, was already laid there. He died only six days before the King, and was buried on 12th February. The two little long-dead Princes, Alfred and Octavius, had been brought from Westminster Abbey and reinterred in the royal vault at half past two on the morning of 11th February.[11]

15

THE GOTHIC REVIVAL

King George III's illness had caused the Gothic restoration of the Castle to be laid aside. It was left to King George IV to complete the alterations and at the same time provide himself and his successors with a modern palace. A stay of two months after his state entry on 1st October, 1820, convinced him of the need for extensive improvements. Eight Commissioners were appointed to select an architect, and after a competition they chose the plans submitted by Jeffry Wyatt, nephew of James Wyatt. Parliament voted £300,000 for the work, but the eventual cost amounted to more than a million pounds. Of this, a quarter was spent on new furnishings.

The chosen plan was in some ways pompous and theatrical, but it produced a majesty of effect which is among the wonders of the modern world. The principal change made by King George IV was his removal into private apartments on the east front, where he had lived as Prince of Wales. He thus left the old royal suites on the north to serve as State Apartments. Henceforth they were used for large gatherings and for the state visits of foreign sovereigns. They also formed, and still form, a superb setting for the display of paintings and other works of art in the royal collection.

The east and south fronts had changed little since the fourteenth-century rooms were remodelled in King Charles II's reign, and were still linked only by narrow passages. The new plan provided for a spacious Grand Corridor, 550 feet long, to be erected along the inner side of these two fronts. It was designed to open on the upper storey into the newly arranged suites, and to provide extra offices on the ground floor.

Work began on these two fronts in June 1823. At about the same time orders were given for the demolition of Queen's Lodge, which was taken down in the autumn. The public road between the Lodge and the South Terrace had been closed since 1818, when it was diverted to a route further away from the Castle. After the death of King George III some of the old pleasurable spirit had revived. Boys played again in the Little Park, and every day except Tuesday and Saturday the band played to a happy audience on the East Terrace. It was a sad blow when on 4th August, 1823, King George IV closed the entire Terrace to the public except on Sundays.

In June 1824, when Wyatt's plans were finally adopted, the King ordered Mr. Tebbott, the royal builder, to complete two models of the Castle, prepared on a scale of one-eighth of an inch to a foot, one showing it as it then stood, the other with the projected improvements.[1] Two months later, on 12th August, he celebrated his sixty-second birthday by laying the foundation stone of King George IV Gateway, the new entrance into the Castle from the Long Walk. It replaced the old Rubbish Gate further west, which was blocked up. The architect flanked his archway with the twin York and Lancaster Towers, the former of which was new while the latter dated in part from King Henry II's reign. The inscription on the foundation stone referred to him, not as Wyatt, but Wyatville. This was the name he had asked leave to take in honour of his appointment. "Veal or mutton," the King is said to have agreed, "call yourself what you like."

He himself supervised the work from the Royal Lodge, his private home three miles away in the Great Park, from which he used to drive over in his pony phaeton wearing Windsor Uniform and, in summer, a straw hat. Wyatville was on the spot, for he was living in Winchester Tower, which was later granted to him as a residence for life.

Along the east front of the Castle, beginning at the northern end, Wyatville placed the Private State Dining Room, the Crimson, Green and White Drawing Rooms, and the King's private suite. The Queen's tower at the southern end was also remodelled, although there was no Queen to occupy it. Apartments for the use of visiting royalty and other guests were on the south side. The new Grand Corridor not only provided a link all the way round, but formed a noble gallery for the display of pictures and furnishings. To so keen a patron of art as King George IV this was an added recommendation.

Wyatville's work on these two fronts proved more difficult and costly than had been foreseen, because the stripping of the walls revealed unsuspected decay. Many were cracked through, and numerous holes were found. Some of the damage dated from the previous century, when the apartments were parcelled out to tenants. Wyatville found that they had cut into the walls, making little extra closets and enlarging rooms according to their fancy. The roof was in equally poor condition. As it had to be removed, the opportunity was taken to add an extra storey for the accommodation of servants.[2]

Despite setbacks and increased expense, this part of his work was completed in the space of five years. On the afternoon of 9th December, 1828, the King drove from the Royal Lodge to the new Grand Entrance of the Castle to take possession. Wyatville delivered up to him in a crimson bag the master keys of his new suite and was knighted.[3] The King made Christmas the occasion for a housewarming party. His guests found him in high spirits, and well pleased with the elegance, warmth and comfort at his command.

He was surrounded not only with luxurious new furnishings and his superb private collection of pictures, but also by the latest devices. Although the rooms included no bathrooms as we know them today, hot and cold baths had been installed. Gas light was another novelty. This benefit the Castle shared with the town, where the official torchbearer had lit the first gas lamps three months earlier, on 6th September. A third feature which was much talked about was the plate glass in Wyatville's great new bay windows along the east front.

Below these windows a new scene met the eye. The old Bowling Green which had been there since King Charles II's reign had gone. In its place Wyatville had laid out the East Terrace Garden. As the Little Park was still open to the public, this enclosure of lawns and statues met the growing royal desire for privacy. In the decorative Orangery on the north side of the garden grew thirty-four fine orange trees, a gift to King George IV from the King of France. Wyatville had also contrived an elegant public approach to the North Terrace, which had hitherto been reached by winding wooden stairs descending under Queen Elizabeth's Gallery. The gate leading on to the Terrace near Winchester Tower was among the many improvements made by him in 1828.

On the south front he had rebuilt the Terrace as far as King George IV Gateway. The archway of the new entrance was said to be the largest in any castle in England,[4] and opened on to one of the noblest vistas in Europe. Although the Frogmore road still cut across the top of the Long Walk, the removal of Queen's Lodge and other intervening houses had removed visual barriers, and the eye could now travel uninterruptedly along the avenue to its limit three miles away.

To close the view King George IV was planning to set a gigantic statue of his father on Snow Hill. This had been in his mind long before the alterations in the Castle were begun. The *Reading Mercury* of 15th January, 1821, announced: "His Majesty has ordered a full-length statue in bronze of George III to be erected on the top of Snow Hill, Windsor Park, with his hand pointing towards his favourite residence, Windsor Castle."

The statue was executed by Sir Richard Westmacott, who began work on it at his London foundry in 1824, and received a total payment of £18,712.[5] Its planned relation to the Castle accounts for its colossal size. Horse and rider stand $25\frac{1}{2}$ feet high. The towering base is also 25 feet high. The latter was designed by Wyatville at a cost of £5,000. Tradition says that it was built to resemble the base of Peter the Great's statue in the Decembrists' Square in Leningrad (then St. Petersburg), "but of many pieces of stone instead of one block of granite."[6]

The King laid the foundation stone on his birthday in 1829. It was a piece of granite weighing four tons, already inscribed with the words *Georgio Tertio Patri Optimo Georgius Rex* ("King George to George III, best of fathers"). He did not see the completed statue, which was not ready until more than a year after his death. It took a month to assemble. Early in September 1831 the horse was despatched on a truck from Westmacott's foundry. Its enormous weight caused the wheels to sink into the road leading to the summit of Snow Hill, with the result that the truck overturned and one of the legs was broken. Repairs were carried out at the roadside. Before it was raised on to the pedestal, Mr. Maynard, later keeper of Queen Victoria's private kennel, and fifteen others "got inside the horse, where they partook of a luncheon of bread and cheese, and concluded their repast by drinking the health of King William IV, and singing 'God save the King'."[7]

It has long been called "The Copper Horse", though no one knows how the name originated. Queen Victoria is said to have rebuked a guest who unthinkingly replied, when asked how he had spent the afternoon, that he had walked to the Copper Horse and back. "You mean," she said coldly, "the equestrian statue of our Grandfather."

After completing the alterations on the south and east fronts, Wyatville began remodelling the faded palace of King Charles II on the north. Many of the beautiful ceilings painted by Verrio were in poor condition, and he removed all but three. Those that remain are the ones in the King's Dining Room and the Queen's Presence and Audience Chambers.

He extended the Queen's Guard Chamber to cover his new Grand Entrance from the Quadrangle, which masks the remains of *La Spicerie*, the gateway built by King Edward III. The King's Guard Chamber he made into the Grand Reception Room, and the King's Presence and Audience Chambers into the Garter Throne Room. St. George's Hall he extended by demolishing the private chapel at its western end, thus making it into a gallery 185 feet long. Verrio's paintings on walls and ceiling were replaced by a Gothic interior. On the panelled ceiling Wyatville displayed the arms of the Knights of the Garter from the foundation of the Order in 1348.

Over Horn Court next door he built the Waterloo Chamber. It was reported in August 1828 that the King "meant to form a magnificent collection of pictures to be called the Waterloo Gallery", which would be open to the public. Although it was not finished in his lifetime, this was George IV's memorial of the battle of Waterloo. The chamber was specially designed to hold Sir Thomas Lawrence's portraits of the sovereigns, statesmen and generals who helped to defeat Napoleon. Since it was constructed between four walls and therefore windowless, Wyatville designed a picturesque lantern roof to admit light.

Apart from these changes and the building of a more spacious Grand Staircase in Brick Court, the State Apartments retained the pattern of King Charles II's palace. They do so still, though the

Queen's Bedchamber and Queen Elizabeth's Gallery were made into the Royal Library by King William IV in 1832.

On the outside of the Castle Wyatville's work stands out boldly. In the course of his alterations he completed the replacement of King Charles II's windows by Gothic ones. His uncle had used Portland stone for those on the Star Building and the Queen's state apartments. This was expensive to work, and probably for reasons of economy Wyatville employed freestone, which can be cut with a saw. Their respective windows may be picked out at a glance. The inferior freestone has taken on a harsh yellowish tint while the Portland stone remains pale and elegant.

Apart from the remodelled windows on the Star Building, the north front was still as King Charles II left it. To break the flatness Wyatville built the octagonal Brunswick Tower at the north-east corner, and the Cornwall and King George IV Towers. The former allowed an extension of the new Grand Reception Room, formerly the King's Guard Chamber, while the latter contained a great bay window lighting the King's state Drawing Room. It was in this bay that the body of King George IV lay in state after his death in 1830.

Before the alterations the outline of the surviving medieval battlements around the Upper Ward was unassuming. Wyatville adopted a striking invention to give greater importance to it. While working on the south and east fronts he finished the York and Lancaster Towers and the Queen's Tower with projecting battlements supported by corbels. The massive construction of this device may be judged by the fact that the Queen's Tower carries over a thousand tons of stone. He used the same ornamental feature on his lofty Brunswick Tower and the drum towers flanking the Norman Gateway.

He completed the effect by raising the Round Tower 33 feet and crowning it with a projecting battlement supported on arched corbels. The original height was thus doubled, raising it to 128 feet above the level of the road. The scheme was applauded as daring and skilful, since the tower stood on an artificial mount, lacking the solidity of the ancient portions of the Castle based on solid chalk. Wyatville found it necessary to increase the thickness of the lower wall considerably before adding the upper part.

Previously the flag had risen "out of the centre, as it were accidentally". Wyatville provided a flag turret 25 feet high, and so the

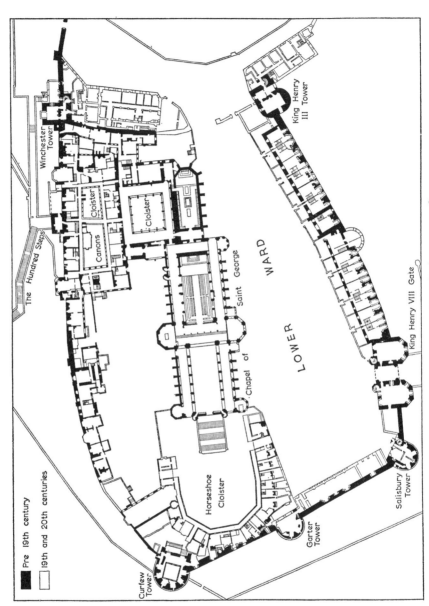

Windsor Castle, Lower Ward in its present form

Pre 19th century

19th and 20th centuries

Winchester Tower

The Hundred Steps

Cloister

Canons

Cloister

Chapel of Saint George

LOWER WARD

King Henry III Tower

King Henry VIII Gate

Horseshoe Cloister

King Henry VIII Gate

Salisbury Tower

Garter Tower

Curfew Tower

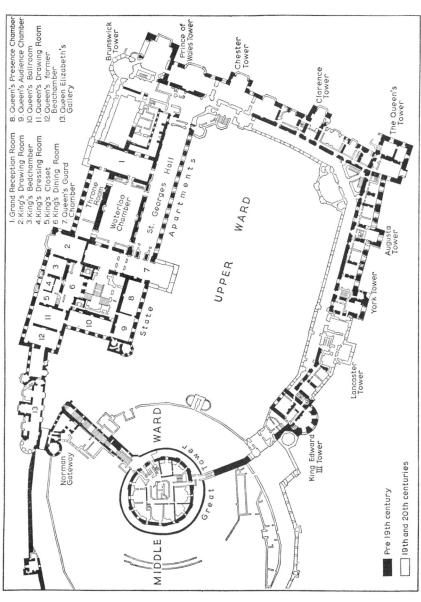

1. Grand Reception Room
2. King's Drawing Room
3. King's Bedchamber
4. King's Dressing Room
5. King's Closet
6. King's Dining Room
7. Queen's Guard Chamber
8. Queen's Presence Chamber
9. Queen's Audience Chamber
10. Queen's Ballroom
11. Queen's Drawing Room
12. Queen's former Bedchamber
13. Queen Elizabeth's Gallery

Brunswick Tower

Prince of Wales Tower

Chester Tower

Clarence Tower

The Queen's Tower

Throne Room

Waterloo Chamber

St. George's Hall

State Apartments

UPPER WARD

Augusta Tower

York Tower

Lancaster Tower

MIDDLE WARD

Great Tower

Norman Gateway

King Edward III Tower

■ Pre 19th century

□ 19th and 20th centuries

Windsor Castle, Middle and Upper Wards in their present form flag has since flown at a height of 203 feet above road level. The Royal Standard is hoisted whenever the Sovereign is in residence. At other times the Union Flag takes its place. Whichever one it is, it flies day and night.

The first stone of the addition to the Round Tower was laid on the King's birthday in 1828 by his brother, Adolphus Duke of Cambridge, and his nephew, Prince George of Cumberland, later the Blind King of Hanover. It was completed in 1832, the builder being Mr. Thomas Bedborough, of the local firm of Tebbott and Bedborough.[8]

Wyatville also turned his attention to the eastern side of the mount, which the filling-in of the ditch in 1779 had rendered featureless. By the removal of 13,000 cubic feet of top soil from the Quadrangle he had lowered its surface by three to six feet, and he now made the Moat Path at the foot of the mount, placing in front of it Ibach's equestrian statue of King Charles II, which he raised on a stone pedestal flanked by water basins. For some years the public had not been admitted to the Quadrangle, but the opening of this footway in 1832 allowed them to circulate and enjoy a full view of the buildings. It curves round the green slope, which in springtime turns golden with daffodils, to reach St. George's Gate, another of Wyatville's innovations, at its southern end.

Winchester Tower, his own home, he made into a miniature palace with suites of rooms opening off a great spiral stone staircase.

---

17. The Horseshoe Cloister, *c.* 1770; from the coloured drawing by Paul Sandby in the Royal Library, Windsor Castle

The white-washed houses and gabled roof of the Chapter Library are overlooked by the Curfew Tower, surmounted by King Edward IV's belfry and the "Garter" clock. The wall across the cloister, separating private gardens from a public pathway, dated from the Restoration.

18. The Horseshoe Cloister today

The trim houses as they were remodelled in 1870. The wall in front of them, shown in Sandby's drawing, survived until this period. The Chapter Library was reconstructed at the same time as the houses. The Curfew Tower had assumed its modern appearance seven years earlier, when the original bell-cage and dome were enclosed in the additions of 1863.

The principal rooms on the north front he dignified with the name "State Apartments", in imitation of the royal galleries. Outside he carved the name "Winchester Tower", and in continuation, across the north front, the words which had so displeased King Edward III, and which he found almost worn away—*Hoc fecit Wykeham Anno Domini 1356*.[9]

The red-brick house next door, with "The Royal Standard" and the old guardroom beside it, were not grand enough neighbours for Wyatville's stately residence. The inn and the guardroom he swept away, replacing them with the present Lord Chamberlain's Offices, but the house he remodelled to form an addition to Winchester Tower. The two were connected with a first-floor gallery. By the time he had finished, the pretty domestic outline of the house was lost, for Wyatville clamped on to it a grey stone front which made it look like a lesser tower.

His work continued throughout the reign of King William IV and into Queen Victoria's. The final stage in the modernization of the palace was the erection of the Royal Mews, which was built to his plans. It occupies four acres on the south side of the Castle, and covers the gardens of Queen's Lodge and the neighbouring houses

---

19. The Albert Memorial Chapel, looking west

Like the Mausoleum of Queen Victoria and the Prince Consort at Frogmore, the Albert Memorial Chapel embodies the richest expression of nineteenth-century design, though in this instance the artistry is enshrined in an older setting. The architectural traditions of the chapel go back even further than 1494, when King Henry VII rebuilt the one originally erected by King Henry III. Mr. John Harvey has pointed out that the plan of the Albert Memorial Chapel, with its polygonal eastern apse and windows of early Perpendicular form, probably derives from the alterations made by King Edward III when he adapted the chapel for use by the Order of the Garter. Today its splendour centres on the cenotaph of the Prince Consort, surmounted by his effigy in white marble. This is seen in the foreground of the picture, and behind it is the magnificent unfinished tomb by Sir Alfred Gilbert, R.A., of Prince Albert Victor, Duke of Clarence (1864–92), elder brother of King George V. Beyond that (but unseen in the photograph) is the white marble tomb of Prince Leopold, Duke of Albany (1853–84), youngest son of Queen Victoria. The west window is blocked up with mosaic pictures of eminent persons and benefactors whose names are memorable in the history of the College of St. George.

which once stood in St. Albans Street. Only Lower Lodge survived the change, and this was cased and stuccoed to resemble stone, so that it should not look out of place in its grey Gothic surroundings.

The foundation stone of the Royal Mews was laid on Monday, 19th August, 1839, "a few yards only from the palings on the west side of the Home [or Little] Park." To Wyatville was accorded the honour of carrying out the ceremony, but the shadow of death was already beside him as he stood waiting in the rain, and feeling himself unequal to the effort he handed the silver trowel to the mason, Mr. Noel. It was a melancholy climax to his achievement. Because of the weather the Queen was not present, and barely a dozen spectators saw the stone laid.[10] On 18th February, 1840, Wyatville died in London. His body was brought to Windsor and buried in a vault in St. George's Chapel. George Villiers, 5th Earl of Jersey, Master of the Horse, took formal possession of the completed mews on 24th October, 1842.

16

QUEEN VICTORIA AND THE PRINCE CONSORT

On Tuesday, 1st August, 1826, Princess Victoria of Kent was taken to visit King George IV at the Royal Lodge. She was seven years old and accompanied her mother, the Duchess of Kent, and her grown-up half-sister, Princess Feodore of Leiningen.

When they arrived the King took Princess Victoria by the hand, saying "Give me your little paw." Then he told her he was going to give her something to wear. It was his portrait set in diamonds, and she felt very proud when it was pinned to her shoulder on a blue ribbon.

To amuse the little Princess he desired two of his guests, Lady Maria Conyngham and Lord Graves, to take her for a drive through the Great Park. With her governess, Miss Lehzen, she accompanied them in a carriage drawn by four grey ponies to Sandpit Gate where the King had his menagerie. There she saw a wonderful collection of animals, including wapitis, gazelles and antelopes.

That afternoon the King and his house party of royal and distinguished guests drove to Virginia Water, the ornamental lake on the southern edge of the Great Park. A handsome barge was in readiness, and they all cruised up and down for two hours, while a band played in a second barge. At 5.30 a sumptuous banquet was served in the Fishing Temple beside the lake.

The pleasures of this brief holiday were among the Princess's earliest and most treasured memories. Long afterwards, in 1872, when she was the widowed Queen of England, she jotted them down.[1] By that time the precise course of events had become confused in her mind, but the details remained clear. One incident which stood out in her memory happened unexpectedly, probably on the Wednesday morning. With her mother she was walking in the Park when they met the King, driving in his phaeton with his sister, Princess Mary, Duchess of Gloucester. He called out "Pop her in", and Princess Victoria was lifted up and placed between him and the Duchess. Aunt Gloucester held her firmly round the waist, but Mamma looked much frightened as she saw her precious little daughter whirled away.

The King drove round the prettiest parts of Virginia Water, and afterwards the Princess went with Miss Lehzen to visit Whiting the page, who had been in her father's service. He lived at a cottage close to the lake. Here, she recalled, "I had some fruit, and amused myself by cramming one of Whiting's children, a little girl, with peaches."

On the Wednesday afternoon the King drove with his guests, including Princess Victoria, to see the new works in progress at the Castle.[2] They returned to the Royal Lodge for dinner, and afterwards she went to hear the band play in the conservatory, which was lit up by coloured lamps. It must have been then that a charming conversation, related by her in 1897, took place. The King entered the drawing-room, holding his little niece by the hand. "Now, Victoria," he said, "the band is in the next room, and shall play any tune you please. What shall it be?" "Oh, Uncle King," quickly replied the Princess, "I should like 'God save the King'." Before she left the Royal Lodge on the following morning he asked her what she had enjoyed most during her visit. "The drive I took with you, Uncle King," was her answer.[3]

George IV died at Windsor Castle on 26th June, 1830, and William IV on 20th June, 1837. Both were buried in the royal vault under "Wolsey's Tomb House". Queen Victoria, aged eighteen, made her state entry into Windsor on Saturday, 26th August, 1837, two months after her accession.

Like so many royal cavalcades of the past, her carriage procession left London by the Great West Road, but for the final part of the journey took a new route. It followed the riverside path across Runnymede, entered the Great Park at Old Windsor and drove up the Long Walk. At the top of the avenue it turned under a triumphal arch into Park Street, continued along High Street and went up Castle Hill to King George IV Gateway.

In the early evening came the most applauded side-show of this exciting day. It was the ascent of Mrs. Graham, "the celebrated and only female aeronaut", in her "Victoria" balloon. The inflation of the machine from a gas-pipe had begun on the previous Monday. With Mrs. Graham standing in the attached car, the monster balloon was loosed and made a slow and graceful ascent under the eyes of the Queen. She had chosen to occupy the same tower as her grandmother, Queen Charlotte, and watched Mrs. Graham's feat from the window of her sitting-room. The balloon floated away over the trees of the Little Park and came to earth again nine miles away.[4]

Two years later, on 10th October, 1839, the Queen welcomed at Windsor her first cousin, Prince Albert, younger son of the Duchess of Kent's brother, Ernest I, reigning Duke of Saxe-Coburg and Gotha. Both were twenty years of age, the Prince being three months younger than the Queen. Their marriage had been planned when they were babies, but after her accession the Queen had begun to feel undecided about her feelings. The moment she saw Prince Albert again all her doubts vanished. He could not propose to her, since he was of lower rank, and so it was she who had to introduce the subject of their marriage. On the fifth morning of his visit she received him alone in her sitting-room. After a little conversation she came nervously to the point. He must be aware, she said, why she had asked him to come, and then added, with tears in her eyes, "Could you forsake your country for me? It would make me *too happy* if you would consent to what I wish."

After their marriage at St. James's Palace on 10th February, 1840, the royal couple drove to Windsor for their honeymoon. The Queen wore a white satin bonnet with a white feather round it, and looked very young and very pretty. At Eton College the carriage slowed down for the boys to cheer her. Then it drove on over Windsor Bridge into a fairyland of lights, while in the Curfew Tower and Parish Church the bells proclaimed their joyous greeting.

Next morning the Queen and the Prince were out early on the Terrace, accompanied by Eos, the greyhound which the Prince had brought from Coburg. That very day the Queen wrote to her uncle, King Leopold I of the Belgians who had always wished for the marriage, to say that she was the "happiest, happiest Being" that ever existed. In the following November she gave birth to Victoria,

Princess Royal, later the German Empress Frederick, and a month later the royal family went to Windsor for Christmas. Prince Albert's biographer, Sir Theodore Martin, records that this was his favourite festival, and "he clung to the kindly custom of his native country, which makes it a day for the interchange of gifts, as marks of affection and good will. The Queen fully shared his feelings in this respect, and the same usage was then introduced into their home, and was ever afterwards continued. Christmas trees were set up in the Queen and the Prince's rooms, beside which were placed the gifts with which each took pleasure in surprising the other."

It was not the first time that this charming German custom had been observed in England. It will be remembered that Queen Charlotte delighted local children with her illuminated yew tree in 1800. Queen Adelaide, wife of King William IV, had Christmas trees hung with gilded fruits at her parties at Brighton Pavilion. Queen Victoria herself as a girl always had a Christmas tree decorated with lights and sugar ornaments, and surrounded with presents for herself and her spaniel, Dash, who once received two balls and some gingerbread. It was thus popular in the royal circle before her marriage, but not widely known outside. After 1840 it began to establish itself in the hearts of the nation. A print published in 1858 entitled "The Family Christmas Tree" shows how quickly it was adopted in English homes. Barracks, schools and institutions had Christmas trees, often presented by the Queen or other members of the royal family. Thus all classes had a chance to become acquainted with its joys. Within thirty years the Christmas tree was completely acclimatized. We have the Queen's own word for this. "She rejoices," she wrote to Major (later Sir) Howard Elphinstone on 16th January, 1865, "to think that the Prince and herself are the source of Christmas trees being so generally adopted in this country."[5]

For many years the royal Christmas was spent at Windsor, where decorated trees were the centre-piece of exciting gaieties. Apart from those set up for the Queen, Prince Albert and the Duchess of Kent, the royal children shared one around which their presents were placed. There were others for the Queen's ladies in waiting and the servants. Three small ones stood in the dining-room, where the sideboard supported the traditional baron of beef, weighing some 400 pounds, the historic boar's head and immense game pie. The tallest and most splendid of the trees was placed in the drawing-room. All were lit with dozens of little coloured candles and decorated with gingerbread. Its rich smell mingling deliciously with that of the firs was one the Queen particularly loved. Gifts were unwrapped on Christmas Eve, and then the candles were put out, to be relit at dusk on Christmas Day. They were lit again on New Year's Day and Twelfth Night.

Queen Victoria's second child, Edward Prince of Wales, later King Edward VII, spent his first Christmas at Windsor when he was six weeks old. A month later, on 25th January, 1842, he was baptized in St. George's Chapel. At that time the Queen was still travelling to and from Windsor in a horse-drawn carriage, but soon afterwards a royal train was added to her means of transport. She did not use it until Prince Albert had tested the new railroad and satisfied himself that it was safe for her to do so. With him at her side, she set out from Windsor Castle to take her first train journey on Monday, 13th June, 1842.

Their destination was Paddington. The Western Region line had reached Slough in 1838, but there was still no branch line to Windsor. It was not opened until October 1849, two months before the Southern Region line from Waterloo, and so their train journey began at Slough.

The Queen and the Prince left the Castle in a carriage procession escorted by a detachment of the Royal Horse Guards. The royal train standing in Slough Station was made up of four coaches. The one behind the engine was for luggage. The royal saloon, which had a crown on top, came next. The last two were for the gentlemen in waiting and other attendants. At the back were trucks on which the six carriages were placed.

The Master of the Horse inspected the train, and the Queen's coachman began to climb on to the engine. Dismayed officials finally persuaded him to travel on the pilot engine which steamed ahead to test the line. At the end of the journey he found his scarlet livery and white wig covered with smuts, and never pressed his claim again.

The train steamed out of Slough station as the clock struck noon. It was driven by the great engineer who had built the railroad, Isambard Brunel himself. At five and twenty minutes past twelve it was greeted by cheering crowds at Paddington. As the Queen stepped down, a smiling and graceful little figure in her light summer dress and bonnet, she declared herself "quite charmed" with the experience. The motion of the train had been slight, and much easier than that of a carriage, and she had experienced no discomfort from dust and heat. Altogether, she recorded in her journal, it was quite delightful, and so quick.

The new mode of transport made Windsor still more agreeably accessible. As a royal home the Castle offered every immediate advantage, for so completely had King George IV transformed the palace of his ancestors that little remained for his successors to do. The only attribute it lacked within its walls was a domestic chapel to replace the one taken by Wyatville into St. George's Hall. During the early years of her reign the Queen attended mattins at St. George's Chapel every Sunday, but found the Royal Closet "dreadfully cold" and the services "terribly long".[6]

It was Prince Albert who saw the possibilities of the old "Prince of Wales's Guard Chamber" at the east end of St. George's Hall, which was now buried away behind George IV's new corridor and the Visitors' Entrance. Although deprived of its window overlooking the Quadrangle, it had been made by Wyatville into a music room for the King's private band, and was 34 feet long, 26 feet wide and 26 feet high, and irregular in shape. Under the Prince's direction Edward Blore competently turned it into a chapel which was consecrated on 19th December, 1843. Being plain and still rather dark it was altered in 1852, when it was refitted with richly carved oak panelling and plaster mouldings and tracery, the new style of decoration being described as a light perpendicular Gothic of the period of King Henry VII. At the same time the wall adjoining St. George's Hall was partly removed and converted into a gallery, in which a fine organ was erected.[7] Services were regularly held in this private chapel, and a number of royal christenings, confirmations and weddings took place there.

The Castle still lacked one amenity which every sizable house in the country enjoyed. It had no "pleasure grounds". It had no grounds at all, if by the term one means an enclosed acreage for the exclusive use of the royal family. The concept that royalty had a right to a private life was still too new to have become wholly effective.

King George IV's East Terrace Garden allowed a modicum of exercise in the fresh air, but there was nowhere to walk or drive without being seen. The 500 acres of the Little Park were still open to the public, and apart from a few cultivated areas it was rough and wild, with tall grass growing up to the Castle walls.

Its development into a private royal park was Prince Albert's outstanding contribution to the majesty of the Castle. "One who remembers what the Home Park at Windsor was at the Queen's marriage," wrote the Hon. C. Grey in *The Early Years of the Prince Consort* (1867), "the public road winding round it under a high brick wall—its fashionable 'Frying Pan' walk, and the low public houses opposite—the footpath leading across the Park close to Adelaide Cottage, and totally destructive of all privacy, to the old Datchet bridge—and the slopes so overgrown with trees, dark, gloomy, and damp—will readily admit how much Windsor, as a residence for the Queen, owes to the Prince." It was a formidable task, even for a patron of the arts who was in his own right an acknowledge master of landscape gardening. To begin with, three public roads had to be diverted—the two which circled round William III's wall and met at Datchet Bridge, and, far more important, the highway through Frogmore to Old Windsor. The latter had served as a thoroughfare to London since 1816, when as a result of the Enclosure Acts local development began and Frogmore was linked with the new Straight Road through Old Windsor to Runnymede. Public coaches used it and went to and fro past the entrance to Queen Charlotte's colonnaded mansion, which was still a royal home. Princess Augusta had lived there until her death in 1840, after which it became the residence of the Duchess of Kent. Queen Victoria used to go through a little gate in William III's wall, at the end of a mulberry avenue, and cross the road to visit her mother.

The diversion of this road was a matter which also gave concern to Mr. Robert Tighe, the manager of Nevile Reid's brewery adjoining the North Slopes. He was acutely conscious of the traditions and potentialities of Windsor, and later collaborated with Mr. James Davis, a Welsh barrister, in producing the great *Annals of Windsor*, which was dedicated to Queen Victoria and published in 1858.[8] This belonged to the future: his immediate solicitude was for royal prestige and convenience. He too thought that the Queen should be accorded greater privacy, and embodied several suggestions in his printed *Letter to the Earl of Lincoln* in 1845. The Earl was First Commissioner of Woods and Forests, and in his official capacity controlled much of the land in Windsor. Mr. Tighe reinforced his argument by recording that he had seen parties with their carriages drawn up against William III's wall at Frogmore, "to enable them to lean on it, and thus gratify their curiosity with a view of the Queen when Her Majesty is walking in the enclosure."

He did not dilate on the enclosure, but it could only have been the sunken garden, just within the wall, which had once belonged to a mansion occupied by the Ranger of the Little Park. The house was gone, and the garden was overlooked by the Queen's aviary and the royal dairy. Like her grandfather, she enjoyed visiting the dairy, which she rebuilt. We do not know what King George III's was like, but Queen Victoria's is still there, romantic and enchanting with its stained glass windows and flower-patterned tiles. Not far away were the royal kennels, which were specially designed to afford maximum comfort and hygiene for the Queen's numerous pets.

Along the road, towards the town, but near enough to Frogmore to qualify for the status of neighbours, were the two "low public houses", the "Hope" and the "Horns". At this point a swing gate opened on to the footpath leading across the Little Park to Datchet Bridge. It had been in use since 1818, when the old road alongside the South Terrace was closed, and led past the "Frying Pan", an oval shrubbery about an acre in extent where fashionable society liked to walk on Sundays. The path was carried on a causeway over Shakespeare's fairy dell, which by this time had lost its haunted mystery. During Wyatville's restoration of the Castle all the rubbish had been dumped there. Charles Knight, for whom it held the illusions of childhood, revisited the beloved spot in 1845 and found the hollow almost entirely filled in, his favourite thorns buried, and the ancient roots of trees covered up.[9]

From the dell the pathway continued to Mother Dodd's Hill, and skirting the garden of the lodge where Queen Charlotte once enjoyed her eggs and bacon, continued as of old across the lower park to the bridge. Queen Adelaide, with the same desire for a rural retreat, had converted the lodge into a *cottage orné* in order to give luncheon parties and drink tea there, and it has ever since been called Adelaide

Cottage. In the garden Queen Victoria buried Dash, the companion of her girlhood, whose epitaph she herself is said to have composed:

Here lies DASH
The favourite Spaniel of Her Majesty Queen Victoria
By whose command this memorial was erected.
He died on the 20th December 1840,
In his ninth year.
His attachment was without selfishness,
His playfulness without malice,
His fidelity without deceit.
Reader,
If you would live beloved and die regretted,
Profit by the example of
DASH.[10]

The task of creating the private royal park took eleven years. A commentary on its progress is provided in the journal of Miss Margaretta Brown, whose sister Fanny was the wife of Dr. Keate, Head Master of Eton and from 1820 until his death in 1852 a canon of Windsor.[11] Miss Brown was very fond of walking in the Frying Pan, which she mentions as early as 1802. In 1843 she found "great alterations" in the Park, where the Prince had begun laying out lawns and drives and turning the North Slopes into sylvan "pleasure grounds". In 1849 "Maestricht" was cut up to make way for the Southern Region railway line from Waterloo, to the great disgust of Miss Brown, who detested the railways. It was bad enough when the "vile" Western Region extension from Slough was opened on 8th October, 1849, and the train began "screaming with its vile whistle", and an additional cross when on 18th October she saw the "vile cutting-up of the Home Park" (as the Little Park was by this time generally known).

The Southern Region line reached its terminus opposite the North Slopes, and since the station was to stand within view of the State Apartments its design was carefully supervised. With the Prince's approval it was built in red brick in a style at once prim and purposeful. On the side facing the Castle it presents a long, curving wall broken by twelve entrances. This was the royal platform. Along the outside the crowned monogram VR and PA, and the date 1851, may be seen worked in black bricks among the red. The first train for Waterloo left the station on 1st December, 1849.

While it was being built a trout stream was brought underneath it from the Thames into the Home Park. It flows under stone bridges and willows to re-enter the river by the Royal Boat House opposite Datchet, pursuing a charming course broken by a waterfall and a heronry. This artificial stream, called the Broad Water, was completed by 1851, when the riverside route to Datchet Bridge was closed and William III's wall pulled down. A fragment of the wall remains opposite the station. The Victoria Bridge, which with the Albert Bridge replaced the one originally built by Queen Anne, carried a new road which divided the northern reach of the Little Park. All the parts lying between the road and the river were given by the Queen and Prince Albert, who was Ranger of the Parks, for public recreation. It forms the beautiful stretch called the Home Park Public. The remainder became the Home Park Private, which was concurrently being enlarged on the south by the diversion of the Old Windsor road and the inclusion of Frogmore and the adjacent royal fruit and flower gardens laid out in 1843. The erasure of the ancient Frogmore road removed the last barrier between the Long Walk and the Castle, and allowed the drive through the trees to be taken up to King George IV Gateway. Since 1851 the Home Park Private has been reserved for the use of the royal family.

"Such altered views all around us," mourned Miss Brown as she looked out of her window in the Canons' Cloister. There was more than changed topography to record. A new and awesome dignity surrounded the monarchy, and while this may be partly attributed to the guiding instinct of Prince Albert, it was also inevitable. The old local atmosphere had gone. The coming of the railways, with their speed and their excursion tickets, gave all but the very poorest a chance to visit the Castle, and the Long Walk and North Terrace were even more crowded on Sundays and Good Fridays than in King George III's reign. In the town there were desperate clashes between the shopkeepers, who wanted to remain open, and the "Sunday Trading Abolition Humbug Gentry", but in the Castle rules were strict almost to the point of regimentation. A visitor who so much as lit his pipe on the terrace would find the sentry at his elbow, ordering him to put it out.[12] Another sign of the times was the presence of the Metropolitan Police patrolling the grounds. They had taken up their duties on 30th August, 1839, in place of the Bow Street officer of earlier days.

Well behaved as the crowds were, the Queen did not walk among them as her grandfather had done, and as she herself did at the beginning of her reign. One particular occasion chronicled by the *Windsor and Eton Express* serves to establish the more rigid pattern imposed on royalty. On Easter Sunday 1858 it was reported, "the Royal Family walked on the private promenade on the East Terrace for half an hour. The Prince of Wales appeared for the first time in public in the Windsor Uniform."

The new royal park included several miles of drives and avenues, and the Queen already possessed some charming vehicles suitable for the kind of leisurely touring it afforded. When she and Prince Albert visited King Louis Philippe at the Château d'Eu in 1843 they did their sightseeing in a royal char-a-banc, which so delighted the Queen that the French king had one specially built for her. The gift arrived at the Royal Mews at Windsor in September 1844. It was an open carriage, covered only by a fringed canopy and curtains of biscuit and cream silk, and stood some five feet above the ground. A flight of iron steps had to be climbed to get into it. The four seats, each designed to take two passengers, looked forward. In this majestic carriage, drawn by four horses, the Queen and the Prince often took their guests to Frogmore, and sometimes continued through the Great Park to Virginia Water.

This char-a-banc is now in the carriage museum at Buckingham Palace, with other historic vehicles which once bore royal personages through the Park at Windsor. They include the latticed gold and black sleigh lined with scarlet which the Prince designed and launched at Brighton in February 1845. It was never used there again, but it often came out at Windsor on days when the deer were wading knee-deep in snow, and the Castle took on the illusion of a fairy citadel in a frozen world. As it flashed through the Park, the music of innumerable little bells rang out. They hung from the network over the gay red harness of the ponies Keith and Kintore— small circular bells mounted with white feathers, and larger ones which produced three different tones. The royal children diverted themselves in their own sleigh, and, as the season yielded to summer, and roses and peonies brightened the Castle walls, played in a miniature barouche covered with a scarlet sunshade and drawn by a Shetland pony. The barouche was a gift at Christmas 1847 from Queen Adelaide, whose perpetual pleasure it was to endow with happiness all the children she knew.

Side by side with this march of domestic achievement in the Castle glitters the sequence of formal Court life. One state visit above all others exemplifies the marshalling of balls and banquets, concerts, plays, military reviews and operas which imposed their gloss on the Queen's long reign. It was that of the Emperor Napoleon III and the Empress Eugenie in April 1855. The Queen herself wrote an account of it, and her words summon up a vision of the old-fashioned town, full of flags and flowers and illuminations, and packed with excited crowds as the time of arrival drew near. In the State Apartments regal perfection awaited the imperial guests. Queen Charlotte's gold bed, enlarged and hung with violet satin curtains embodying a flowering profusion of antique needlework, stood in the State Bed-chamber, where it has remained ever since.[13] The colour of the curtains implied a delicate tribute, for violets were the flower of the Bonapartes. Queen Anne's gold mirror and toilet service, used by every succeeding Queen of England, was set out for the Empress: they surmounted a dressing-table composed of festoons of Honiton lace looped with gold. Every detail, Queen Victoria recorded, had been most carefully attended to. A magnificent new grand piano in the Empress's drawing-room, suggesting that her musical skill was appreciated by a Queen she had never yet met, proved how sincere was the royal desire to please her.[14]

On the second day of the visit a military review took place in the Great Park, and the Emperor rode "a very fiery beautiful chestnut called Philips", on which he charged with the Cavalry. Next day, in the Throne Room, the Queen formally announced to him that he was elected a Knight of the Garter, and invested him with the Garter and Riband. In less formal moments he walked in the private park, admiring the grass and saying (as the Queen recorded all foreigners did) that it never grew like that on the Continent. The Empress's gaze strayed often to the Round Tower, which claimed her greatest admiration. She glanced up at it when she was leaving, and then, taking a last look around her, said wistfully, "*C'est si beau, c'est si poétique? il n'y a rien de si beau.*"

The parting left the Queen herself in a reverie of sweet regret. Old wounds had been healed, new friendships born. One by one the impressions which so touched her glimmer up in recorded memories of the visit. Each makes its own vivid impact: the statuesque beauty of the Empress and the accentuated circuit of her crinolined skirts— the first seen in England—which the Queen thought charming; her emeralds gently vying with the Queen's rubies, or her pearls with the Koh-i-Noor; the resplendence of the gold plate; the swirl of floating silk in the ballroom, and the Queen thinking how strange it was that she, the granddaughter of King George III, should be dancing with the nephew of his mortal enemy.[15]

17

THE WIDOWED QUEEN

The maturing panorama of the Queen's reign was crushed half way through its course by the death of the Prince Consort. The title was accorded him in 1857, and he died in 1861 at the age of forty-two. Several years later it re-emerged, and rolled on, irrefrangible in its cumulative majesty, to the triumph of the Queen's jubilees in 1887 and 1897. Even then the destinies of her reign were in a sense controlled by the dead Prince. Although, against her hope and expectation, she survived him for so long a span, he remained her lifelong inspiration in every sphere of duty.

It was only after he died that his dedicated work in the public interest was fully realized. He had given himself unsparingly to his adopted country, and his last act of service was to avert its involvement in the American Civil War. The danger began when the British ship *Trent*, carrying among her passengers two envoys from the Confederate States to the British and French Courts, was stopped by a Federal warship and the envoys forcibly removed. News of this violation of British neutrality was only received when the *Trent* reached Southampton on 27th November, 1861. At once 8,000 troops were despatched to Canada. On the evening of 30th November a brusquely worded Foreign Office note to Washington was submitted to the Queen at Windsor. The Prince realized that it would almost certainly result in Britain's entry into the war. He was already ill with the onset of typhoid fever, but early next morning he rewrote it and at eight o'clock took his amended draft to the Queen, remarking that he could hardly hold his pen. His tactful suggestion that the Federal captain must have misunderstood orders was accepted by Washington, and the crisis passed.[1]

The Prince's illness lasted for a fortnight. As he grew weaker his mind sometimes wandered, and once he told the Queen that when he heard the birds singing he thought of those he had heard in his childhood at the Rosenau. On 13th December even his favourite picture of the Madonna failed to catch his notice. That evening he rallied, and the Queen, who had been praying and weeping in a frenzy of grief, began to hope again. Next morning at seven o'clock she went as usual to the Blue Room, where he lay. It was the one in which both King George IV and King William IV had died, and overlooked the East Terrace and the Park. There was a sad look of night watching about it, and the candles were burnt down to their sockets, but the morning was bright, and the sun shining into the room. Ten years later, when at last the Queen nerved herself to write down her memories of that dreadful time, every detail was still clear in her mind. "I went in, and never shall I forget how beautiful my darling looked, lying there with his face lit up by the rising sun, his eyes unusually bright, gazing as it were on unseen things." In the afternoon she saw a dusky hue on his face and hands, and then the Prince began to speak about the railways, and to arrange his hair, as he used to do when dressing. The Queen knew that these were bad signs. It was as if he were preparing for another and a greater journey. That night, almost as the Castle clock struck a quarter to eleven, he died.[2]

As early as 1843 he and the Queen had agreed not to be buried in the royal vault in St. George's Chapel, like her grandfather and uncles, but in a mausoleum specially designed for them. Their choice accorded with the tradition of the Saxe-Coburg family. His paternal grandparents, who were also the Queen's on her mother's side, lay in a Greek-temple mausoleum surrounded by lawns and trees in the Hofgarten at Coburg. For his father the family had erected an Italianate mausoleum which the Prince himself helped to design.[3]

His wish was to be buried in Queen Charlotte's beautiful garden at Frogmore. Here he had skated on the lake, and planted lilacs and rhododendrons, and the azaleas and syringa which scented the summer air. The Duchess of Kent was already buried there. She had died on 16th March, 1861, and was interred in a circular, domed temple overlooking the lake. Four days after the Prince's death the

Queen chose the site of their own mausoleum at the south-west end of the garden. The building was to take the form of a cross, with a central octagonal chamber covered with a dome. The architects were Albert Jenkins Humbert, who had designed the Duchess of Kent's temple, and Professor Ludwig Gruner, of Dresden, the Prince's adviser on the purchase of old masters. To the latter was entrusted the design of the sombre but splendid interior in the Italian cinquecento style.

On 17th December, 1862, the unfinished mausoleum was consecrated, and early next morning the Prince's body was removed from St. George's Chapel to a temporary sarcophagus there. The building took another six years to complete. The Queen wished it to be a memorial of her husband's interest in the natural products of the world, and so the materials were obtained from many lands. The woodwork was of Indian teak and the roofs of Australian copper. Wales and Scotland contributed a variety of marbles, Scotland and the Channel Isles supplied granite, and England was represented by her Portland stone, her granite from Devon and Cornwall, and her Cornish serpentine. Belgium, France, Italy, Greece and Portugal also furnished marble to enrich the interior.

The great dome represented a blue night sky strewn with golden stars and held aloft by gilded angels. Immediately below it was placed the Prince's tomb, designed by Baron Marochetti. The sarcophagus was a double one, made from a complete block of dark grey Aberdeen granite from the Cairngall quarries. It was said to be the largest flawless block of granite in existence. The plinth of polished black marble was a gift from King Leopold I of the Belgians. At each corner of the tomb knelt a bronze angel with great wings outspread.

On 26th December, 1868, the Prince's body was laid in this magnificent tomb, and upon it was placed his recumbent statue in white marble—Baron Marochetti's last work before his own death earlier that year. At the same time he had carried out the companion figure of Queen Victoria so that when this should eventually be required it would accord with that of the Prince.

To be at Windsor on the anniversary of her husband's death was a sacred obligation which the Queen observed throughout the forty years of her widowhood. Only once did she fail, and that was when the Prince of Wales lay gravely ill at Sandringham in 1871. She always began the day by visiting the Blue Room, and it was a consolation to her if she found it bright with sunshine, as on the morning of her husband's death. No one ever used this room, and few people apart from the royal family ever entered it. It was preserved as a holy and inviolate shrine, where time stood still, and nothing was ever altered or renewed except the flowers on the bed. After the Prince's death the Queen ordered that all his rooms were to be kept as he left them. Not only that, but fresh clothing was to be laid each evening upon his bed, and hot water poured into the basin, as if he were still alive. Until she herself died this rite continued without variation.[4]

Such an observance was unintelligible to English people, who attached a morbid significance to it but the Queen was only following a royal custom familiar in Germany. It had been carried out for the Prince's own father, Duke Ernest of Saxe-Coburg and Gotha. She had seen his rooms when she paid her first visit with Prince Albert to Coburg and Gotha in 1845. In her original journal, quoted by Sir Theodore Martin, she wrote: "These are left just as they were at that sad time. The wreaths, which decorated his room for his birthday, are still there, and there is that sad clock, which stopped going just before he died." Similarly, in the bedroom of her aunt, Queen Frederica of Hanover, the sheets were still being turned back, slippers laid out and hot water brought, ten years after the royal lady's death in 1841.[5] It was therefore an accepted German tradition which until the end of the nineteenth century laid its funereal spell on Windsor.[6]

Every year on 14th December, after the Queen had laid fresh flowers on the Prince's deathbed, and knelt in prayer beside it, she and other members of the royal family attended a memorial service in the Mausoleum. Between 1862 and her own death in 1901 this service was only once cancelled. It was in 1878, when, on the very morning of the anniversary of the Prince's death, their second daughter, Princess Alice, Grand Duchess of Hesse, died at Darmstadt. She had contracted diphtheria while nursing her husband and children. Her four-year-old daughter, Princess May, had died previously of the disease. The Queen's grief was as awed as it was intense. To commemorate mother and child she commanded Sir Edgar Boehm to make for the Mausoleum a statue of the Grand Duchess, lying upon a marble tomb and clasping to her side the figure of "the fever-stricken Child beside whom She had Watched".

Until the last summer of her life, when "by a strange, pathetic, almost prophetic coincidence, she assumed white attire", the Queen never laid aside the mourning she adopted when the Prince died.[7] Always she was dressed in black, relieved on occasions by a white cap and veil, and the Garter Riband and Star. For some years she withdrew from public life. When the loveliest Princess in Europe, Alexandra of Denmark, came across the North Sea to marry the Prince of Wales, she attended the ceremony but remained almost unseen. It took place in St. George's Chapel on 10th March, 1863, and the Queen watched from behind heavy blue velvet curtains in the Royal Closet.

No one saw her enter or leave the chapel. She drove on to the North Terrace, and, using the route accorded to the Chapter by King Charles II, went into the Deanery through a private garden. From the drawing-room, now the Dean's study, she stepped out on to the leads of the Cloister roof. A pathway had been specially constructed across it a few weeks earlier, and this brought her into the Royal Closet by a door beside the great east window. The window was a new one erected by the Dean and Canons in memory of the Prince Consort. It replaced Benjamin West's "Resurrection", and was designed, in the words of the Dean, the Hon. Gerald Wellesley, who had been at the Prince's deathbed, to illustrate his "virtues and actions". A new reredos also made part of the memorial, which was completed only just before the wedding. The sight of this tribute to her husband brought comfort to the Queen's stricken spirit, for it made her feel that *"His* image" was present.[8]

Despite her personal grief, the wedding was the most glorious ever celebrated in St. George's Chapel. The morning had been perversely clouded after springlike weather, but as the assembly waited, pale sunshine strayed into the candlelit choir, illuminating its packed radiance. At the entrance of the bride a quiver of emotion passed through the ranks of onlookers. She was eighteen, and very beautiful, and though pale and trembling, as the Queen compassionately noted, wore with memorable grace her regalia of jewels and crinolined profusion of Honiton lace and orange blossom under a silver moiré train. She was followed by a gathering of bridesmaids in billowing gowns of lace and tulle touched with rosebuds. It was many years since the great west door had been used on a state occasion, and as there were no fit steps leading to it, the bridal procession entered and left through an immense "Gothic Hall" built out into the Horseshoe Cloister. Though used only for the wedding, it was an imposing structure of oak, with waiting-rooms for the Prince and Princess to use before the ceremony. The Princess's boudoir was a fairyland of Nottingham lace and rose-pink silk garlanded with roses, orange blossom and lilies of the valley.[9]

To remedy the lack of steps Sir George Gilbert Scott presently designed the modern ceremonial approach to the west door, consisting of twenty-one steps built of Yorkshire marble with balustrading of Bath stone. It was used for the first time on 21st March, 1871, when Queen Victoria's third daughter, Princess Louise, married Lord Lorne, later Duke of Argyll. On this occasion the Queen drove with the bride to St. George's Chapel and ascended the new staircase.

The path across the leads in the Dean's Cloister, which was made permanent in 1865, skirted the north wall of "Wolsey's Tomb House". No lasting use had been found for this chapel. The idea of converting it into a chapter house for the Order of the Garter had been revived by King George IV, and again by King William IV, but although Wyatville gave it a new groined roof and entrance porch, the plan was never realized. Queen Victoria undertook its restoration in memory of the Prince Consort, and later in 1863 work began under the direction of Sir George Gilbert Scott.

The interior was transformed with a variety of coloured marbles. A floor of marble and mosaic was laid down, and the walls were panelled with large pictures of Biblical scenes in inlaid and coloured marble work. Mosaic panels filled the interspaces of the ribbed vaulting of Wyatville's roof. Before the altar was placed a marble tomb surmounted by a white marble figure of the Prince Consort in fluted armour. It was sculptured by Baron H. de Triqueti, from whose designs the marble pictures and other mosaic work were executed by M. Jules Destreez. The white marble medallions decorating the borders of the pictures were the work of a woman, Miss Susan Durant. When this costly memorial was finished in 1874 it was renamed the "Albert Memorial Chapel".[10]

18

RESTORATION OF THE LOWER WARD

For centuries the growing claims of the palace had tended to obscure those of the rest of the Castle. This was true when Wyatville carried out his great restoration. King George IV had planned to remove every building that adjoined the Castle domain, and in 1828 Queen Elizabeth's Gate and the remaining houses on Castle Hill were removed.[1] Apart from this, the Lower Ward and its periphery remained unaltered, although parts of it were ruinous. Not until Queen Victoria's reign was it made a fit match for the Upper Ward.

Fire had already cleared away some of the houses lining the ditch. The saddler's shop and several others on the corner of Castle Hill were burned down in May 1823. Another fire which began in a grocer's shop on a June night in 1836 left a blackened gap in Thames Street, immediately below Garter Tower. One of the apprentices had gone down to the cellar, when the shop closed at ten o'clock at night, with a lighted candle which set fire to some straw, and soon after the family had retired to bed the house burst into flames. Greedily feeding on the grocer's stock of butter and bacon, the fire leapt from storey to storey. Water was not readily available, for no one knew where to find the fire plugs until the turncock arrived from his home at Eton. In the meantime, the Castle fire brigade, aided by Princess Augusta's brigade from Frogmore, ran a pipe over the top of Garter Tower, which was roofless, and while they poured a thin stream of water into the inferno the townsfolk turned out with bucketfuls. The grocer and his wife and a maid escaped, but the three apprentices trapped in the high-pitched garrets were doomed. All that could be scraped together for the inspection of the jury at the inquest was a sackful of charred bones. The public conscience was deeply stirred by this tragedy, and as a result the royal borough formed its own fire brigade.[2]

In June 1851 workmen began taking down the rest of the houses. They completed their task early in 1852, when the ancient Crispin Tavern at the foot of the Hundred Steps was demolished. It was the last of the houses in Lower Thames Street, some of which were so disreputable that they belonged to no one, but were occupied under what was called "keyhold".

A week or two later a momentous discovery was made in the ditch under the west front. The removal of some old houses which formed part of the Horseshoe Cloister had caused the drainage to be cut off. At the request of the Dean and Canons the Commissioners of Public Works began tracing the course of a large cesspool, which burrowed under the Castle wall between the Curfew and Garter Towers and continued across the ditch, and during the digging an opening was made into a forgotten sally-port six feet below.[3]

As the name implies, this was one of the features of the medieval fortifications. The word comes from *porte*, a gate or exit, through which troops could *sally* or rush out. Although only three are now traceable, the Castle once had a number of them, and we have already seen how Engelard de Cygony's raiding parties made use of these outlets during the siege of 1216.

The newly discovered sally-port was of later date. Its construction showed that it was made during the building of the west front in 1227–30. Sightseers who climbed down into the ditch found a short ascent of chalk steps, six feet wide, in a chalk tunnel ten feet high. The steps led towards the Castle wall until they reached a handsome stone arch. Here the tunnel passed through the wall and turned northwards. Forty more steps led up to another arch where the doorway was blocked.

People thought that this doorway led into one of the cellars in the Horseshoe Cloister, but were proved wrong. Beyond the arch a third flight of steps climbed up into the Curfew Tower. The mouth of this inner end of the sally-port is now covered by a trap-door, but it is seldom entered because the steps are worn and dangerous.

There is no evidence to show why they were used so much. As the sally-port was not made until about 1227, and the Castle saw no serious fighting after 1216, it was never needed for a military purpose. A suggestion has been made that long ago royal servants went in and out that way. It may also have been a boon to gentlemen who lived in the Castle to avoid arrest for debt. Under the old laws they were safe in a royal residence. As late as King William IV's reign fashionable debtors had rooms in the Curfew Tower and Cloisters. Although they only went out openly on Sundays, when they were safe from arrest, they may often have crept down the steps and into the town on dark nights.[4] No such romantic use has been attributed to the sally-port discovered in 1855 between the York and Augusta Towers, which must have played its part in the siege warfare, since it dates from Norman times. Here a narrow, vaulted passage ran steeply down through the solid chalk for nearly 100 feet, reaching its outlet in the old bottom of the ditch which was filled in in 1676. The remains of a third sally-port exist under the east front.

The removal of the houses in Lower Thames Street helped to improve the outlook immediately below the windows of the canons' houses high up in the north wall. The canons did not enjoy the most agreeable of views on this side. When cholera broke out, as it did with exceptional severity in 1853, they could see carts collecting the dead from the riverside slums. Always, too, the powerful smell from Nevile Reid's Brewery by the Chapter Garden drifted into their rooms. Anthony Salvin, who began to reconstruct the exterior of the Lower Ward in 1860, could do nothing about these incidentals, but he gave the canons more ornate windows out of which to look. All this north side was gothicized to match the continuing line of the Castle further east, and its inconsequential domestic features reduced to majestic order. At the same time, Salvin rebuilt the Hundred Steps (of which there are actually 134). Like so much of the material used for the Castle in past centuries, the granite blocks arrived by water and were unloaded on the wharf below Windsor Bridge. The Prince Consort laid the first step on 3rd April, 1860.[5]

Along the west front Salvin found much to do. As long before as 1677 Sir William Dugdale, Garter King of Arms, had described Garter Tower as being "much out of repair". By 1859, when the ditch was filled in and the new levels turfed, it was a hollow ruin, with wild flowers growing in its walls. The Salisbury and Curfew Towers had fared better, but the latter needed refacing on the street side. Salvin used too soft a stone, with the result that in 1885 all three towers had to be recased with heath stone from High Wycombe. The prim evenness of their modern dress contrasts with the picturesque antique masonry in the connecting wall.

In 1863 the townsfolk had to accustom themselves to a drastic change in the appearance of the Curfew Tower. The clock-case and dial which had done service since 1756 were removed, and King Edward IV's bell-cage and dome enclosed within the pointed hood which still surmounts the tower. This foreign-looking roof is the twin of the slightly earlier one on the Tour de la Peyre at Carcassonne in southern France. The Emperor Napoleon III was repairing Carcassonne in 1855, when he and the Empress Eugenie paid their state visit to Windsor. He must have spoken about his work there to the Queen and Prince Albert, and it is generally agreed that the Curfew Tower owes its modern appearance to the French emperor's taste.

Ever since it became the belfry of St. George's the Curfew Tower has contained a clock. The first two wore out. The third, made in 1689, is still there. It was the work of John Davis of Windsor, son of King Charles II's blacksmith. Windsor people never had any quarrel with the clock itself, but when Salvin started his work they had long been dissatisfied with the dial. It was supposed to represent a Garter Star, and had hands which could only be told with difficulty. They were pleased when the *Windsor and Eton Express* announced on 29th July, 1865, "The Curfew Tower now has a new clock face, with proper hands and figures on a dark blue ground."

Not only eyes, but ears, too, had long been taxed. Every three hours, at three, six, nine and twelve, throughout the day and night, a tuneless sound was chimed by the old bells in the tower. With the exception of the Great Bell, which was renewed in 1633, they seem to have been the original ones brought from the earlier belfry in 1479, though all had been recast at varying times. The sound for which they were responsible was a particular annoyance to the organist of St. George's Chapel, Dr. (later Sir) George Elvey, who lived just below in the cloisters. The chimes were worked by the clock, and during Salvin's restoration were silenced. While this was in progress Elvey applied himself to the task of finding out what tune they ought to play. On examining the chime-barrel he found that several pegs were missing. These he supplied, and the tune was rendered intelligible. On Queen Victoria's birthday, 24th May, 1865, Windsor heard the strain renewed, but not until the chimes were completely renovated in 1874 was full justice done to it.[6] It is the old hymn-tune *St. David*, followed by what bell-ringers call the "King's Change", and the clock, not content with setting the bells in motion every few hours, puts them through the melodious performance three times.

Within the Lower Ward Salvin demolished Crane's Buildings and erected the present guardroom between the Salisbury and Garter Towers, incorporating the latter in it. One of the last things the Prince Consort did before his fatal illness was to inspect the guardroom, which was finished in 1862. Salvin completed his work at Windsor by rebuilding Wyatville's Grand Staircase in the State Apartments in 1866, placing the new ascent so that it was reached from the Grand Entrance through Edward III's vault, which henceforth served as the State Entrance Hall. These various improvements were partly paid for by the sale of Queen Elizabeth I's bake-house, last heard of when it was repaired for King Charles II in 1687. The Windsor Castle (Bakehouse) Bill, enabling the Crown authorities to dispose of the "Old Royal Bakehouse in Peascod Street", received the Royal assent in 1862.[7]

Changes both social and architectural took place in the cloisters a few years later. When we last met the minor canons they were moving into the Horseshoe Cloister built for them by King Edward IV in 1475, and taking their meals together in a hall erected sixty years earlier. "Old Commons", as it was called, has been identified as the hall which makes part of the organist's residence.[8] It was turned into a school for the choirboys in 1550. A stone fireplace put in at the time has carved on it several names, including that of "H. Walker" (probably Henry Walker, a minor canon between 1586 and 1596). Someone—we like to think it was a mischievous choirboy who knew Walker—has added underneath it "is a knave".[9]

Until about 1870 the minor canons continued to live in the Horseshoe Cloister, which at some period had been covered with white lath and plaster. It had become shabby, and the whole foundation was tumbledown. There were fewer clergy to serve the chapel by this time. Some of the canonries had been suspended by Act of Parliament in 1840, which meant that more residences were available on the north side of the chapel. The minor canons, who were themselves reduced in number, moved with their families into these houses, leaving the Horseshoe Cloister for the lay clerks, or singing-men, and the vergers.

The lath and plaster were cleared away, and the houses restored by Sir George Gilbert Scott in the half-timbered, red-brick construction of earlier days. He also restored in this warm and agreeable style the organist's house, "Marbeck", which stands against the north wall and includes the lovely "Old Commons". It was reopened in 1872 as a boarding school for the choirboys, and so continued until the choir school moved down in 1894 to the quarters of the disbanded Naval Knights. Now, once again, the hall where the minor canons once ate, and where Marbeck and other composers later worked and trained the choristers, is a music room used for choir practice. After his reprieve from the stake Marbeck returned to this house, to which he has given his name, and continued writing religious books almost until his death in about 1585.

There was another communal dining chamber nearby which did not survive. It was built in 1519 on part of the site of the old Great Hall of the Castle by Canon James Denton, later Dean of Lichfield, and known as "New Commons" or "Denton's Commons". The good canon had been concerned for the welfare of the chantry priests, for since they did not belong to the royal foundation they did not share its privileges. They lived in little houses attached to the chapel, or in rooms inside, including the crypts at the west end, and took their meals in the town. The choristers, too, led "a wandering and unquiet life". It was to provide them and the chantry priests with a dining-hall that Denton raised his pleasant building, which reached almost to the old well under the chapel wall and enclosed a portion of the hill above it. Besides the dining-hall it was equipped with a kitchen, pantry, buttery, larder, pastry and cook's chamber. Although St. George's was specially exempted when chantries were abolished by law after the Reformation, the appointment of priests gradually ceased, and by about 1570 "New Commons" had outlived its original purpose. It was made into a canon's house and finally demolished in 1859.

In the Canons' Cloister improvements were effected without loss of picturesque detail and tradition. A new descent made in 1862 to

the Hundred Steps under the tower commanding them did not minimize the validity of a fanciful name applied to this spot. "Kill-
Canon-Corner," affirmed Sarah Lady Lyttelton, the royal children's
former Governess, in a letter written on 3rd January, 1851, "is in its
worst dank dismal miseries; and going through it, blown before a
dark winter gale every night, is dangerous to all but the famous
hardy spinsters" (whoever they were).[10] Lady Lyttelton may have
thought of the name "Kill-Canon-Corner" herself, but more likely
it derives from some ecclesiastical humorist of earlier days. His
invention explains itself. A north gale racing up into the cloister,
ready to tear away the heavy door from human grasp, still lends
colour to it.

The Dean and Canons closely followed the royal pattern in introducing domestic amenities. Piped water was brought up from the
Thames at Chapter expense in 1698, sixteen years after Morland
perfected his system for King Charles II, and supplied "to every
house except the Poor Knights houses". A deep well in one of the
three little courtyards which were then enclosed within the Deanery
buildings was probably covered over soon afterwards. The one in the
Canons' Cloister, faithfully represented in Norden's survey, remained for a time as a picturesque adjunct in that little realm of
apparently timeless antiquity. Norden shows a wheel under a tiled
roof throwing water into a bucket, and it seems always to have
continued as a draw-well, for there is a story on record that in about
1738 a drunken soldier fell into it and was killed. After this it was
stopped up and paved over.[11]

The soldier's spectre was supposed to walk the Cloisters, and so
the unfortunate man adds a morsel of supernatural tradition to the
history of the Castle. For a place so full of the diversity of human
life, and so rich in kinship with the past, it is disappointingly poor in
ghost-lore. Apart from King George III and Queen Elizabeth I, who
was reputed even in Queen Victoria's reign to haunt her Gallery,
documented ghosts hardly exist. Bickham in 1742 tells us that the
reason the Devil's Tower had been so named was "a receiv'd Notion
that formerly it was haunted by evil Spirits", but adds: "For many
Years, however, it has been inhabited, without the least Interruption
or Disturbance, as we can find, from such aerial Visitors."[12]

The few uncertain phantoms that continued to impose their aura from the unlit centuries were the familiars of old servants tattling round winter fires, and lack even an incorporeal quality. The premise that many supposed hauntings were the fruit of excited fancy is still demonstrable in the Castle. Even now, the atmosphere-laden shadows of an alley, or the gloom of a staircase twisting between stone walls, offer a clue to the background from which sprang the complexes of more limited days. When gas light was introduced into the precincts by command of George IV in 1829, the locale became unfavourable for the less well-defined ghosts. They nevertheless retained a tenuous influence, especially in the Canons' Cloister. The gossips long recalled the raw young sentry whose hat suddenly vanished from his head one black night (in the days when sentries patrolled the cloisters), causing him to take to his heels in horror. But the ghost that played this trick, it was knowledgeably alleged, was only a cook relieving the tedium of the canonical kitchen by putting her hand through the window as the sentry went by.

19

END OF AN ERA

Eight centuries of building and rebuilding brought the architectural progression to a halt. By the middle of Queen Victoria's reign the Castle had achieved its modern majesty of form and outline, and henceforth no outstanding changes of feature were called for.

If some of its medieval attributes had from time to time been sacrificed, others were only lost beneath the deposits of changing taste and convenience. One of these was the Norman well in the Round Tower. Whatever the merits of Mr. Gray's water-raising engine in 1784 may have been, it was soon discarded and the well covered up and forgotten. Towards the end of Queen Victoria's reign, when Sir John Cowell tried to locate it, even the oldest servants could tell him nothing. As Master of the Royal Household, Sir John's responsibility included the care of every part of the Castle. He was also an engineer officer who had served at the siege of Sebastopol in 1855, and his military training led him to infer that the Round Tower had once contained a well.

Eventually he found an ancient person who remembered hearing of a well under a bedroom floor. On 24th August, 1886, Sir John had the flooring raised, and an inch or two below the joists discovered some stones. The story may be continued in the words of the *Illustrated London News* of 11th June, 1887. One stone was "a large one, with two iron rings let into it, which was moved with some difficulty, for two sides of it were bevelled like a voussoir; and when it was lifted, one ring drew, and the stone vanished into a black space beneath—the distance it fell being indicated by the time which passed before the echoing thud was heard before it reached the bottom." Sir John had found the well, and a splendid relic it proved to be. It was 6½ feet in diameter, and beautifully lined with stone for the first 60½ feet, where it passed through the earth of the mount. The remaining 104 feet continued down through the solid chalk.[1]

The Round Tower no longer served as the residence of the Governor. It had ceased to be required when Prince Albert was appointed to this office in 1843. Although the apartments had been closed to the public, an increasing number of people liked to climb the great flight of steps and continue up the Tower stairs to the battlements. On their way they passed the giant Sebastopol Bell hanging in the well of the upper staircase. It was one of a pair, said to have hung in the clock tower of the Church of the Twelve Apostles at Sebastopol, which were brought to England after the Crimean War and exhibited with other trophies at Woolwich Arsenal. Queen Victoria and Prince Albert saw them there on 19th February, 1856.

One of the monster bells went to Aldershot and was placed in a wooden frame on Gun Hill, where a sentry posted at this point struck the hours on it. It was re-erected in 1879 in the clock tower of the Cambridge Hospital at Aldershot.[2] The Windsor bell was set up on the North Terrace[3] until in 1868 Mears and Stainbank, bell founders, of Whitechapel Road, London, hung it in the Round Tower. A translation of the Russian inscription around it says that it was cast in Moscow at the manufactory of Nicolas Samtun and weighs 54.4 poods (17 cwt. 21 lb.).

This bell added its mourning note to that of the Curfew Tower bell during the funeral of Queen Victoria. Her reign, the longest in English history, ended with her death at Osborne on 22nd January, 1901. After a long procession by sea and land her body reached Windsor for burial on Saturday, 2nd February. The final part of the journey was made by train from Paddington. At Windsor Central Station a Royal Artillery gun carriage drawn by horses waited to bear her body to St. George's Chapel. The coffin, covered with a white satin pall and surmounted by the Crown and the regalia and insignia of the Garter, was placed upon it, but whether through the intense cold, the roll of muffled drums, or the boom of cannon, the horse on the off-side nearest the wagon suddenly became restive. The driver was unable to control the animal, which lashed out his heels furiously and eventually caught one of his hind legs in the pole-bar, and fell on his knees. The traces were smashed, not once but twice.

It is reported that in this terrifying situation one of the Queen's aides-de-camp stepped forward. He was Captain the Hon. Hedworth Lambton, popularly known as "Powerful Lambton", one of the heroes of the siege of Ladysmith. "Let the horses be taken out," he suggested, "and the bluejackets forming the guard of honour have the supreme honour of drawing their dead mistress to St. George's Chapel."[4]

So it came about that sailors in blue uniforms and straw hats pulled the gun carriage through the hushed streets, while in the Castle the Curfew Tower bell and the Round Tower bell were tolled.[5] It was because of this unrehearsed incident that England's sovereigns are now always drawn by sailors to their burial in St. George's Chapel.

After the funeral service Queen Victoria's body was laid in the Albert Memorial Chapel until Monday, 4th February. Then, to the renewed tolling of the two great bells, it was borne to Frogmore and interred with the Prince Consort's. Since that time the Sebastopol Bell has always been tolled on the death of the Sovereign, and again during the funeral procession. It is never heard on any other occasion.

20

THE MODERN CASTLE

The funeral usage of the great bell was one among several traditions engendered during the twentieth century, which saw, too, the revival of some ancient customs. In 1901, the year of his accession, King Edward VII restored the medieval practice of admitting royal ladies to the Order of the Garter by bestowing the honour on his consort, Queen Alexandra. King George V, in turn, appointed Queen Mary a Lady of the Garter when he succeeded to the throne in 1910. In 1937 King George VI similarly honoured Queen Elizabeth.[1]

A more exclusive dignity is accorded to modern Ladies of the Garter than was granted to those of the Plantagenet period. Stalls are assigned to them in the choir of St. George's Chapel, and their banners displaying their coats of arms are hung above.

Early in King George V's reign the chapel began to show signs of possible collapse. It was four hundred years old, and although the interior had been restored in King George III's reign, the fabric never received more than cursory attention. Sir Christopher Wren's measures in 1681 had played their part in preserving it, but repairs alone were no longer adequate to counter the progressive decay. A survey made by Sir Harold Brakspear in 1918 revealed that the great oak tie-beams of the roof, given by Bishop Beauchamp when the chapel was built, were hardly long enough for their purpose and did not rest sufficiently on the walls. Moreover, the death-watch beetle had taken its toll. The vault was cracked and in danger of falling in, the flying buttresses were crumbling, and in parts the very foundations of the chapel were insecure.

Restoration began in 1930 and took ten years. In the course of a superb architectural feat, the vaulting of both choir and nave was removed, bay after bay, repaired, cleaned and reassembled. To give extra support, buttresses were added for the first time to the north and south transepts. Upon the pinnacles, where Wren had wanted to put pineapples, was set a new galaxy of Royal Beasts, seventy-six in all—Lancastrian along the south side and Yorkist along the north, in reference to the tombs of King Henry VI and King Edward IV. The choir was reopened just before Easter 1927. The repair of the nave followed, and on 4th November, 1930, a day of bright autumn sunshine, King George V and Queen Mary, with other members of the royal family, Knights of the Garter and distinguished guests, attended a service to inaugurate the reopening of the fully restored chapel.

The cost of the restoration, which amounted to £170,000, was borne by the King, the Knights of the Garter, and a host of other donors, some of whom gave princely sums. To secure the future maintenance of the chapel two societies were formed: "The Association of Descendants of Knights of the Garter", and, in 1931, "The Association of the Friends of St. George's." In 1934 they were amalgamated, and King George V became Patron of the joint organization, whose full title is "The Society of the Friends of St. George's and the Descendants of the Knights of the Garter".

The Chapter itself no longer had means to meet the expenses imposed by the needs of so precious a structure. Originally St. George's had been one of the richest foundations in England, but in 1867 the properties with which it was endowed were appropriated by the Ecclesiastical Commissioners in return for a fixed income, which became more and more markedly inadequate as time passed. The Society of Friends and Descendants may be likened to a modern counterpart of the medieval benefactors of the chapel, since it is through the members that its treasures are maintained and fresh assets added. Their influence is more than national. In a world where the commerce of society transcends continental limits St. George's is a universal vision, and English-speaking countries recognize their share in it. Friends and Descendants in the United States of America have their own special organization for the pursuit of historical and genealogical interests.

The funeral of King George V, who died at Sandringham on 20th

January, 1936, took place at Windsor in bitter weather eight days later. His burial in St. George's Chapel confirmed its status as the reliquary of the reigning house. King Edward VII was already interred there, not in the royal vault, but in a tomb on the south side of the high altar. Queen Alexandra, who died in 1925, shares it with him, and their recumbent effigies lie side by side, together with that of the King's beloved terrier, Caesar, who reposes beneath his master's feet. King George V was buried in a splendid sarcophagus of Clipsham stone at the end of the nave, where the sunset glow of the west window enfolds it. When Queen Mary died in 1953 her body was laid beside the King's, and her marble effigy placed with his on the tomb.

During the later years of King George V's reign there were in Windsor Great Park two royal homes on which the eyes of the world were soon to turn. The historical background of the Park and Forest may be recalled at this point. The old haunted fastness of the Forest had yielded in 1813 to the movement for wholesale enclosure and consequent release of land for agriculture. At that time it comprised 59,000 acres and embraced parts or the whole of seventeen parishes. Today it is a curving belt of woodland fringing the Great Park, and both together only measure about five miles from north to south, and some three miles across, but they are still a princely inheritance, offering residential pleasures as abundantly as in the remoter past. When King George V died, Fort Belvedere on Shrubs Hill, originally a triangular tower built by William Duke of Cumberland, son of King George II and Ranger of the Great Park, was the country residence of the new King, Edward VIII. At the Royal Lodge, near the Copper Horse, the Duke and Duchess of York customarily spent week-ends with their two young daughters, Princess Elizabeth and Princess Margaret.

This was an ideal family home, for the house stood like a pale pink gem in its own sylvan grounds, and all around were the miles of grass and pool and woodland, the rhododendron glades, the commemorative trees planted by royal hands, the landmarks which Norden depicted, and the memorials which recall history and legend. The house was no longer as King George IV had known it. Most of the original Royal Lodge was demolished after his death, but King William IV spared a panelled Gothic dining-room which had only just been completed. In the graceful home created for themselves by the Duke and Duchess of York, this apartment became the centre of family life and the commanding feature of the charming terraced front. George IV's private chapel, which was detached from the house but within the grounds, had been rebuilt by Queen Victoria in 1866 as the Chapel of All Saints. It was intended for the use of people living and working in the Great Park, and the Duke and Duchess and the two Princesses joined the congregation every Sunday morning.

After reigning only eleven months, King Edward VIII ceded his throne to the Duke of York, since only by this action was he able to marry the lady of his choice, the American-born Mrs. Wallis Simpson. The Instrument of Abdication was signed at Fort Belvedere on 10th December, 1936. On the following day, at ten o'clock at night, he broadcast to the nation from a room in the Castle, before leaving England to live abroad. He took the title Duke of Windsor, and in exile married Mrs. Simpson, who thus became the Duchess of Windsor.

On the accession of King George VI his elder daughter, Princess Elizabeth, aged ten, assumed the status of Heiress Presumptive to the throne, and a new responsibility rested on her young shoulders. From babyhood she had visited the Castle as a welcome guest, beloved and petted by her grandparents: now she had to learn to know it as its future Sovereign. During the formal Court residences at Easter and Ascot the royal sisters had a new part to play, and even before the Second World War broke out they received some indication of the vast traditions which it was their task to uphold.

When war began in 1939 the Castle reverted to its role of fortress. The precincts were closed to the public, and all its defences organized. The great west window of the chapel was dismantled and stored in the vault of the Curfew Tower. Bombs fell all around, but the Castle was miraculously preserved, and throughout the war stood unscathed and sure, a stronghold in reality, since it had become once again, in literal truth, the *Domus Regis*—the "King's home". During the worst of those troubled years the royal family lived within its walls. An observer of their daily routine placed on record the King's devotion to duty. He "went to work" at eight in the morning as regularly as any factory or office worker, arriving back at the

Castle at six or seven in the evening, after a day of "climbing bomb damage, visiting poor distressed bomb victims, walking through endless miles of factories, inspecting endless miles of ranks of soldiers, walking endless miles of training grounds, travelling endless miles of railways."[2]

The writer of these words was Mr. Hubert Tanner, Master of the Royal School in Windsor Great Park, which Queen Victoria founded in 1845 for the education of children on the Crown Estate. He knew how the royal family faced the strain of war because it was he who produced the famous pantomimes in which Princess Elizabeth and Princess Margaret headed a cast of his own schoolchildren. However harassing the King's day had been, he would always watch the rehearsals of these pantomimes, which were performed in the Castle and raised hundreds of pounds for charity. The audiences were privileged to see the contrasting personalities of the royal sisters revealed in their acting. Princess Margaret was always charmingly confident, loving what she called "The Claps", while Princess Elizabeth was more nervous, but with that dedicated instinct which became so marked when she succeeded to the throne, sank all thought of herself in the part she was playing.[3]

By contrast with its embattled front, a floodlit Castle celebrated the return of peace. The silvered towers proclaimed their ascendancy across many counties, and within the grounds, shafts of colour fathomed the depths of the Moat Garden, picking out lawn and rose walk and plashing stream in delicate relief among the shadows. Presently a sunlit picture imposes itself on the post-war scene. The year 1948 brought the 600th anniversary of the founding of the Order of the Garter, and with it a resurgence of ancient pride. Although services for the members of the Order had occasionally been held in St. George's Chapel after 1805, not one Knight of the Garter had been installed since that time, and the ceremony of installation had lapsed. For some years all that had happened was that a new Knight was summoned to Buckingham Palace, where the insignia were handed over to him privately. To commemorate the 600th anniversary King George VI commanded the Knights to assemble at Windsor for a chapter and service on 23rd April, 1948, and on this occasion the ceremony of installation was revived. In the procession that passed through the grounds to the chapel were the Heiress Presumptive, Princess Elizabeth, Duchess of Edinburgh, in the robes of a Lady of the Garter, and her husband, Prince Philip, Duke of Edinburgh, who was installed as a Knight of the Garter.

During the rest of the King's reign the Royal Lodge continued to be his favourite home, the Castle serving again as a palace to which the Court moved from London for the Easter and Ascot residences. Since the war the 4,800 acres of the Great Park had included a 2,000-acre farm, and during the last years of King George VI's life it was enriched with model tokens of its rural vitality. To house some of the hundreds of people who work there a village was built about a mile south of the Royal Lodge, and equipped with the traditional attributes: a green and a general shop and post office, which has above its doorway a medallion bearing the King's cypher and the date, 1949, in gold on a blue ground. From the shop door the handsome village hall on the other side of the cricket field appears to be built in pale yellow bricks: in reality, they range from soft lemon to plum, and provide a unique document in design, for they came from bombed sites in London.

The King himself opened this community centre, which is named the York Hall, not long before he died. In his speech he referred to the man who had planned the village, Sir Eric Savill, Deputy Ranger of the Great Park and Deputy Surveyor of Windsor Woods and Forest, and to his other great achievement, the woodland gardens on the eastern edge of the Great Park. It was in accordance with a wish expressed by the King on this occasion that the enclosed landscape of lake and lawn and flowers created by Sir Eric was named the Savill Gardens. It links up with the Valley Gardens, where glades of azaleas and rhododendrons descend in winding paths to the shore of Virginia Water.

At 1.27 on the afternoon of 7th February, 1952, the Sebastopol Bell began to toll for King George VI, who had died in his sleep at Sandringham. It sounded fifty-six times, once for every year of his age, at one-minute intervals. Again during the august majesty of the funeral procession it was heard, this time tolling 113 times at half-minute intervals. Meanwhile, Queen Elizabeth II had been proclaimed according to the ancient style, at "The Cross", the bridge and within the Castle. Not the least moving sight in the great funeral

procession to St. George's Chapel were the mourning figures of the
two veiled Queens, the young Queen Regnant and Queen Elizabeth
the Queen Mother, in their carriage.

Two years later the promise of the new reign was being demonstrated in full and winning dignity. On her accession the Queen
became Sovereign of the Order of the Garter, and on 14th June,
1954, held her first installation service. It was the more memorable
because the personage honoured on this occasion was Sir Winston
Churchill, who brought his own grand and popular bearing to
enhance the vitality of the traditional scene. His presence was a
reminder, if one were needed, that the Order founded by King
Edward III within the narrow sphere of militarism had reached its
climax as the "supreme Order of Merit for the whole nation".

The Queen now customarily holds a Garter ceremony every year
on the Monday in Ascot Week. The procedure has been simplified,
but with no loss of historic effect. The service takes place in the
afternoon, and when a Knight elect is to be installed the proceedings
open with his investiture in the morning. The Sovereign and Knights
Companions assemble in the Throne Room. At the Sovereign's
bidding Garter and Black Rod and two of the Knights go out to
summon the Knight elect, who returns walking between them. With
the assistance of the two supporting Knights the Queen buckles on
the Garter, places the Riband with the Lesser George over his left
shoulder, affixes the Star and invests him with the Mantle and
Collar. As he receives the insignia, the Prelate pronounces the
ancient Admonition appropriate to each piece. The presentation of
the Mantle is accompanied by these words:

> Receive this Robe of heavenly colour, the Livery of this Most
> Excellent Order, in Augmentation of thine Honour, ennobled with the
> shield and red Cross of Our Lord, by whose power thou mayest safely
> pierce troops of thine enemies, and be over them ever victorious, and
> being in this temporal warfare glorious, in egregious and heroic actions,
> thou mayest obtain eternal and triumphant joy.

Equally glorious and inspiring is the exhortation when the Collar
is put on:

> Wear this Collar about thy Neck, adorned with the image of the
> Blessed Martyr and Soldier of Christ, Saint George, by whose imitation

provoked, thou mayest so overpass both prosperous and adverse encounters, that having stoutly vanquished thine enemies, both of body and soul, thou mayest not only receive the praise of this transient Combat, but be crowned with the Palm of Eternal Victory.

The Oath is then administered to the newly invested Knight, and the Company, led by the Sovereign, passes in procession out of the Throne Room. The traditional banquet is represented by a luncheon party in the Waterloo Chamber, where the gold plate mirrored in the gleam of a mahogany table calls back ancient splendours. Afterwards the procession is marshalled in the same order as of old. The Military Knights walk at its head, in their scarlet uniform of "Unattached Officers and Officers on half-pay" which King William IV chose for them in 1834, and which they alone now wear. Next come the Officers of Arms—heralds and pursuivants—wearing their tabards and "looking rather like knaves of hearts", and then the Knights of the Garter attired in their sweeping mantles of deep blue velvet and plumed caps, and walking, as anciently decreed, two by two. Royal Knights and Ladies of the Garter walk last, followed by the Officers of the Order—the Gentleman Usher of the Black Rod, the Secretary, the Register, Garter, the Chancellor and the Prelate—in their scarlet robes.

Finally comes the Queen in a jewelled gown of white satin under her velvet mantle, accompanied by the Duke of Edinburgh and followed by two scarlet-coated Pages of Honour bearing her train.

In this order the procession passes through the Castle grounds and ascends the great staircase to the west door of St. George's Chapel. Installations take place at the beginning of the service. The Sovereign will announce, "It is Our Pleasure that the Knight Companion be Installed", and at this bidding the Chancellor calls the name of the new Knight, who is conducted to his stall, and the brief ceremony ends with the prayer which is read daily in St. George's: "God save our gracious Sovereign and all the Companions, living and departed, of the Most Honourable and Noble Order of the Garter."

The choice of the Monday in Ascot Week for the Garter ceremony completes the calendar of public events which crown the social year. On the four succeeding days the Queen drives through the Great Park to a point near its south-west boundary, from which she continues in a carriage procession on to Ascot Racecourse. It happens that 18th June, the anniversary of the Battle of Waterloo, normally occurs in Ascot Week, and in a private ceremony the Duke of Wellington delivers to the Queen the banner by virtue of which he holds Stratfield Saye. The Waterloo Day banquet, informally founded by King George V in 1914 and resumed after the First World War, takes place that night in the Waterloo Chamber.

In these and other ways tradition is being constantly fulfilled and replenished. While the Court residences at Easter and Ascot continue in accustomed state, the Queen has also made the Castle her private home. At Christmas and during week-ends throughout the year, the Queen's Tower is occupied by its Sovereign Lady, and the grounds offer peace and pleasure to the royal family. Since 1964 the Castle has also had a resident Governor, as in earlier times. When Lord Freyberg, V.C., Deputy Constable and Lieutenant Governor, died in 1963, he was succeeded by another distinguished soldier, Viscount Slim, a Knight of the Garter, who was appointed a year later to the office of Constable and Governor (vacant since the death of the Earl of Athlone in 1957). In this capacity he continues to live at Norman Tower, the house at the foot of the Round Tower steps which embodies the original Lieutenant Governor's residence, and in which three distinct periods blend. The old house was enlarged in about 1760 by the building of a pedimented annexe in the Moat Garden, on the site of the "Tulip Garden".[4] Paul Sandby shows it in one of his drawings, but its separate identity was lost to view when Wyatville faced it with grey stone. Finally, after Queen Victoria ceased to appoint State Housekeepers, the apartments allotted to those ladies was added. As they included the "Prisoners' Room", this now fittingly makes part of the Governor's official residence. The Moat Garden—a flowering oasis to which now and then the nightingale returns—was laid out anew by Sir Dighton Probyn, V.C., Keeper of the Privy Purse to King Edward VII, who made the rockeries and waterfall, and imported the sandstone boulders from the neighbourhood of Sandringham.

In the Lower Ward, as in the Upper, the challenge of a changing and practical world is being met. Presage of an international role was given in St. George's Chapel on Sunday, 1st December, 1963, when mattins took the form of a memorial service for President John

Kennedy, and Julia Ward Howe's heroic Battle Hymn was sung there, probably for the first time, and with as fitting effect as any Tudor anthem. In 1965 the chapel became the centre of a movement designed to meet "the urgent need for a fresh partnership of laity and clergy in the mission of Christianity". Two of the large cloistral houses were united to form St. George's House, a residential centre for meetings of the clergy, and for "consultations between church representatives and prominent people in Parliament, the professions, the Civil Service, commerce, industry and the trade unions".[5] St. George's House was opened by Queen Elizabeth II on 23rd October, 1966. Soon afterwards the Royal Closet in St. George's Chapel, originally King Edward IV's chantry, was made into a chapel for the particular use of men and women attending courses there.

Thus from the founts of the past the Castle endows and inspires the future. As a Royal Palace and Fortress under the direct control of the Sovereign, as a religious centre and a museum of history and the arts, it represents a compelling force to which the whole world turns. The site where once the white chalk dust rose as labourers hacked at the virgin cliff has become common ground for all races and all tongues.

21

THE ROYAL BOROUGH

The matrix of the royal borough of Windsor lies in that core of cobbled streets which stands opposite the Castle gate. Within this small area were rooted the dominant features of corporate life: the Parish Church, the old Guildhall (now the "Three Tuns"), the Town Hall, and anciently the Market Cross, the pillory and the stocks.

Windsor received its first charter from King Edward I in 1277, when it was finally separated from Old Windsor and became the borough of New Windsor. Its medieval existence, both mercantile and religious, was governed by "The Fraternity of the Holy Trinity", from which the Town Council was recruited. Mayors were being elected by 1361. In 1518 "a new house" was built for the Trinity Guild.[1] It was identified by the sign of "le three tuns", and "lovyng drynkyngs" among the brethren point to the convenience of the arrangement. Corporation business was conducted in a large upper room overlooking the Butchers' Shambles in High Street.

Proclamations were made at the Market Cross or Round Market House, originally erected, according to Ashmole's *Antiquities of Berkshire*, by John Sadeler in 1380.[2] It stood in High Street, near if not actually at the point of juncture with Castle Hill and Peascod Street. The only known representation of it appears to be in one of the views annexed to the picture showing the death of the Windsor Martyrs in Foxe's *Actes and Monumentes*. Three men indicted for perjury in the Martyrs' case were condemned to "ride about Windsore, Reading, and Newbery, with papers on their heads, and their faces turned to the horse tails", and Foxe's artist shows their enforced tour with the Market Cross in the background. He depicts the building as an open structure, its roof supported by a central shaft and six encircling pillars, and surmounted by a cross.[3]

Norden, in 1607, did not include the Round Market House in his topographical view of the Castle and town. He showed in preference the "new market house" which the Corporation decided to erect in 1586.[4] It was placed in front of the Butchers' Shambles, on the site of the present Town Hall, which in form it closely resembled, for it had an upper chamber supported on wooden pillars. When the building was finished in 1597 the upper floor was let to Thomas Chapman, "inhowlder", at a rent of £3 a year, and farmers sold their corn, meat and other produce in the open exchange below.[5] An insight into the aspect of the town centre is provided in 1629, when High Street was paved "from the north end of the Corne Market House, and from the upper end of Peascod Street" to the Castle gate.[6] More revealing of the human background is the enactment of 1635–6, which proclaimed that dunghills must be removed from the streets and lanes, pigs deterred from wandering loose about the market place, and washing kept out of the public thoroughfares.[7]

About this time many cities were rebuilding or beautifying their market crosses, or so it was maintained by Dr. Godfrey Goodman, Bishop of Gloucester and a canon of Windsor. Their civic zeal put him in mind, he said, "of an ould Crosse in Windsor ready to fall", and he took upon himself in 1635 to restore and adorn Sadeler's Cross in a manner which offended the strong puritan element in the town.[8] William Prynne, the pamphleteer, described the Bishop's choice: "On one side there is a large statue of Christ in colours (after the Popish Garbs in foraigne parts), hanging on the Crosse, with this Latin inscription over it, *Iesus Nazarenus Rex Iudaeorum*, in great gilded letters; on the other side, the picture of Christ rising out of the Sepulchre." In vain the Mayor pointed out to the Bishop that it was unlawful to erect a crucifix in a public place without licence. He was unmoved, and the ornamentation continued for a few years to violate the feelings of "the purer Saints of those Times, by whose Endeavours," Ashmole supposed, "it was demolished in the most impious Rebellion, begun 1641."[9]

The Round Market House itself survived until the present Town Hall was built. It was in 1687 that the Corporation decided to demolish the wooden-pillared market house and build a guild hall or town hall instead. Sir Thomas Fitch, Surveyor of the Cinque Ports, designed the handsome new building and superintended its erection until he died in January 1689, leaving it to be completed by Sir Christopher Wren. On 17th October, 1689, the Corporation recorded its decision to desert the chamber at the "Three Tuns" and move into its new quarters.[10] There was only one misgiving. The fine upper room, later known as the "Banqueting Room and Justice Chamber", was supported by stone pillars placed around the outer sides of the open corn exchange, and since it was to be used for concerts and assemblies, the Corporation wanted complete assurance of its safety. Lady Elvey tells the traditional story in spirited vein:

> The burgesses, fearing for their august persons, lest they should find themselves on the flags below one fine night, after or during a dance or some other festive gathering, requested the illustrious architect to place equally strong pillars in the centre as a measure of precaution. Failing to satisfy these good men and their merry wives that the structure was perfectly safe as he designed it, he reluctantly consented to set up pillars in the required position; but he privately ordered them to be made four inches shorter than the real supports. Generations of happy aldermen lived and died in ignorance of this fact till the ceiling of the yard below had to be repaired, when the workmen discovered that the centre uprights had never touched the beams on which the room rested.[11]

Soon after the Corporation had moved, the market place (represented by the Round Market House) figured in a parliamentary dispute. In 1690 Sir Christopher Wren and Mr. Baptist May were returned as members on one indenture by the mayor, bailiffs and burgesses, and Sir Charles Porter and Mr. William Adderley on another indenture by the inhabitants paying scot and lot. The return of Wren and May was challenged, not only by Porter and Adderley, but by the townspeople, on the grounds that it was "the right of the general inhabitants to elect at the Market Cross" instead of the election being made "at the Guild Hall by the mayor, bailiffs, select burgesses and common council."[12] A report by the Committee of Privileges and Elections upheld the mayor, but the House of Commons disaffirmed the resolution and decided that Porter and Adderley were duly elected.[13]

Although the Round Market House, being ruinous, was taken

down in 1691, together with the adjacent pillory,[14] its traditional significance continued to dominate the annals of Windsor. Pote stated in 1749 that since the dispute "the Election of Members to serve Parliament for this Borough has constantly been openly made" at the Market Cross by the mayor, bailiffs, burgesses and all the inhabitants paying scot and lot, and this continued until the passing of the Reform Act in 1832.[15] The site was still known as "The Cross" when Sir Edgar Boehm's statue of Queen Victoria was placed on Castle Hill to commemorate her jubilee in 1887. As late as 1930 gay little stalls continued to hold their own every Saturday in the old market place between the Town Hall and "The Cross".

In the market place on 2nd March, 1764, Thomas Watkins was hanged "for the murder of Miss Hammersley's maid".[16] He was the last person to be executed there. His body was afterwards gibbeted in Gallows Lane, a hollow road branching off the route between Frogmore and Datchet Bridge, and one of the expeditions relished by local youths was a walk to see "Watkins hanging in chains". When James Brindley prepared his profile of the river for the Thames Commissioners in 1770 he unquestioningly accepted "Watkins's Gibbet" as a landmark, like the royal waterworks and the wharf below Windsor Bridge, and the name appears in his published work. The dangling skeleton remained a feature of the riverside landscape until it disintegrated, for human bones were dis-interred in 1816, when Gallows Lane was swallowed up in the new road to Old Windsor and Staines.[17] The spot where the gibbet stood is now within the Home Park Private.

The old Butchery is brought back to mind by the pretty sight of "Market Cross House" next to the Town Hall—a little crooked house built in 1718 on the site of an earlier one. When William Bradbury bought the property in 1656, it was stated to be "an house or tenement used for a Butcher's shop and a Dwelling house near the Markett house." It was still a butcher's shop when William's great-grandson, Silas Bradbury, decided to rebuild it. Workmen had just dug the foundations when Thomas Rutter, Mayor of Windsor, came on 18th February, 1718, "with Constables Tything men and Labourers and violently filled up the Foundation that had been digged and threatned to send the Labourers there working for Mr. Bradbury to Goal, pretending the ground where the premises stood belonged to the Corporation." To leave his intentions in no doubt, Mr. Rutter put a cordon of railings around the site. Mr. Bradbury's lawyer went to counsel, and counsel opined that Mr. Bradbury had an undoubted title and might break down the rails with which Mr. Mayor had enclosed the property, provided "he dos itt not in a Tumultuous or Riotous manor".[18]

The outcome was that Mr. Bradbury built his house, which continued for many years as a butcher's, and then became a beer-house called "The Royal Standard"—probably in succession to the tavern of that name which formerly stood in the Castle. Its six little rooms stand piled in pairs over the chalk-lined vault which workmen were excavating when Mr. Mayor so unfeelingly interrupted them in 1718.

The Parish Church of St. John the Baptist, like the Town Hall, was rebuilt on the templet of its predecessor. After serving Windsor for some seven hundred years, the original church became so decayed "as to render the performance of Divine worship within its walls in some degree perilous", and the foundation stone of the new one was laid on 20th September, 1820. It was erected by the royal builders, Tebbott and Bedborough, "to the design of Mr. C. Hollis, but under the superintendence of Mr. Wyatt [later Sir Jeffry Wyatville]." The entrance porch was enriched with handsome monuments from the old church, and the royal pew enclosed by a screen carved with "pelicans feeding their young and rising from their nests supported by festoons of fruit and foliage". It originally formed the altar rail in St. George's Chapel and was stated to be the work of Grinling Gibbons. The new church was opened in 1822.[19]

Both the educational and medical traditions of Windsor stem from the town centre. The graceful Masonic Hall to the north-east of the Parish Church was its first school building, erected in 1726 to house the "Free" or "Charity" School founded on 3rd November, 1705 (and still active). Sir Christopher Wren is said to have been the architect. The narrow width of a cobbled lane separates the hall from the original premises of the "Royal General Dispensary" opened in 1818 "for the Relief of the Sick Poor", and removed in 1834 to Bachelors' Acre, where the first two wards for in-patients were added in 1857. The new Dispensary and Infirmary was formally opened on 1st January, 1858. It was the first institution visited by Queen

Victoria after the death of the Prince Consort; she went there with the newly-married Princess of Wales on 21st April, 1863.[20]

On 22nd June, 1908, King Edward VII laid the foundation stone at Spital of the fine hospital which is called after him. As its name implies, the site was associated with care of the sick. It was here that the twelfth-century Hospital of St. Peter provided sanctuary for "leprous brethren and maidens". The establishment attracted the bounty of King Henry III, who endowed it in 1251 with an area of adjoining land. It had a warden, chaplain and two sisters in charge, and its primitive provisions suggest standards more nearly allied with those of its modern successor than are traceable in the intervening centuries. The organized relief of the leper hospital contrasts favourably with the shunned isolation of the plague settlement in later years. Sufferers from plague were banished to cottages and "hutches" scattered about the common fields until 1604, when a "pest house" was built at the bottom of Sheet Street. It was little more than an ante-room to the grave, and the inmates found scant comfort there. "Some infected, in the anguish of their desese, broke out of the pest-house", came naked into the town, and had to be "forced back".[21]

The plague-carriers from London in 1563, whose reception by a new pair of gallows has already been noted, would probably have made their demented way by water rather than by road. The river was for centuries the great highway, and the "Keeper of the Legg of Windsor Bridge", as he was styled in Queen Elizabeth I's reign, had the "oversight of the said bridge, together with ye receipt of the toll or customs thereof as well by land as by water."[22] The erection of the earliest bridge is believed to have followed immediately on the founding of the Castle, though reference is not made to one until 1273. Since it was formerly always a wooden structure, it must have been rebuilt countless times before the iron bridge which now spans the Thames was erected. Frederick Duke of York, High Steward of Windsor, laid the corner stone on 10th July, 1822, and it was opened on 1st June, 1824.[23]

News was still being transmitted by water in 1681, when fire destroyed Shakespeare's Garter Inn, for it was the Windsor barge that took the intelligence to London, but already a nightly post and a regular coaching service were speeding the flow of life. They had been introduced by 1679, and under the pressure of this gathering impulse the first phase in the modern history of Windsor began to develop. One grace which remains immutable is the association of town and Castle. When Windsor's right to the rare designation of "Royal Borough" was confirmed in 1922, it was an appropriate sequel to King George V's proclamation on 17th July, 1917, that "Our House and Family shall be styled and known as the House and Family of Windsor." Queen Elizabeth II in turn ratified the choice for herself and her children.

The inaugural opening of Frogmore House to public view on 8th August 1990, with continuance on stated days in August and September, then and in the following years, commemorated not only Queen Charlotte, creator of royal Frogmore, and her second daughter, Princess Augusta, to whom she bequeathed her *Paradis Terrestre*, but also later royal personages who found peace and pleasure there.

Queen Charlotte comes instantly to mind in her Colonnade, 'that Sweet retirement in the summer all Dressed out with Flowers' and overlooking her beautiful lake, and in The Mary Moser Room, named by her in honour of the gifted flower painter who was drawing mistress to the Princesses and a founder member of the Royal Academy, and who painted the walls and ceiling of the room for her with garlands of the flowers she loved and studied.

Names and interiors of rooms may have changed, but many remain endowed with royal personality. The Duchess of Kent's Sitting Room, formerly the Bow Drawing Room, retains the memory of this royal lady who took so leading, if unforeseen, a part in the regal destiny of England. Born Victoria, Princess of Saxe-Coburg-Saalfeld, she was the widow of Emich-Charles, Prince of Leiningen and a mother when, with some hesitation, she accepted Edward, Duke of Kent and Strathearn, fourth son of King George III and Queen Charlotte, in marriage on 11th July 1818. She was again a widow when on 24th May 1820 her daughter reached her first birthday. That daughter was the future Queen Victoria.

When Princess Augusta died in 1841 the young Queen gave Frogmore House to her mother, Duchess of Kent, who lived there until her death in 1861. Her remains had already been removed from the entrance of the Royal Vault in St George's Chapel 'for interment in the New Mausoleum in the Grounds of Frogmore' when, as that stricken year drew to its close, Albert Prince Consort died, on 14 December. His remains were removed on 18 December 1862 to the 'Royal Mausoleum in the grounds of Frogmore', where in 1901 the body of Queen Victoria, who had died at Osborne, was conveyed. Thus this closely related family – for the Duchess of Kent was sister to the Prince Consort's father – remained together in their beloved Frogmore as they had in life, the Queen and Prince in their Mausoleum, the Duchess in hers.

Queen Mary's Flower Room commemorates the consort of King George V and great-granddaughter of Queen Charlotte, who when Princess of Wales wrote of Frogmore, 'It is too divine here . . . the house charming & fresh & the garden & grounds a dream.' Here, as in the Castle, Queen Mary founded a private museum of royal *memorabilia*, including the lock of hair, 'a pale-Brown, more than Cendré', that the future Queen Charlotte sent from Mirow to her unknown King when she learned that she was to become Queen of England.

Frogmore House enshrines many such precious memories.

Retrace one's steps from Frogmore and the private Home Park to Windsor town and here is an ancient Borough with a modern designation. The Royal Borough of Windsor, where the seven hundredth anniversary of the granting of its first Charter was celebrated in 1977, is now the Royal Borough of Windsor and Maidenhead, a change effected only with royal sanction, as officially recorded:

> By the Charter of Incorporation granted by Her Majesty the Queen the Windsor & Maidenhead District Council became incorporated as the Royal Borough of Windsor & Maidenhead with effect from 1st April 1974.

So read the first minutes of the new Borough. The first Mayor, Cllr C.S. Aston, presented the Council with a silver sculpture he had commissioned.

Time, as always, brings changes to the town centre, but Windsor cherishes its historic past. The Guildhall, Bachelors' Acre, the Theatre Royal, founded in 1791, retain their storied interest – the Acre saved in 1972, by the resolute campaign led by 78-year-old

Miss Doris Mellor, of Windsor, from becoming a car park. (It was there that on 28 May 1977 Windsor celebrated the granting of its first Charter with a Medieval Fair that the Queen and the Duke of Edinburgh visited that evening.) And the Windsor Local History Publications Group, founded in 1976 from a small group of WEA students and tutors, and of which the President is the Honorary Archivist of the Royal Borough of Windsor and Maidenhead, Mr Gordon Cullingham, flourishes with ever-increasing success in its recording of an incomparable past.

22

THE FIRE – 1992

The fire that on Friday 20th November 1992 flamed through the north-eastern heights of the Upper Ward of Windsor Castle sent tremors of shock across the world.

'The Chapel', 'The Palace', 'The State Apartments', 'St. George's Hall' – as the fire blazed on, like a ravenous dragon bent on engorgement, and not immediately controllable, names began to emerge, often confusedly. St. George's Chapel, shrine of the Order of the Garter and burial place of kings and queens, erected between 1477 and 1528, was endangered according to some of the initial media reports. This was not so. The Queen's Free Chapel of St. George in the Lower Ward, separated from the Upper Ward by the Middle Ward and William the Conqueror's grassy mound crowned by the Round Tower, lay beyond the path of destruction.

The doom-laden Chapel, of which the very existence may have been unknown to reporters as to many others, was the Chapel Royal adjacent to the Private Apartments of the Sovereign. It was Edmund Blore's competent conversion of the music room of St. George's Hall, under the direction of Albert, Prince Consort, consecrated on 19th December 1843 and refitted with richly carved oak panelling in 1852.

There, obscurely, the fire had started. The time was a few minutes after 11.30 in the morning. And from there the flames swept rapidly north, east and south, and westward into the many-windowed St. George's Hall overlooking the Quadrangle – built by King Edward III in 1362–5 as the banqueting hall of the Knights of the Garter, the western half of which had been the Chapel Royal until King George

IV demolished it and Sir Jeffry Wyatville panelled the extended hall for him.

Next in the imperilled State Apartments was the resplendent Grand Reception Room adjoining St. George's Hall and overlooking the North Terrace from the Cornwall Tower. In the full range of threatened majesty other names stand out that document the centuries of building, rebuilding and cumulative grandeur: The Waterloo Chamber; The Garter Throne Room overlooking the North Terrace, where Knights Companion of the Order assemble and the Queen invests new Knights before their Installation at the annual service in St. George's Chapel in June; The Queen's Ballroom, remodelled from a medieval nursery wing by King Charles II for his consort, Queen Catherine; The King's Dining Room, which in earlier times, when the principal meals of the Sovereign were a ceremonial formality to which privileged members of the public were admitted as spectators, was known as 'The King's Public Dining Room'; The King's Drawing Room; The King's State Bedchamber with its magnificent eighteenth-century domed and gilded bed, placed there by Queen Victoria for the occupation of the room by the Emperor Napoleon III and the Empress Eugénie on their state visit in 1855; The King's Closet, once a retreat of privacy next to The Queen's Drawing Room, properly 'The Queen's Withdrawing Room'; The Queen's Guard Chamber; The Grand Vestibule; The Grand Staircase.

Intrepidity, determination, endurance have never been wanting in the defence of the Castle. Nor were they wanting now, either in the teams combating the fire as it pierced the mysteries of those centuries of building and rebuilding, blazed 50 feet in the air and glowed over Windsor town, the royal Parks and the Thames Valley, or in the Castle residents and countless friends who immediately gave untiring help in removing its treasures to safety. One of the first rescuers was Prince Andrew, Duke of York, who was in the Precincts and joined the police and soldiers on duty when the alarm sounded.

All this the Queen saw when that afternoon she went to the Castle to view the afflicting spectacle. Half a century earlier, living there during the Second World War, and familiar with the sound of falling bombs and the alarm that summoned her and Princess Margaret to the royal air-raid shelter within its walls, the Queen had known the

Castle both as palace and embattled fortress. A rare experience and one of which the rapidly organised defences against the fire may have been reminiscent.

Lest the fire should spread through the Long Corridor of the Private Apartments, which overlook the East Terrace and King George IV's Garden from the Queen's Tower at the south-eastern corner of the Upper Ward to the Prince of Wales's Tower and the Brunswick Tower at the north-eastern, pictures and furniture had been immediately removed and a fire-break established. These are the Apartments celebrated in that joyous 'Royal Housewarming' early in 1805, which in turn leads one back to the life story of the King who loved a home of his own: George III and his supremely happy union with the consort he had never before met when on the afternoon of Tuesday 8 September 1761 she came to him out of the mists and gales of the North Sea, he a 23-year-old Sovereign, she a Princess of 17, to be married to him that same evening. He began by acquiring Buckingham House, The Queen's House or 'Palace in the Park', leaving St. James's Palace the official seat of majesty. At Windsor, unused since the death of Queen Anne in 1714 and a monument of neglect, The Queen's State Bedchamber was hastily brightened to welcome the young Queen Charlotte, already mother of a Prince of Wales, when she and the King stayed there for his Installation on 22nd September 1762 as Sovereign of the Order of the Garter.

What are now the Private Apartments having been parcelled out as offices and grace-and-favour residences for Court ladies and privileged friends, years were to pass until with the King's customary kindness accommodation having been found for the occupants during the restoration of the Castle, which began in 1778 (regarded as perhaps the most important date in its history after 1066), he and the Queen could vacate their comfortable country home, The Queen's Lodge, opposite the South Front, presently to be demolished, and in 1805 move as he had so long desired into the newly appointed home in the Castle; Queen Charlotte into the Watch Tower, later 'The Victoria Tower', and now 'The Queen's Tower' (the name was suggested to Her present Majesty and graciously adopted), and the Princesses into adjacent suites on east and south.

The King had, as always, accorded his Queen the palatial upper storey and for his personal use he chose those unpretentious apartments beneath the Queen's State Bedchamber where, in time, he was to spend the last sad decade of his life and from which his wraith was to salute the guard as it proceeded along the North Terrace. But although it was left to King George IV to perfect the new private domain, he himself had endowed the Castle with the primacy of place among the Royal residences that war could not impair, nor fire destroy.

Not for long was bleakness imposed on the Long Corridor, Wyatville's imposing two-storeyed gallery added for King George IV, and the historic apartments to which it leads. Within little more than a week furniture and pictures had been replaced and the Queen and the Duke of Edinburgh could return to their rooms.

The immediate and unavoidable threat on the outbreak of fire had been to two of the magnificent Drawing Rooms, the Green Drawing Room in the Chester Tower and the Crimson Drawing Room, and to the State Dining Room in the Prince of Wales's Tower, all nearer the Chapel. These might perhaps be described as the Private State Apartments. Here the Queen could entertain guests on less formal occasions than those held in the State Apartments.

The Green Drawing Room was damaged by smoke and water (more than a million gallons, it was said, were pumped from the Castle mains and the River Thames). The Crimson Drawing Room, epitome of gilded splendour, and the State Dining Room were devastated. The gold and white Chapel, serenely beautiful with its stained glass and above it, in the gallery, the early Victorian organ with duplicate keyboards that it shared with St. George's Hall and on which the Prince Consort used to play, was lost.

But nowhere in this stricken region had the fire found more inviting prey than the timber roof of St. George's Hall, dating back to the fourteenth century, and Wyatville's wooden ceiling, profusely adorned along its entire length with shields of arms of Knights of the Garter from the foundation of the Order in 1348. First the ceiling, then the roof, collapsed, crashing down in mountainous heaps and leaving the Hall bared to the sky.

Extensively damaged too were the Grand Reception Room, once King Charles II's Guard Chamber, but adapted and glorified by Wyatville, the great Kitchen and all the ground-floor domestic region, though much was saved. China had been removed and glass remained untouched.

Such was the magnitude of this north-eastern area encompassed by flames, smoke and water, and within which the fire crews valiantly aimed to retain the fire. But the paramount threat was not here.

From the immediacy of blaze and burning roofs the fire crept stealthily over the rest of the State Apartments. It was moving towards Queen Elizabeth's Gallery and the Norman Tower, residence of the Constable and Governor of Windsor Castle, where at the Norman Gate the Upper and Middle Wards meet. And towards priceless and irreplaceable treasures of the Crown.

Queen Elizabeth's Gallery had been built by the first sovereign Elizabeth as a 'cul-de-sac' out of her bedchamber suite. It was that same suite that some two hundred years later welcomed the young Queen Charlotte on her first visit to Windsor. Memories of his parents, both of whom loved books, may have been very much in King William IV's thoughts when one day he was walking through these apartments. As a charming story relates, the King remarked that he was the only Sovereign in Europe to have no library (the original royal library having been presented to the British Museum). There and then he resolved to have one, 'And I will have it here'.

In Queen Elizabeth's Gallery he founded the Royal Library, which was to extend into those apartments, upper and lower, reminiscent of his parents and, together with its wealth of books in this unique setting, to hold the world-famed royal collection of drawings, Italian, Flemish, English, French, Dutch, inclusive of such names as Leonardo da Vinci, Canaletto, Holbein, Paul and Thomas Sandby. Here the fire imposed its deadliest threat.

So swiftly had it crept westward over the roof timbers of the State Apartments that before anyone could know it was coming it was only two rooms away. Help came instantly and with it the Royal Librarian and his staff were able to save the thousands of books and the Old Master drawings.

This grim peril past, the story reverts to where it began and to the fate of the octagonal Brunswick Tower, most north-easterly point, where in the afternoon the floors collapsed and in the evening lurid flames lit the sky as it was engulfed.

Another day dawns, the great fire dies. The tale moves on to a considered view of the havoc, first pausing to reflect momentarily on the tragic irony of invasion by fire just as St. George's Hall was about to be rewired and fire breaks installed in the roof spaces to obviate the risk of such a calamity. There was one consolation. Only the day before the outbreak the pictures and armour had been removed in preparation for the work. And it happened too that all the damaged apartments had been prepared and emptied of pictures and furniture. The only losses were a heavy sideboard and a large picture of King George III on horseback by Sir William Beechey.

Review of the fire brought too the reassuring conclusion that, horrific as had been the devastation, the worst had in effect been limited to the structure of those north-eastern apartments, and principally to the roofs: but it was far-reaching and restoration must be estimated in terms of many years and millions of pounds. Even in this there was a note of hopefulness. Windsor oak there would be, for the monstrous gales in recent years had blown down many trees in the royal Parks.

Nearly one thousand years of Majesty had created the Castle. Majesty would take the lead in maintaining it. The opening, for the first time, of the State Apartments of Buckingham Palace to a fee-paying public in August and September, when Her Majesty would be at Balmoral Castle, was a gracious gesture towards the sight-seeing world and a declared practicability in raising means to meet the cost of restoration.

At Windsor the Precincts were open again within three days. And presently visitors could again enjoy the unforgettable tour to view Queen Mary's Dolls' House, the Picture Gallery and the range of the State Apartments – or those of the State Apartments as remained undamaged, or only minimally, by fire and smoke. Of well-wishers there was no lack, as the founding of a public fund testified. So high was the mounting cost of restoring the damaged splendours, and so encouraging the opening of Buckingham Palace, that in January 1994 an entry fee of £8 to the Castle precincts was introduced (Windsor residents being accorded a free pass).

The mode of such a restoration as the fire had imposed brought the stimulus of envisaging contemporary architecture and arts in relation to august tradition. A special Castle Restoration Committee with the Duke of Edinburgh as its Chairman and the Prince of Wales as its Vice-Chairman, and a Sub-Committee concerned with the architectural renaissance and with the Prince of Wales as its Chairman, were formed to represent Sovereign interest and commitment.

'The story always old and always new' – Robert Browning's words have nothing to do with a calamity at Windsor Castle, but they come irresistibly to mind. The Castle is no museum of disaster. It is a living Palace and a living home and its future is as inviting as its past.

SOURCE NOTES

In these notes the following abbreviations are used:
Anstis: *The Register of the most Noble Order of the Garter from its Cover in Black Velvet usually called The Black Book*, ed. John Anstis, Garter King of Arms, 2 vols., 1724.
Ashmole: Elias Ashmole, Windsor Herald, *The Institution, Laws and Ceremonies of the Most Noble Order of the Garter*, 1672.
Ashmole (Berkshire): Elias Ashmole, *The Antiquities of Berkshire*, 3 vols., 1719.
Beltz: G. F. Beltz, Lancaster Herald, *Memorials of the Order of the Garter*, 1841.
Bickham: George Bickham, *Deliciae Britannicae, or the Curiosities of Hampton-Court and Windsor-Castle*, 1742.
Cal.S.P.D.: Calendar of State Papers Domestic, Record Publications.
Cal.T.B.: Calendar of Treasury Books, Record Publications.
Camden: William Camden, *Britannia*, first published 1586.
Complete Peerage: The Complete Peerage, by G.E.C., new edn., revised, enlarged and edited by the Hon. Vicary Gibbs, etc., 12 vols., 1910–1959.
Elvey: *Life of Sir George Elvey*, by Lady Elvey, 1894.
Evelyn: *Diary of John Evelyn*, ed. S. de Beer, 6 vols., 1955.
Fiennes: *The Journeys of Celia Fiennes*, ed. Christopher Morris, 1949.
Fortescue: The Hon. Sir John Fortescue, late librarian to the King at Windsor Castle, *Author and Curator*, 1933.
Gernsheim: Helmut and Alison Gernsheim, *Queen Victoria. A Biography in Word and Picture*, 1959.
Hall: Edward Hall (d. 1547), *The Union of the Noble and Illustre Families of Lancastre and York*.
Harwood: T. Eustace Harwood, *Windsor Old and New*, privately printed, 1929.
Hedley: publications by the present writer are so indicated.
Hentzner: Paul Hentzner, *A Journey into England in the Year MXXCVIII*, printed at Strawberry Hill, 1757.
Holinshed: Raphael Holinshed, *Chronicles* (1577), planned by him and known by his name, but written by several hands.
Hope: W. H. St. John Hope, *Windsor Castle. An Architectural History*, 2 vols., published by *Country Life*, 1913.
Hughes: G. M. Hughes, *A History of Windsor Forest, Sunninghill and the Great Park*, 1890.
Knight: Charles Knight, *Passages of a Working Life during Half a Century*, 3 vols., 1864.
Luttrell: Narcissus Luttrell, *A Brief Historical Relation of State Affairs 1678–1714*, 6 vols., 1857.
Menzies (1864): William Menzies, Resident Deputy Surveyor, *The History of Windsor Great Park and Forest*, 1864.
Menzies (1904): William Menzies, Winsor Park and Forest [1904].
Morshead: Sir Owen Morshead, Librarian to H.M. the Queen, *Windsor Castle*, second, revised edition, 1957.
Papendiek: *Court and Private Life in the Time of Queen Charlotte: being the Journals of Mrs. Papendiek, Assistant Keeper of the Wardrobe and Reader to Her Majesty*, 2 vols., 1887.
Poynter: Ambrose Poynter, "An Essay on the History and Antiquities of Windsor Castle," prefixed to Wyatville's *Illustrations of Windsor Castle*, 1841.

Pyne: W. H. Pyne, *The History of the Royal Residences of Windsor Castle, St. James' Palace*, etc., 3 vols., 1819.

Pote: Joseph Pote, *The History and Antiquities of Windsor Castle*, 1749.

Sandford: Francis Sandford, Lancaster Herald of Arms, *A Genealogical History of the Kings of England*, 1677.

Tighe: R. R. Tighe and J. E. Davis, *Annals of Windsor*, 2 vols., 1858.

Whitelock: *The Anglo-Saxon Chronicle*, revised translation, ed. Dorothy Whitelock, 1961.

Wyatville: *Illustrations of Windsor Castle, by the late Sir Jeffry Wyatville, R.A.*, ed. Henry Ashton, 2 vols. bound in one, 1841.

CHAPTER 1

1. q.Hope, 2
2. Harwood, vii & 81
3. Orderic, q.Hope, 6
4. Hope, 12
5. Whitelock, 172–3; *Complete Peerage*, IX, 706
6. Ibid, 165
7. Gervase, *Acta Pontificum* (Rolls Series 73), ii, 378, q.Hope, 13; *The Chronicle of Robert of Gloucester* (Rolls Series 86), ii, 646, q.Hope, 14; Whitelock, 181; Tighe, I, 29
8. Whitelock, 192
9. T. Rymer, *Foedera*, etc. (London, 1816), I, i, 18, q.Hope, 13
10. Peter of Blois, q.Trevelyan, *History of England*, 1947, 141
11. Hope, 568
12. Fabyan, q.Tighe, I, 33

CHAPTER 2

1. Benedict of Peterborough (Rolls Series 49), ii, 101; Chronica Magistri Roger de Hoveden (Rolls Series 51), 136, 141, 207; Gervase of Canterbury, *Opera Historica* (Rolls Series 73), i, 515; q.Hope, 23–24
2. Annals of Margam; *Histoire des Ducs de Normandie et des Rois d'Angleterre* (Société de l'Histoire de France), Paris, 1840, q. Tighe, I, 45–46; Hope, 26
3. Tighe, I, 47
4. Lord Denning, Master of the Rolls, "Runnymede, Fount of English Liberty", *The Times*, 9th June, 1965
5. Hope, 26–27; *Histoire des Ducs de Normandie*, 177, q.Tighe, I, 56
6. Hope, 27; Tighe, I, 56, 63
7. The significance of the change from square to D-shaped towers at Windsor was pointed out by Sir Owen Morshead in his *Windsor Castle*, 1951, 15
8. Liberate, Close and Pipe Rolls, q.Hope, 49–50
9. *Chronica Majora* (Rolls Series 57), V, 263, 264, q.Hope, 65
10. Liberate and Close Rolls, q.Hope, 67, 69
11. Ibid, q.Hope, 61, 89
12. Liberate Roll, 24 Henry III, q.Tighe, I, 65; Ibid, 25 Henry III, part ii, m.15, q.Hope, 61
13. Fabyan, q.Tighe, I, 85–87
14. These and other medieval features came to light in 1964–5 at No. 25 The Cloisters, and are described by P. E. Curnow in "Royal Lodgings of the 13th Century in the Lower Ward of Windsor Castle: some Recent Archaeological Discoveries", Friends of St. George's Report, 1965, 218–228
15. Kidson, Murray & Thompson, *A History of English Architecture*, 1965, 94
16. Close Rolls, 27 Henry III, m.5, q.Hope, 56; Madox's History of the Exchequer, q.Tighe, I, 70
17. *Flores Historiarum* (Rolls Series 95), ii, 481, q.Hope, 73
18. *Archaeologia*, XVII, 297, q.Tighe, I, 107–8

CHAPTER 3

1. *Adae Murimuth Continuatio Chronicarum*, ed. Edward Maunde Thompson (Rolls Series 93), 155, 156, 231, 232, q.Hope, 111–112
2. Hope, 111–116; Archaeologia, XXXI, 6, q.Tighe, I, 140
3. Tighe, I, 143
4. Documented evidence for this account of the founding of the Order is fully set forth in "Joan of Kent and the Order of the Garter", by Margaret Galway, in the *University of Birmingham Historical Journal*, I, 1947, 13–51

5. Rymer, *Foedera*, q.Tighe, I, 301–3
6. Wardrobe Accounts, *Archaeologia*, XXXI, q.Tighe, I, 144
7. Pat.22 Edward III, pars.2, m.6, q.Tighe, I, 155; Ashmole, 152–167
8. Treasurer's and Precentor's Accounts, q.Hope, 374
9. Ashmole, 547; see also p. 209
10. Beltz, lxxviii
11. Dr. E. H. Fellowes, *The Knights of the Garter 1348–1939*, Appendix I, "The Ladies of the Garter" (p. 102)

CHAPTER 4

1. Hope, 501
2. Maurice F. Bond, "Some Early Windsor Seals", Friends of St. George's Report, 1951, 22–28
3. Dr. Anthony Deane, *Time Remembered*, 1945, 207

4. Pipe Roll, 41 Edward III, m.41, q.Hope, 201
5. Camden, edn. 1607, trans. by Richard Gough, 1739, I, 152; see also 15, No. 9 below
6. Hope, 195
7. q.Tighe, I, 193

CHAPTER 5

1. Galway, *op. cit.* (3, No. 4, above)
2. ibid.
3. Tighe, I, 257
4. Froissart, q.ibid, I, 257
5. *Chronique de la Traison et Mort de Richard Deux, Roy Dengleterre*, ed. and trans. for the Historical Society by Benjamin Williams, 1846, q.Tighe, I, 258–61
6. British Museum, Sloane MS. 1776, cited Tyler, *Life of Henry the Fifth*, q.Tighe, I, 271
7. Tighe, I, 272; *Complete Peerage*, VIII, 450, note (g)
8. Hilaire Belloc, *Avril*, 1931, 21; the poem appears under the title, "The Complaint", pp. 26–28
9. British Museum, Cotton MS., Julius, B1, *The Chronicle of London*, ed. by Sir H. Nicolas, p. 159, q. by Canon J. A. Fisher, "Saint George the Martyr", Friends of St. George's Report, 1960, 12–19; (Black Book) Anstis, II, 65
10. Tyler, *Henry the Fifth*, I, 327–8, q.Tighe, I, 290

11. Hall, Holinshed, q.Tighe, I, 286
12. Kidson, Murray & Thompson, *op. cit.* (2, No. 4 above), 150
13. Hope, Plate XVIII (opp. p. 230), which shows "Part of the Stair (restored) up to the Donjon or Great Tower as rebuilt in 1439–40". See also 9, No. 2 below.
14. British Museum, Add. MS. 6113, f. 103b, pr. with introduction and notes by Sir F. Madden, *Archaeologia*, XXVI, 275, q.Tighe, I, 367 *et seq.*
15. W. J. Thoms, *The Book of the Court*, 1838, 160
16. Ashmole, 549; Stow's *Annals*, edn. 1631, 429, q.Tighe, 373–4
17. Patent Roll, 15 Edward IV, part ii (No. 536), m.18, q.Hope, 376
18. See 2, No. 14, above
19. S. Bentley, *Excerpta Historica or Illustrations of English History*, 1831, 366, 367, 372, 373, q.Hope, 376–7
20. Thomas More's narrative, printed in Holinshed's Chronicle, edn. 1808, III, 331

CHAPTER 6

1. Ashmole, 518–519, 594; Anstis, II, 225; Sir H. Nicolas' *Memoir of Elizabeth of York*, 83, q.Tighe, I, 412
2. P. C. C. Blamyr, 13, 26, q.Hope, 384
3. Mr. Philip R. Lee, "Master Masons" (letter), *The Times*, 10th Feb., 1964
4. British Museum, Cotton MS., Vespasian, C, XII, f. 236–249, q.Tighe, I, 434–441; Ashmole, 337, 559
5. Hall, Holinshed, q.Tighe, I, 470
6. q.Tighe, I, 492
7. Ashmole, 338
8. Ibid, 560, 603; Anstis, II, Appendix, ii–xix
9. Stow's *Annals*, edn. 1631, 513, q. Tighe, I, 484
10. Hall, q.Tighe, I, 488
11. Mills' "Catalogue of Honour", 42, q.Tighe, I, 503
12. Bodleian Library, Rawlinson MSS, D.776, f. 85, D.780, f. 62, D.781. f. 156, q.Hope, 250–252
13. Tighe, I, 506
14. Canon H. W. Blackburne & Maurice F. Bond, *The Romance of St. George's Chapel*, 1956, 12
15. Dr. E. H. Fellowes, *Organists and Masters of the Choristers of St. George's Chapel*, 1939, 19
16. Quoted by Dr. Anthony Deane, *Life of Thomas Cranmer*, 1927, 235
17. The illustration appears between pp. 1398 and 1399
18. Canon S. L. Ollard, *Deans and Canons of Windsor*, 1949, 59–60
19. Strype, q.Tighe, I, 508–509
20. Hope, 478–484
21. q.ibid, 484
22. Sandford, 463–464

CHAPTER 7

1. J. G. Nicholas, *Literary Remains of King Edward VI*, 1857, I, cxxxi
2. Statues, printed in Anstis, II, App. no. xiv, q.Tighe, I, 578
3. Hope, 257–258
4. Stow's *Annals*, q. Tighe, I, 507
5. Hope, 259: Dr. E. H. Fellowes, The Military Knights of Windsor, 1944, xxvii-xxxiii
6. q.Harwood, 221
7. *Cal.S.P.D.*, Elizabeth, Vol. 136, No. 83, q.Hope 268; ibid, Vol. cxi, f. 51, q.Hope, 274; Account of George Woodward Esq., Clerk of the Works (1580), Audit Office (Declared Accounts) Works, Bundle 2477, Roll 257, q.Hope, 275; Cal.S.P.D., Eliza-beth, Vol. cl, No. 62, q.Hope, 275. The story of Queen Elizabeth and the cold dinners is quoted (with sources) by Tighe, I, 646; a woodcut showing the remains of the "Royal Oven" at the bakehouse in Peascod Street appears on p. 665
8. Hope, 255; *Cal.S.P.D.*, Elizabeth, Vol. CIX, No. 31, q.ibid, 273
9. Bickham, 199
10. Hentzner, 68–78 (visit to Windsor); 48–53 (Queen Elizabeth)
11. q.Harwood, 116
12. Hedley, "Shakespeare's Windsor", *Berkshire Archaeological Journal*, Vol. 61 (1963–1964)

CHAPTER 8

1. Documents transcribed from originals and copies in the archives of St. George's Chapel, q.Hope, 287–289
2. See "Royalist Prisoners in Windsor Castle", by Sir Owen Morshead, *Berkshire Archaeological Journal*, Vol. 56 (1958) on which p. 98 is based
3. C. V. Wedgwood, *The Trial of King Charles I*, 1964, 66
4. Ibid, 203
5. William Jones, *Crowns and Coronations*, 1883, 312; Tighe, II, 236
6. *An Account of what happened on opening the Coffin of King Charles I*, 1813
7. Dr. E. H. Fellowes, *Memoranda concerning King Charles I*, 1950; Commander C. J. M. Fellowes, R.N., "The Opening of the Tomb of King Charles I in 1888", Friends of St. George's Report, 1965, 229

8. E. G. O'Donoghue, *The Story of Bethlehem Hospital*, 1914 (various references); *Notebooks*, Walpole Society, XVIII; *The Journal of James Yonge* (1647–1721), 1963, 158
9. Hope, 302; Tighe, II, 252; Hughes, 151
10. Dr. E. H. Fellowes, *The Military Knights of Windsor*, 1944, xxxvi–xxxix
11. Ashmole MS. No. 1126, q.Tighe, II, 294
12. Pote, 40
13. Menzies (1864), 32
14. Ibid, 15; Tighe, II, 253–255

CHAPTER 9

1. Day's Book, Ashmole MS. No. 1126, q.Tighe, II, 289
2. Hentzner, 72; see 5, No. 13 above
3. Luttrell, I, 111
4. Hist.MSS.Comm., MSS. of Duke of Rutland, II (1889), 37
5. Bickham, 159
6. Pote, 424
7. Hope, 326
8. Ibid, 318, 327
9. Ibid, 313
10. Bickham, 142
11. King's Warrant Book, 311–312, and Warrants not relating to Money, 247, q. in *Cal.T.B.*, vi (1679–1680), 533–534, cited by Hope, 330
12. Fiennes, 277
13. *London Gazette*, q.Tighe, II, 389
14. Hope, 323
15. Bickham, 137
16. *Cal.T.B.*, 1717, 315
17. Tighe, II, 419
18. Ibid, II, 471–472
19. Wren Society, XVIII, 91
20. Tighe, I, 35, II, 472, 536
21. Original report in the archives of St. George's Chapel, q.Hope, 386–388
22. Hedley, *Round and about Windsor*, 1949, "Dorney Court" (227–236)

CHAPTER 10

1. Hope, 305
2. Ashmole, 502
3. Ibid, 548
4. Ibid, 203–204, 211, 215, 221, 547–551, 563–566, 574
5. Ibid, 500, 588–593
6. Ibid, 609
7. Evelyn, III, 479
8. *Complete Peerage*, II (App. B), 581; ibid, X, 159, note (k), quoting Hist. MSS. Comm., Polwarth MSS., I, 42; Beltz, cxxxv

CHAPTER 11

1. *Autobiography of Sir John Bramston*, Camden Society, 1845, 231, q.Tighe, II, 426
2. Pote, 62–63
3. Knight's *Windsor Guide*, 1783, 35
4. Poynter
5. *Cal.S.P.D.*, 1698, 111
6. Hester W. Chapman, *Queen Anne's Son*, 1955, 106
7. Ibid, 140
8. Fortescue, 165
9. *Cal.T.B.*, 1705–1706, 225
10. Ibid, 1704–1705, 289, 373; 1708, 401; Pote, 417 (Queen Anne's Bed)
11. Ibid, 1705–1706, 319; 1706–1707, 242; 1708, 228
12. A. Austin Eagger, *Venture in Industry: the Slough Industrial Health Service 1947–1963*, 1965, 1
13. *Cal.T.B.*, 1706–1707, 110; Declared Accounts (Pipe), Roll 3457, q.Hope, 332
14. Hall Book, q.Tighe, II, 487
15. Ashmole (Berkshire), III, 59; Tighe, II, 485
16. Luttrell, V, 205
17. "A General View of Windsor Park", by Henry Wise, Royal Library, Windsor Castle; there is a photostat copy in the British Museum (188 g.1.10)
18. *Cal.T.B.*, 1704, 32, 51
19. *Cal.T.B.*, 1710, 309, 338
20. Menzies (1864), 26
21. Wise's original plans are in the Royal Library, Windsor Castle; there are photostat copies in the British Museum. See also *Cal.T.B.*, 1708

CHAPTER 11—*cont.*

22. Report of Mr. Robert Stephenson, M.P., *Windsor and Eton Express*, 7th Sept., 1858
23. Hedley, "Queen Anne's Lake", *The Times*, 30th Dec., 1960; "Maastricht Garden at Windsor Castle", *De Maasgouw*, 1961, 139
24. *Cal.T.B.*, 1705–1706, 610
25. Ibid, 1708, 209
26. Tighe, II, 488, 490–494, 656; Harwood, 249–250

CHAPTER 12

1. Tighe, II, 526–527
2. *Passages from the Diaries of Mrs. Philip Lybbe Powys*, 1899, 115
3. Hedley, "A Windsor Mystery", *The Times*, 6th Oct., 1958, and "Gracious Housekeeping". *The Times*, 3rd May, 1960
4. Royal Archives, Georgian Papers 2434, q.Morshead (1957), 71
5. Royal Archives, Georgian Papers 2631, q.ibid
6. MS. volume of "Copies and Extracts", q.Tighe, II, 536 n.
7. Tighe, II, 538
8. Knight's *Windsor Guide*, in *Les Délices des Chateaux Royaux* [1785], 37
9. Morshead (1957), 9, 173
10. Knight's *Windsor Guide*, 1783, 14
11. Ibid, 21; Pyne, I, 161
12. Papendiek, II, 100–101
13. Ernest de Selincourt, *Dorothy Wordsworth*, 1933, 33
14. Hedley, "Court and Chapel, 1760 to 1873", Part I, Friends of St. George's Report, 1960, 20–26
15. Knight, I, 77; Elvey, 130

CHAPTER 13

1. Papendiek, II, 201
2. Knight's *Windsor Guide*, 1825, 15
3. Pyne, I., "Frogmore"; see also Hedley, "Windsor was a Queen's Little Paradise", *The Times*, 30th April, 1963
4. Papendiek, II, 201

CHAPTER 14

1. Harcourt Papers, VI, 83
2. Gentleman's Magazine, 1805, 262–264
3. *Annual Register*, 1805, 379; Beltz, cxxxiii
4. *Complete Peerage*, II (App. B), 566–580
5. Hedley, "Knights of Windsor", *The Times*, 15th June, 1962; Tighe, II, 565–577
6. Gentleman's Magazine, 1805, 374–376, 470–474; Knight's *Windsor Guide*, 1807, 141, and 1825, 189–198
7. *Proceedings of the Committees of Bachelors of New Windsor*, published by Charles Knight & Son, 1817. (A diorama showing the scene on Bachelors' Acre, made by Miss Judith Ackland and Miss Mary Stella Edwards, of Staines, in 1959, and based on contemporary accounts and portraits, is on view in the permanent exhibition in Windsor Town Hall.)
8. Gentleman's Magazine, 1809, 976
9. Morshead (1957), Foreword
10. Knight's *Windsor Guide*, 1825, 177–188; Gentleman's Magazine, 1820, I, 172
11. Fellowes & Poyser, *Registers of St. George's Chapel*, 1957, 249

CHAPTER 15

1. *Windsor and Eton Express*, 7th June, 1824
2. The documented record of Wyatville's alterations will be found in Hope, 254–365, in which the text of his *Illustrations* is quoted

3. *Windsor and Eton Express*, 13th Dec., 1828
4. Ibid, 11th Oct., 1828
5. *The Letters of King George IV*, ed. A. Aspinall, III (1938), 360, 458, 477, 484
6. Menzies [1904], 11

7. *Royal Companion to Windsor Castle* [*c.* 1860], 20
8. *Windsor and Eton Express*, 25th Feb., 1860
9. See 4, No. 4, above.
10. *Windsor and Eton Express*, 24th Aug., 1839

CHAPTER 16

1. *Letters of Queen Victoria*, ed. Benson and Esher, 1837–1843, John Murray, I, 1907, 14–17
2. *Windsor and Eton Express*, 5th Aug., 1826
3. Sir Richard Holmes, *Queen Victoria*, 1897, 23
4. *Windsor and Eton Express*, 2nd Sept., 1837
5. Hedley, "How the Christmas Tree came to the English Court", *The Times*, 22nd Dec., 1958
6. Ibid, "Court and Chapel, 1760 to 1873", Part II, Friends of St. George's Report, 1961, 59
7. *Windsor and Eton Express*, 20th Nov., 1852
8. See Maurice F. Bond, "A Century of Windsor History 1858–1958", *Berkshire Archaeological Journal*, Vol. 57 (1959)
9. *The Pictorial Edition of the Works of Charles Knight*, ed. Charles Knight, *Comedies*, I, 204

10. Royal Companion to Windsor Castle [*c.* 1860], 16
11. "Eton under Keate: Extracts from the Diary of Miss Margaretta Brown", *Etoniana*, No. 69 ff.
12. Elvey, 136
13. The flowers, recently appliquéd to new green satin curtains, were embroidered at Queen Charlotte's Orphan School at Ampthill, and originally formed part of the panoply of a throne in the King's Audience Chamber.
    The curtains, curiously enough, were one tribute which was lost on the Empress. When she revisited the apartments half a century later she was heard to murmur, "Toujours ces affreux rideaux!" (Still those awful curtains): Fortescue, 241
14. *Windsor and Eton Express*, 21st and 28th April, 1855
15. Queen Victoria, *Leaves from a Journal*, 1855, ed. Raymond Mortimer, 1961

CHAPTER 17

1. A photograph of the Prince's draft is reproduced in Gernsheim, 139
2. Royal Archives, Z.142, q.Elizabeth Longford, *Victoria R.I.*, 1964, 298–301
3. The influence of the Saxe-Coburg tradition was kindly pointed out to me by Mr. Winslow Ames, of Saunderstown, Rhode Island, U.S.A.
4. A photograph of a drawing showing the Blue Room appears in Gernsheim, 139
5. Wilhelmina Countess of Munster, *My Memories*, 2nd edn., 1904, 140
6. Hedley, "Where the Prince Consort Died", *The Times*, 13th Dec., 1961,

and letters following, 18th, 22nd and 23rd Dec.
7. *Illustrated London News*, 9th Feb., 1901, 208
8. Hedley, "Court and Chapel, 1760 to 1873", Part II, *Friends of St. George's Report*, 1961, 60–61; Georgina Battiscombe, "Gerald Wellesley: A Victorian Dean and Domestic Chaplain", ibid, 1963, 134–135
9. W. H. Russell, *Memorial of the Marriage of H.R.H. Albert Edward Prince of Wales and Alexandra Princess of Denmark*, 1863
10. Hope, 487–8

CHAPTER 18

1. *Windsor and Eton Express*, 3rd May, 1828

2. Ibid, issues of June and July 1836, *passim*

CHAPTER 18—*cont.*

3. Ibid, 6th March, 1852
4. Elvey, 27
5. *Windsor and Eton Express*, 7th April, 1860
6. Elvey, 226
7. *Windsor and Eton Express*, 26th July, 1862. See 7, No, 7, above

8. Dr. E. H. Fellowes, *Minor Canons of Windsor*, 1945, 25
9. Ibid, 26
10. *Letters from S.L.*, 1873, 460
11. Hugget, Sloane MS. No. 4846, f. 119, q.Tighe, II, 10
12. Bickham, 137

CHAPTER 19

1. See also Hope, 547
2. Lt.-Col. Howard N. Cole, *The Story of Aldershot*, 1951, 54, 323, 333
3. "A Monster Bell has been placed on the North Terrace, presented to Her Majesty, from Sebastopol": Brown's

Windsor Guide (undated, but published between 1857 and 1861), 20
4. *Windsor and Eton Express*, 9th Feb., 1901
5. Ibid

CHAPTER 20

1. Dr. E. H. Fellowes, *The Knights of the Garter* 1348–1939, Appendix I, "The Ladies of the Garter" (p. 102)
2. *Tabs*, April 1948

3. Ibid
4. Tighe, II, 527–528
5. "Windsor Church Centre Plan", *The Times*, 27th Oct., 1965

CHAPTER 21

1. Tighe, I, 480
2. Ashmole (Berkshire), III, 59
3. See 6, No. 17, above
4. Mayor's Book, Ashmole MSS., No. 1126, q.Tighe, I, 650–652
5. Ibid, II, 22; Pote, 12
6. Ibid, II, 111
7. Ibid, *loc. cit.*
8. Ibid, II, 101
9. Ashmole (Berkshire), III, 59
10. Hall Book, q.Tighe, II, 443
11. Elvey, 77
12. *Cal.S.P.D.*, 1700–1702, 546
13. Tighe, II, 449–451

14. Hall Book, q.Tighe, II, 451
15. Pote, 28; Tighe, II, 451
16. Gentleman's Magazine, 1763, 515, and 1764, 143
17. Tighe, I, 473
18. Original deeds, q.Hedley, *Round and About Windsor*, 1949, 96
19. Knight's *Windsor Guide*, 1825, 9
20. J. E. McAuley, *The Hospital at Windsor*, 1960, 2, 7, 15, 29, 35
21. Matthew Day, 1659, q.Tighe, II, 304
22. Tighe, I, 653
23. Knight's *Windsor Guide*, 1825, 22

INDEX